MRS

D1326578

SCHOLASTIC
COLLECTIONS
Compiled by Julia Eccleshare

Five-minute Stories

© 1995 Scholastic Ltd

Published by Scholastic Ltd,
Villiers House,
Clarendon Avenue,
Leamington Spa,
Warwickshire CV32 5PR

Compiler Julia Eccleshare
Editor Sophie Jowett
Series designer Joy White
Designer Lynda Murray
Cover and illustrations Annabel Spenceley

Designed using Aldus Pagemaker
Printed in Great Britain by Ebenezer Baylis & Son Ltd,
Worcester

British Library Cataloguing-in-Publication Data
A catalogue record for this book is
available from the British Library.

ISBN 0-590-53351-7

All rights reserved. This book is sold subject to the condition
that it shall not, by way of trade or otherwise, be lent, hired
out or otherwise circulated without the publisher's prior
consent in any form of binding or cover other than that in
which it is published and without a similar condition,
including this condition, being imposed upon
the subsequent purchaser.

No part of this publication may be reproduced, stored in a
retrieval system, or transmitted, in any form or by any
means, electronic, mechanical, photocopying, recording or
otherwise, without the prior permission of the publisher.
This book remains copyright, although permission is granted
to copy pages where indicated, for classroom distribution
and use only in the school which has purchased the book.

Contents

PAST AND PRESENT

WINNERS AND LOSERS

WHAT MAKES THINGS TICK?

THE WORLD WE LIVE IN

BEGINNINGS AND ENDINGS

Acknowledgements

**The publishers gratefully acknowledge permission
to reproduce the following copyright material:**

Teresa Anderson and the author Diana Ross for 'The house that suits you will not suit me' from *The Golden Hen* (1942, Faber & Faber Limited); A&C Black (Publishers) Limited for 'Thomas Barnardo' from *Dr Barnardo* by Donald Ford (1958, A&C Black); Curtis Brown Group Limited for 'Leaving London' from *Carrie's War* by Nina Bawden (1973, Victor Gollancz Limited); Laura Cecil Agency for 'The voracious vacuum cleaner' from *Stuff and Nonsense* by Laura Cecil (1989, Bodley Head); © 1974 Jean Chapman for 'The awful baby' (Hodder & Stoughton, Australia), © 1976 Jean Chapman for 'The king who wanted to touch the moon' from *Pancakes and Painted Eggs* (1976, Hodder & Stoughton, Australia), © 1974 Jean Chapman for 'Stone soup' from *Tell Me A Tale* (1974, Hodder & Stoughton, Australia) and © 1986 Jean Chapman for 'What we need is a new bus' from *Never Meddle With Magic* (1986, Puffin); CIS Publishers, Australia for 'Mrs Simkin's Bathtub' by Linda Allen previously published in *All the year Round* (Hamish Hamilton); © 1995 Geoffrey R. Clarke for 'On Christmas Eve'; © 1992 Julia Eccleshare for a retelling of 'Wumbulgal' from *Spring Tinderbox* (1992, A&C Black); The Education Company of Ireland (a trading unit of Smurfit Services Limited) for 'Traffic jam' by Frank Murphy from *Links 1* (1976, Education Company of Ireland); Evans Brothers Limited for 'A desire to serve the people' from *Nelson Mandela (Profiles series)* by Mary Benson (1986, Hamish Hamilton), 'Florence Nightingale' from *Florence Nightingale (Profiles series)* by Angela Bull (1985, Hamish Hamilton), 'Mohandas Gandhi' from *Gandhi (Profiles series)* by Kathryn Spink (1984, Hamish Hamilton) and 'Martin Luther King' from *Martin Luther King* by Nigel Richardson (Hamish Hamilton); Faber & Faber Limited for 'January jumps about' from *To Aylsham Fair* by George Barker (Faber & Faber), 'Bedd Gelert' from *Stories for Nine-Year-Olds* edited by Sara and Stephen Corrin (1979, Faber & Faber), 'How the polar bear became' from *How the Whale Became and Other Stories* by Ted Hughes (1989, Faber & Faber), 'The autograph' from *See You at the Match* by Margaret Joy (1987, Faber & Faber) and 'Clever Polly and the Stupid Wolf' from *Clever Polly and the Stupid Wolf* by Catherine Storr (1967, Faber & Faber); Victor Gollancz Limited for 'The bet' from *More Stories Julian Tells* © 1986 by Ann Cameron (1986, Victor Gollancz); © 1988 Doris Harper-Wills for a retelling of 'Raincloud' from *Storyworld* chosen by Saviour Pirotta (1988, Blackie and Sons); HarperCollins USA for 'The fish angel' from *The Witch of Fourth Street and Other Stories* © 1972 Myron Levy (1972, Harper & Row); David Higham Associates Limited for 'By St Thomas Water' from *Union Street* by Charles Causley (Macmillan), 'The elephant's picnic' by Richard Hughes from *Don't Blame Me* by Paul Rogers (Chatto and Windus) and 'Football on a lake' from *A Book of Spooks and Spectres* by Ruth Manning-Sanders (1979, Methuen); John Johnson (Authors' Agent) Limited for 'Hare and Tortoise' by Æsop, adapted by James Reeves, from *A Golden Land* (1958, Constable and Puffin Books); Larousse PLC for 'Hare the hero' by Edward Blishen from *A Treasury of Stories for Seven-Year-Olds* (1988, Kingfisher) and 'The Dragon and Saint George' from *The Kingfisher Book of Myths and Legends* by Anthony Horowitz (1985, Kingfisher); Macmillan Children's Books for 'The girl who loved wild horses' by Paul Goble (1979, Macmillan); Scott Meredith Literary Agency for 'The house' by André Maurois; © 1984 Patricia Miles for 'The borrower' from *Hundreds and Hundreds* by Peter Dickinson (1984, Puffin); © 1993 Brian Moses for 'Uncle' from *All in the Family* compiled by John Foster (1993, Oxford University Press); Orion Publishing Group Limited for 'Cat and Mouse' by Margaret Mahy from *Downhill Crocodile Whizz and Other Stories* (1988, J M Dent and Sons), 'The ghost who came out of the book' from *Nonstop Nonsense* by Margaret Mahy (1988, J M Dent and Sons) and 'The little boy who wanted a flat world' from *The First Margaret Mahy Storybook* by Margaret Mahy (1975, J M Dent and Sons); Oxford University Press for 'Heaven and Earth and Man' from *Chinese Myths and Fantasies* retold by Cyril Birch (1961, OUP); © 1995 Bette Paul for 'Our house sixty years ago'; Penguin Books Limited for 'The incredible shrinking hippo' by Stephanie Baudet (1991, Hamish Hamilton), 'Benny the boaster' by Thelma Lambert (1988, Hamish Hamilton), 'Mouse party' and 'When Pig got smart' from *Rats on the Range and other Stories* by James Marshall (1994, Hamish Hamilton), 'Plain Jack' by K M Peyton (1988, Hamish Hamilton), 'Daedalus and Icarus' from *Heroes and Monsters – Legends of Ancient Greece* by James Reeves (1969, Blackie) and 'Last day' from *Charlotte's Web* by E B White (1952, Hamish Hamilton); Peters, Fraser and Dunlop Group Limited for 'Noah's ark' from *Waving at Trains* by Roger McGough (Jonathan Cape), 'A speck speaks' from 'Nothingmas Day – a poem' from *For Beauty Douglas* by Adrian Mitchell (Allison & Busby) and 'The legend of Ra and Isis of Ancient Egypt' by Michael Rosen from *Kingfisher Book of Children's Poetry* (1985, Kingfisher); Saviour Pirotta for 'The king who was afraid to die' by Indira Rai (Saviour Pirotta) from *Tales from Around the World* (1988, Blackie); Laurence Pollinger Limited for 'Why Noah chose the dove' by Isaac Bashevis Singer (Farrar, Straus and Giroux Inc.); Murray Pollinger Limited for 'Sam plays the trumpet' by Gabriel Alington and 'Slowly does it' by Robin Ravilious from *Animal Stories for the Very Young* by Sally Grindley (1994, Kingfisher) and 'Clive at the dyeworks' © 1995 by Pippa Goodhart; The Post Office Film and Video Library for 'Night Mail' by W H Auden (1935, Post Office); Random House UK Limited for 'A battle' from *Fox's Feud* by Colin Dann (1983, Hutchinson and Arrow Books); Reed Consumer Books for 'My naughty little sister makes a bottle tree' from *My Naughty Little Sister* by Dorothy Edwards (1969, Methuen Children's Books), 'The story of Paka the cat and Pania the rat' by A J Mounteney Jephson from *The Book of Magical Cats* chosen by Margaret Mayo (1978, Kaye & Ward), 'The mouse and the winds' from *Mouse Tales* by Arnold Lobel (1973, World's Work), 'The magic egg' by Marguerita Rudolph (1971, World's Work) and 'Elizabeth' by Liesel Moak Skorpen from *The Silent Playmate* by Naomi Lewis (1991, World's Work); The estate of Ian Serraillier for 'The summit', a passage from 'Everest Climbed' by Ian Serraillier from *The Windmill Book of Ballads* (Heinemann); Walker Books Limited for 'The Greenwood' from *Robin Hood* by Sarah Hayes (1989, Walker Books); A P Watt Limited for 'Black beetles' and 'Your country needs you' from *Lanhydrock Days* by John Bradfield (1991, Victor Gollancz); Watts Group Limited for 'Sea-Woman' from *British Folk Tales* by Kevin Crossley-Holland (1987, Orchard Books) and 'Feather Woman and the Morning Star' retold by Margaret Mayo from *Orchard Book of Magical Tales* (1993, Orchard Books); and Wayland Publishers Limited for 'The day of Trafalgar' from *England Expects* by Roger Hart (1972, Wayland).

Every effort has been made to trace copyright holders. The publishers apologise for any inadvertent omissions.

INTRODUCTION

Long before the printed word, the bound book and the idea of universal literacy, telling stories was the prime means of communication. Ideas of right and wrong, spiritual beliefs, tribal laws and customs, mighty deeds and acts of heroism – all of these were passed down from one generation to another through stories. While details may have been lost, altered or exaggerated, the core or essential nugget would survive many retellings providing a basis for the next version.

Telling stories as a way of comprehending the world in which we live is universal. Creation myths, for example, have come about in all cultures as a way of explaining the complexities of the world as we find it. For the listener, as well as the teller, a story is often the best way of understanding an idea, an attitude or a principle. A straightforward explanation of something scientific or historical may look simple enough but, in reality, it is often hard to remember because the facts relate to each other only if you understand them, not because they are tied together by a coherent narrative.

Stories can provide a framework for conveying information and that is the purpose of this collection. Chosen from a wide range of sources, from different times and different places, they all give the listener a nugget of information and, in doing so, help to foster listening skills.

Listening is an important way of learning in all areas of the curriculum. Hearing these stories will show that science and geography, as much as RE and history, can be comprehended and enhanced by fiction. Hearing stories from so many sources and conveying such different kinds of information develops powers of comprehension and will also inform and develop the listener's own story-telling skills. The different voices in this collection, some first person, some third, some accurate and observational, some fanciful, plus the inclusion of poetry, will expose listeners to a wide range of styles which will, in turn, influence the voice and scope of their own writing.

Based on the idea that listening to stories will add to comprehension of almost all kinds of information, this collection of five-minute stories is loosely designed to support different areas of the curriculum in Key Stages 1 and 2. While not tied to specific topics, the stories have been divided into chapters which broadly fit with the subjects of the curriculum.

Thus in 'Past and present' the stories include a number of accounts of how people lived in other times. Some, like the extract from *England Expects* – an account of the Battle of Trafalgar on 21 October 1805 – are contemporary with the event. The immediacy of the writing makes something from long ago come alive; its drama is as fresh as when it happened. Other stories are more detached and reflective, such as 'Daedalus and Icarus', a story from Greek mythology, which tells not only of man's earliest known attempt at flight, but also demonstrates when confidence takes precedence over obedience.

Biography and autobiography are among the most powerful ways of informing subsequent generations of how it felt to live at certain times and in different countries when conditions were – thankfully – far removed from what they are today. The horrors of slavery as recounted in 'Fifty years in chains' gives a graphic account of what it felt like to be a slave. The complete degradation and total absence of rights could not be more tangible if related as a series of bald facts.

The stories in 'The world we live in' reinforce knowledge about the earth and how it has been formed and conquered at different times. Listening to Ian Serraillier's exhilarating, if overly-patriotic, 'Everest Climbed' evokes the majesty of the enormous mountain and the courage of those who took on the challenge of climbing it.

'What makes things tick?' looks at how things work – or don't! – as in the ridiculous 'The elephant's picnic' in which the elephant and the kangaroo fail to understand what 'boiling a kettle' means. W. H. Auden's rhythmic 'The night mail' evokes the train rattling through the night with letters for one and all, explaining how the post gets – or used to get – delivered across the country. The fanciful 'The king who wanted to touch the moon' emphasises the impossibility of reaching up into space from the ground.

In 'Beginnings and endings' there are varying accounts of how the world comes to be as it is. Every culture needs explanations for mortality, the weather, why people and animals are as they are and for many other wondrous but everyday phenomena.

How skill and courage may be used to overcome adversity or sheer physical strength is the underlying theme of 'Winners and losers'. Some are more amusing than anything else, but some will genuinely inspire listeners to think again about their own behaviour.

Whatever the story, there is always a point to it. Listen carefully, sometimes it is easy to comprehend the facts but hard to grasp the underlying message, which is the real meat of the tale, in the first hearing. The stories may be read aloud many times asking the listener to absorb and reflect on what they hear. In that way they will enhance their understanding of what the stories explain while also enriching their capacity for listening to stories and making them their own.

Julia Eccleshare

WHO AM I?

Sam plays the trumpet

Every day Sam asked the same question.

'Are we going to the park today?'

The park was his favourite place, because right in the middle was a big round bandstand where each afternoon the Brass Band played. Sam sat on the grass in front of all the chairs and listened to the music. It was fine music, loud and exciting. The bandsmen and bandswomen wore red jackets and smart peaked caps. Some of them played trumpets and their bright shiny instruments gleamed in the sun. Sam's mother sat beside him with his small sister, Rosie, till Rosie got bored and had to be taken to see the ducks. Sam never got bored listening to the band. He was going to be a bandsman when he grew up.

'I'll play the trumpet,' he said, 'and I'll wear a red jacket like the people in the band.'

On his fifth birthday, his mother and father gave him a trumpet. It was bright and shiny like the trumpets in the band. Sam took a deep breath and blew into the end, but no sound came out. He tried again, puffing out his cheeks. Still nothing happened. Then his father had a turn. He blew and he blew and his face went very pink, but the trumpet would not make a single toot.

'It needs a lot of practice,' Sam's father said. 'You'll have to keep at it.'

Sam did keep at it. He took the trumpet to the park and blew it all the time the band was playing. But no toot came out. Then one day, towards the end of the concert when the music rose to a mighty peak, there was a moment's pause. The conductor waited with both arms raised, the whole audience held their breath – except for Sam. He went on blowing. And suddenly, to his great surprise, the trumpet gave a TOOT, loud and shrill. TOOT, TOOT, TOOT, it went.

Everyone round him turned and stared.

'Shush,' they all said. 'Shush. Be quiet.'

Sam blushed and stared at his shoes, but he could not help smiling. He had TOOTED his trumpet! He wished his mother would come back from the duck pond so that he could tell her.

When the concert was over, one of the trumpet players in the band beckoned to Sam.

'Me?' said Sam, pointing to his chest.

The Bandsman nodded and beckoned again, so Sam took his trumpet and climbed the steps onto the bandstand.

'That's a pretty nice instrument you've got there,' the Bandsman said.

Sam held out his trumpet. 'You can blow it if you like.'

'We'll swap,' said the Bandsman, handing Sam his.

It was big and very heavy and when Sam blew into it no noise came out. Then the Bandsman tried Sam's. Nothing happened. He tried again – and again.

'It's a bit difficult,' Sam said.

'You show me then,' said the Bandsman, giving the trumpet back to Sam. So Sam showed him. TOOT, TOOT, TOOT.

'That's splendid,' said the Bandsman. 'You'll be a fine trumpeter one day.'

He turned and called the rest of the band. 'Hey, come and hear this.' The others gathered around Sam while he played for them. TOOT, TOOT, TOOT.

When Sam's mother and Rosie came back from the duck pond, they were surprised to see him on the bandstand. Sam waved to them and played an extra loud TOOT. His mother laughed and clapped her hands. Rosie clapped too. And then all the bandsmen and bandswomen clapped as well. Sam blushed again and stared at his shoes.

He felt he would burst with happiness.

Gabriel Alington

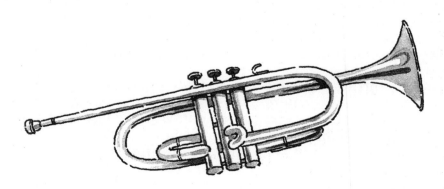

The bet

Gloria and I were in the park. I was in one of those moods when I want to beat someone at something. And Gloria was the only one around.

'Bet I can jump farther than you,' I said.

'Bet you can't,' Gloria said.

We made a starting line on the ground and did long jumps.

'I win!' I said.

'But not by much,' Gloria said. 'Anyway, I jumped higher.'

'I doubt it,' I said.

'I bet you can't jump this railing.' The railing went around the path in the park.

'I'll bet,' Gloria said.

We both jumped the railing, but Gloria nicked it with her shoe.

'You touched it!' I said. 'I win.'

'You win too much,' Gloria said.

She sat down on the grass and thought.

I sat down too. I wondered what was on her mind.

'Well,' Gloria said, 'I guess you can win at *ordinary* things. But *I* can do something special.'

'Like what?' I said.

'I bet you I can move the sun,' she said.

'Bet you can't!' I said.

'Bet I can,' Gloria said. 'And if I win, you have to pay for me to go to the cinema.'

'If you lose,' I said, 'you pay for me. And you're going to lose, because nobody can move the sun.'

'Maybe *you* can't,' Gloria said. '*I* can.'

'Impossible!' I said.

'Well – suppose. Suppose I make you see the sunset in your bedroom window? If I can do that, do you agree that I win?'

'Yes,' I said. 'But it's impossible. I have an east window; I see the sun rise. But the sun sets in the west, on the other side of the house. There's no way the sunset can get to my window.'

'Ummm,' Gloria said.

'What are you thinking about?' I asked. 'Thinking how you're going to lose?'

'Not at all,' Gloria said. 'I'm thinking about what film I want to see.'

'When are you going to make your miracle?' I asked.

Gloria looked at the sky. There were hardly any clouds.

'Today will be just fine,' she said. 'Here's what you have to do....'

It was seven o'clock at night. I was in my room. I had done what Gloria asked. I had pulled the telephone into my bedroom on its long cord.

It was getting dark in my bedroom. There was no way the sun could come back now.

The phone rang. I picked it up.

'Hello, Gloria,' I said. 'The phone isn't the sun.'

'Look out of your window,' Gloria said.

'I don't see anything unusual,' I said.

'O.K.,' Gloria said. 'Now watch your wall, the one opposite the window.'

I watched. A big circle of yellow light was moving across the wall. It floated higher. Then it zig-zagged across the ceiling. Then it floated back down the wall again. It looked just like the sun does coming in the window in the morning. Except the morning sun doesn't dance on the ceiling.

I spoke into the phone. I had to admit – 'It looks like the sun!'

Gloria's voice sounded far away. 'It *is* the sun. Now look out of your window again,' she said. 'Look at my house.'

From the upstairs of our house we can see over lots of garages and gardens to the top floor of Gloria's house.

'See my house?' Gloria asked.

'Yes.'

'See my window?'

'Yes.'

'Look hard!' Gloria said.

And then I saw a person learning out of Gloria's window. It was Gloria. And I saw what she had in her hands – a mirror big enough to move the sun.

'Gloria! You're reflecting the sun into my house!' I said. 'You're sending signals!'

It was a wonderful invention! I didn't know exactly what it was good for, but it seemed as if it must be good for something.

'Of course!' Gloria said. 'I've got to stop now.'

The sun went away. Her voice went away. I guessed her arms were getting tired from holding that big mirror out of the window.

Then I heard her voice on the phone again.

'Did I do it, or didn't I?' she asked.

'Do what?' I answered. I was so excited about the signalling invention I had forgotten about the bet.

'Move the sun!' Gloria said.

'Yes,' I said, 'you did it. You win.'

'Ummm,' Gloria said. Her voice was full of satisfaction.

I knew what she was thinking about – what film she wanted to see.

And I was thinking how I was going to have to do something I never want to do – at least not for years and years and years: treat a girl to a cinema trip.

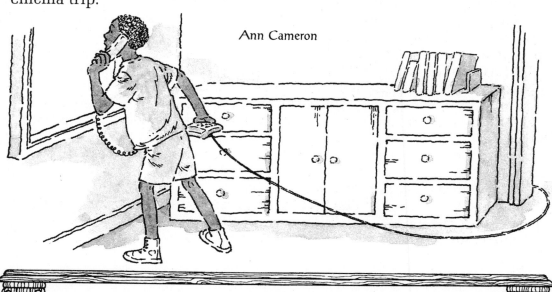

Ann Cameron

Benny the boaster

Benny's school was going to have a Sports Day. Miss Barker told Class 3 all about it. There was going to be an egg-and-spoon race, a high jump, and a special running race for all the fathers.

'My dad's the fastest runner in the world,' boasted Benny to his friend Mark. 'He's sure to win the fathers' race!'

'No, he's not,' said Mark. 'My dad is!'

'We'll see,' said Benny.

Benny and his dad ran all the way home that day. Benny wanted Dad to get in training for Sports Day.

But by the time they got home, Dad was all red in the face and puffed out. And Benny got home first! Benny began to get worried. Maybe Dad wasn't the fastest in the world after all.

On Sports Day the sun shone brightly and everyone had great fun.

Benny came second in the egg-and-spoon race and Rupert won the

high jump. Then all at once it was time for the fathers' race. Lots of dads were taking part.

Mark's dad had come dressed just like a real runner. And he won the race easily!

Benny was dismayed to see that his dad had come puffing in last of all! Benny so wished that Dad had won the prize....

One morning when everyone was coming in to school, Miss Barker was trying to move a piano.

'Oh dear!' she sighed. 'This is much too heavy. I can't move it!'

Benny stepped forward.

'My dad is the strongest man in the world,' he boasted. 'He'll move it easy-peasy!'

But Dad couldn't move the heavy piano.

'I've got this bad back,' he explained to Miss Barker.

Then Jill's dad came in. And he moved the piano with no trouble at all.

Benny felt upset. He so wished Dad had been able to help Miss Barker....

He knew his dad was the best in the world. But how could he prove it to everyone?

Later that day Miss Barker said: 'Class 3, listen carefully. I need someone to take the cooking class next week. Can you ask at home if your mum or dad can do it?'

Benny put up his hand.

'Please, Miss! My dad is the best cook in the world!' boasted Benny. 'He always cooks super dinners. I'm sure he'll do it.'

Miss Barker gave Benny a letter to take home to Dad, explaining about the cooking class.

'Tell him I'm very grateful,' she said. 'And I hope he'll be able to come next Monday.'

Benny put the note in his anorak pocket and forgot all about it.

On Sunday evening, as Benny was hanging up his anorak, the note dropped out.

'This is for you, Dad,' said Benny. 'I told Miss Barker you could do it.'

When Dad read the letter he frowned. 'It's about the cookery class at your school. I'm supposed to be taking it. And, oh help! It's tomorrow!' said Dad, none too pleased.

'What will you teach us to make, Dad?' said Benny eagerly. 'Chocolate fudge like Jill's mum did? Or fairy cakes like Mrs Smith?'

'No,' snapped Dad. 'Those things are far too sweet and sugary. And anyway it depends what we've got in the larder. There's no time to go to the shops now.'

Dad looked in the kitchen and found he had tomatoes, onions and lots of eggs. He got out his cook book.

'I know!' said Dad, brightening up. 'I'll make Spanish Omelette!'

'Oh no, Dad! Not Spanish Omelette!' Benny's face fell. He hated Spanish Omelette and he didn't think his friends would like it either. If Dad made that, no one would think he was the best cook in the world!

'Look, Benjamin,' said Dad. 'You got me into this cooking-at-school lark, so just be quiet and help me all you can!'

The next morning, Benny helped Dad carry all the things they needed for the cooking class: tomatoes, onions and a big box of eggs. Benny couldn't help wishing he was carrying nice things like bags of sugar and cocoa powder!

The six children who were in the cookery class were gathered round the big table in the Cookery Corner. Dad put on his stripey apron.

'Today we are going to make a Spanish Omelette,' he told them. He explained that it was like scrambled eggs with onions and tomatoes chopped in.

'Sounds horrible,' whispered Mark.

'Yucky,' agreed Rupert.

'Now, you can each break an egg into this bowl,' said Dad. He had got an enormous mixing bowl from the school kitchen.

Mark's egg fell on the floor and broke. Rupert's egg ran all over the table top. Only a few eggs ended up in the bowl.

Dad asked Jill to beat the eggs with a wooden spoon.

'Ow!' squealed Jill. 'I've got egg in my eye!'

'Who wants to chop an onion?' said Dad quickly, as he mopped up. Dad showed Mark how to chop an onion carefully. But Mark didn't realise that chopping onions makes you cry!

'Oooh!' sobbed Mark, tears rolling down his face. 'I don't like this.'

Then Rupert cut his finger slicing the tomatoes.

'Aaah!' he screamed. 'Real blood!' Rupert nearly fainted. He couldn't stand the sight of blood.

'Oh dear!' cried Dad. 'My cooking class! It's all going wrong!'

Dad had to stop everything and take Rupert to Mrs Munn for a plaster.

When they came back, everyone had lost interest in the Spanish Omelette. The children were all at the other end of the room, trying to get the caretaker's parrot to talk.

But Dad carried on cooking. He heated up the little stove and soon the omelette was sizzling in the pan. When it was cooked only Benny was still sitting at the table.

Dad put out some little plates. 'Doesn't anybody want to eat this?' said Dad.

But no one seemed interested.

'I think you were right, Benny,' said Dad sadly. 'I should have made fairy cakes after all...'

Suddenly Benny sat up.

'Can I try some, Dad?' he said.

Dad put some of the omelette on a plate and Benny pretended to eat it.

'It's YUMMY!' he cried loudly.

The children came back to the table.

'Is it really yummy?' said Rupert, who loved to eat.

'Er... yes,' mumbled Benny, trying hard to look as if he was enjoying it.

All at once, everyone wanted to taste the Spanish Omelette. And to Benny's surprise, everyone loved it!

'It's delicious, Mr Johnson,' said Rupert, munching at full speed.

'I wish my dad could cook like this,' said Mark, with his mouth full.

'I love the burnt bits,' said Jill.

But when no one was looking, Benny tipped his share of the omelette on to Rupert's plate.

After the cooking lesson, the children went back to their classroom.

Miss Barker asked them how it had gone.

'It was super!' said Mark.

'I'd never had Spanish Omelette before. It was terrific!' said Rupert, licking his lips.

'Well, I told you!' said Benny proudly. 'My dad is the best cook in the world!'

'Yes,' said Rupert. 'And for once, Benny, you were right!'

Thelma Lambert

Plain Jack

Once there were two old mares in a field together, who each had a foal.

One mare had won a lot of races and thought a lot of herself. She spoilt her foal dreadfully. She told him how clever he was and what a lot of races he would win when he grew up.

He was very valuable and called Fire of England.

The other mare was very plain and had won only one small race. Her foal was plain like her and called Plain Jack.

'You will have to work very hard if you are to be a winner, Plain Jack,' she said to him sternly. 'You don't come from a family of great winners like Fire. All the same,' she added tartly, 'he'll come to a bad end if he doesn't behave himself.'

Jack remembered her words, and when they went to the sales he behaved his very best. But he only fetched a small price. He was bought by a man called Bill who lived in the North.

But Fire, in spite of behaving disgracefully in the sale-ring, was sold for an enormous price to a very rich owner, and went to live in the best stable in England.

'I will try very hard to make Bill pleased with me,' thought Jack.

A lad called Barney looked after him and his jockey was called Joe. They liked Plain Jack because he tried. When he was ready to race they took him to Yarmouth. To Jack's surprise he found Fire was entered in the same race.

Fire was ridden by the best jockey in the country. Everyone admired him. But he was very naughty and bucked his jockey off. The crowd booed and someone threw a tomato.

But Plain Jack tried his hardest and came fifth out of twenty-three horses.

Bill and Joe and Barney were very pleased with him.

Every time he ran Plain Jack tried his hardest, and the crowd liked him because he never let them down.

Barney read to Jack from the racing paper: 'Plain Jack is a great favourite with the racing public'.

But on the back page it said: 'Fire of England disappointment'. It said Fire was to be sold because he was no good.

Plain Jack did not see him again until he was sent to run in a race at Epsom.

The racecourse was on the downs, and people were picnicking and playing cricket. Some children were riding along by the rails.

One of the horses was a very thin, poor chestnut. When it saw Plain Jack going down to the start of the race, it put up its head and whinnied. Jack got a great surprise, recognising his old friend Fire.

Jack did not want to race, he wanted to stay with Fire. When the race started Jack hung back. Joe did not know what was wrong with him. Fire bucked his rider off just like old times, jumped the rails and chased after the race. He ran like the wind.

'Look at that thin old nag!' everyone laughed. 'He's the fastest of the lot!'

But at the end Fire was caught and led away in disgrace.

Plain Jack had come last and Bill and Joe and Barney were very disappointed with him. It was the first bad race he had ever run.

They took him home but Plain Jack would not eat and stood with his head in the corner thinking of poor Fire.

He got very thin. Bill called the vet but the vet could find nothing wrong with him.

'I don't understand it,' said Bill. 'Ever since Epsom –'

Barney had an idea. He told Joe to go to Epsom to try to find out about the thin chestnut horse who seemed to have upset Jack so. Joe searched all the riding stables and found Fire at last in a grotty shed with no food and no water. He was thinner than before and very miserable.

Joe examined him carefully.

'Why! You're Fire of England – I recognise you! The day the guv'nor bought Jack, you were sold for half a million pounds! But you're not worth tuppence now.'

Joe told Bill and Bill bought Fire from his nasty owner. Joe fetched Fire home. When he walked in the yard, Plain Jack put his head out of his box and whinnied with excitement.

Bill laughed. 'So that was the trouble! Put him in the box next to Jack, and get them each a good feed! I can use Fire for my hack.'

Barney brought two big feeds. Both horses ate up every oat – and wanted more!

So Fire of England came back into a racing stable and grew fat and happy again. Plain Jack went on running races, trying his hardest and never giving in, and the racing public loved him because he never let them down, except that one time.

When Fire and Jack got old and were retired, they were turned out in a field together. They stood under the trees in the shade, swishing their tails – the horse with a great talent who never used it, and the horse with little talent who used it all.

K. M. Peyton

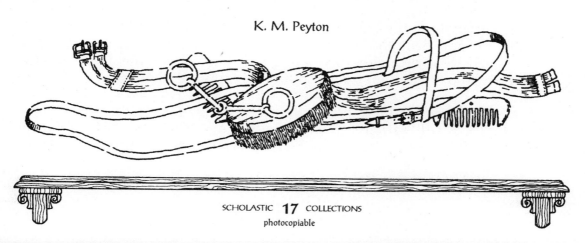

The awful baby

Once, even before breakfast, even before Richard was dressed, things were passed over the fence from next door. First came a big basket. It was full of baby napkins, baby bottles, jars of baby food and baby clothes. Next came a car seat. Then came the fat baby, Liza, who usually lived next door.

'She's our baby for today,' said Mummy. 'Her mother has to go to town.'

Richard didn't want the fat baby, not for a whole day. She couldn't talk. She couldn't walk. She pulled things about and she crawled. And the first thing she did was to crawl across the kitchen floor to the cupboards. *Clatter! Crash!* Liza pulled out saucepans.

'Oh, you busy one,' laughed Mummy, not at all cross. She gave Liza a wooden spoon to bang.

Liza threw the spoon away. Richard gave it back to her. She threw the spoon right across the kitchen. Richard ran to fetch it and Liza crawled off, plop-plop, out of the kitchen. She crawled into the bedroom. Into the bathroom. Into the sitting-room. She grabbed at the coffee table trying to pull herself upright. It wobbled. It fell. Liza yelled.

Mummy came rushing in and gathered her into her arms, kissing her cheek, crooning to her. Then and there, Richard decided that Liza was awful, but he watched while Mummy bathed her. When she tried to wash Liza's toes she kicked out her feet. *Splash!* Richard was wet on his face and his arm and his shirt. And when he tried to dry Liza's toes she curled them away, then squirmed and wriggled so he couldn't catch them. Later, she grabbed and pulled at him when he sat in his own car seat and she sat in hers on the way to the supermarket. She wanted his teddy. Richard held Ted tightly. Liza yelled until the car stopped.

Oh, botheration! Mummy had forgotten to bring Liza's stroller. So she put Liza on one hip, flung her bag over one shoulder and they went into the supermarket. 'Fetch me a trolley, please, Richard,' Mummy said.

Richard wheeled the trolley and Mummy took what she needed from the shelves and dropped them into it. Liza took things which Mummy didn't need. She dropped them in the trolley, or on the floor. It was Richard who picked them up and put them on the shelves. She really was an awful baby!

Near the soap powder shelves, Mummy sat Liza on the trolley's baby seat. She liked riding there. She swung her legs. She waved her fat arms and smiled at everyone. People looked and smiled back at Liza, even when she made grabs at them. No one looked at Richard.

They stopped at the deep-freeze cabinet. Richard held the door open so that Mummy could stretch in and take out a chicken and some margarine. Liza stretched the other way. She tugged at a pink carton on top of a display stand. Pull, pull, pull! It slid towards her then toppled down. Its flap dropped open. *Plop! Smash! Splosh!* Broken eggs splattered the trolley and Liza and the floor. She yelled.

Mummy snatched Liza up out of the trolley into her arms. Now Mummy was sploshed with sticky egg, its yellow yolk and white bits of shell. Liza screamed. She buried her head in Mummy's shoulder. People rushed to help. Someone mopped up Mummy. Someone mopped up Liza. Someone mopped up the trolley. Someone mopped up the floor. No one noticed Richard.

He wheeled the trolley to the cashier's desk. 'We'll pay for the broken eggs,' said Mummy.

'That's all right,' said the cashier. 'It was an accident. Your baby has had a nasty fright.'

Liza hiccupped.

'She's *not* our baby,' said Richard.

The cashier hadn't heard him. She said, 'Just pay for what you need.'

Mummy fumbled for her shoulder bag. She couldn't find it. She didn't have it. Everything was in it – money, wallet, car keys. Where could it be? She remembered locking the car door, putting Liza on a hip and the bag over one shoulder. Yes! She remembered that. Where was the bag now?

'Should anyone find a shoulder bag, please bring it to the desk,' said the cashier into her microphone. Everyone in the supermarket heard the announcement. Richard certainly did. He was running back to the soap powder shelves. Mummy had put Liza into the trolley there, but she hadn't left her bag. And it wasn't by the cereals, or the bread, or honey. He looked in the stand where the egg cartons were stacked. No bag there either.

Richard turned to the refrigerator cabinet. He stood on his toes and opened the door to look in. Mummy's bag was on top of the margarine. Stretching, stretching he could grasp its strap. He pulled gently. Down came an icy-cold bag and some margarine as well. Back went the margarine into the freezer and off went Richard with the shoulder bag, icy cold and flapping against his legs all the way to the cashier's desk.

'You're a clever boy to find Mummy's bag,' she said.

'I don't know what I'd do without Richard, specially today,' said Mummy. 'He's my best help, isn't he, Liza?'

Liza smiled and babbled baby-talk to Richard and stretched out her fat little arms to him, putting egg on his shirt.

'Your baby thinks so, too,' said the cashier.

'She's not our baby,' Richard said but the girl didn't listen because she said, 'Your baby's put egg on you, too.'

So they took Liza home and gave her another bath. And Richard had a bath. And Mummy had a shower while Richard minded Liza. She crawled very close to him and tried to pull herself upright on his leg. He gave her a hug and they both fell over in a heap. They laughed and laughed. She really was a nice, fat, cuddly, crawly baby – Richard's baby for that day.

Jean Chapman

The incredible shrinking hippo

It was Sunday when Simon found the hippopotamus. It looked like a big grey rock in the middle of the lawn.

'What are you doing here?' he asked.

'Looking for some mud,' said the hippopotamus.

'There's no mud in our garden,' said Simon. 'I could put some water in the bath and you could splash around in that, but you're too big.'

'Oh, that's no problem,' said the hippo. 'I can shrink. Just say the word "tiny".'

'Tiny,' said Simon.

The hippo got smaller and smaller until Simon could hold him in the palm of his hand.

'Brilliant!' laughed Simon. 'You can be my pet now!'

'I don't want to be a pet!' squeaked the tiny hippo.

'Oh, please!' said Simon. 'I'll take you everywhere with me and put you in the bath every day.'

'All right, but you must keep me a secret,' said Hippo. 'I don't like being stared at.'

'I promise,' said Simon.

'And another thing,' said Hippo. 'If anyone says the word "hippopotamus", I'll immediately grow back to my normal size.

Simon nodded, only half listening.

'To make me shrink again,' went on Hippo, 'you must say any word which means "tiny", but you can only use the same word once.'

'OK,' said Simon. He knew several words which meant 'tiny', but he was sure he wouldn't have to use them. 'Come on, let's go and play in the bath.'

Next day Simon took Hippo to school. He stood Hippo behind the curtain on the classroom window sill.

'What are you doing there, Simon?' shouted Suzie Marks.

'Can I swap seats with you for today, Suzie?' asked Simon.

'No, you can't,' she said. 'I like sitting by the window.' And she lifted her chair down onto the floor with a clatter.

Miss James came in and everyone hurried to their places.

'Good morning, children,' she smiled. 'Last week we were talking about animals found in Britain. Today we're going to talk about animals found in Africa. The first animal has a funny name which means "river horse".'

She unrolled a big poster and pinned it to the cork board. 'It's a hippopotamus.'

Simon gasped and looked towards the curtain. Just behind Suzie's head, the curtain was bulging out and growing fatter and rounder and lumpier.

'Little!' he yelled, making everyone jump.

Miss James looked startled. 'Please don't shout out like that, Simon! Hippos certainly aren't little anyway.'

The class sniggered. Simon went red. It wasn't easy having a hippo for a pet.

After school Simon's mum took him to the dentist. He was a nice man with red hair and a white coat.

'Come and sit here, Simon,' he said. 'And let's have a look at your teeth.'

Simon climbed onto the chair and lay back. On the far wall was a big picture. It was of an animal, grinning widely and showing two rows of very big teeth.

A hippopotamus!

The dentist looked up. 'Lovely teeth they have, hippopotamuses,' he said.

Squeak! Creak! Simon's schoolbag began to burst at the seams.

'Schnor!' said Simon, his mouth still open as the dentist poked at his back teeth.

There was a ripping sound and a small grunt.

'Small!' shouted Simon.

'Yes, that's all,' smiled the dentist. 'Your teeth are fine – just like our friend the hippo's.'

Simon picked up his torn bag and went out. Having a pet hippo did have its problems.

At home Simon went to the bookshelf and took down his dictionary. He turned to the 'T's. There it was. Tiny. He's said that. And small. And little. There was only a big word left. He sounded it out carefully and hoped he could remember it.

Then he went into the bathroom and put Hippo in the basin for a wallow.

'Wonderful!' gurgled Hippo, his flabby top lip slapping the surface of the water. 'I could stay here for hours.'

'You can't,' said Simon, fishing Hippo out. 'Dad'll be coming in to wash his hands for dinner soon.'

The next morning Simon left Hippo in his bedroom while he went down for breakfast.

'Something has walked right across the butter!' said Mum.

'Walked?' said Dad, pouring milk on his cornflakes. 'Don't you mean nibbled or licked or poked their finger into?'

'I mean walked,' said Mum. 'Look. Footprints.'

Simon's dad stared at the butter. Simon stared too, remembering how he'd come down in the night for a drink of water – and put Hippo on the kitchen table while he filled the glass.

'Not a mouse,' said Dad, looking closely at the butter. 'Not a spider either. These are round footprints – like those of an elephant or a hippopotamus.'

'A hippopotamus!' cried Mum in a loud voice.
Simon gasped.

A creaking sound came from above.

What was that big word he'd found in the dictionary?

Then there was a grunt and the ceiling above cracked under the great weight.

What was that word?

'What's that?' said Dad, jumping up. 'It sounds as if there's an elephant in your room, Simon.'

Then Simon remembered.

'MICROSCOPIC!' he yelled.

The creaking and grunting stopped.

'Just a game,' grinned Simon.

Inside he didn't feel like grinning. If that word was said once more there'd be real trouble. Hippo had to go. Hippopotamuses were definitely no good as pets.

But what could he do with a hippopotamus? Take it to the police station? Or a pet shop? It was too far to take it to Africa. The next best thing, he thought, was the zoo, but there was no chance of going there soon.

Simon climbed slowly upstairs, thinking hard. He looked out of his window into the street.

A big van stopped next door and two men jumped out. They opened the back doors wide. The van was empty. Simon remembered his mum had said their neighbours were moving today. This must be the van to take their furniture to their new house.

The two men went into the house and Simon stared at the van. It was very tall. It was very wide. A big strong van that could carry a lot of heavy furniture. He smiled, picked up Hippo and ran downstairs and out of the front door.

The men were still inside the house. Simon walked quietly up to the van. Then he reached inside as far as he could and stood Hippo on the floor.

'Goodbye Hippo,' he said. 'It's been fun playing with you. These men will take you to the zoo where there's plenty of mud and water to wallow in, and you can be your normal size all the time. I'll come and visit you when I can.'

'Goodbye,' said Hippo.

Simon shut the big doors and then ran quickly back to his garden and hid behind the hedge.

The two men came out of the house carrying a piano. Simon watched them struggle with it down the path and into the road. He watched their look of surprise and their cross shouts when they found the van doors closed.

The piano jangled as they put it down in the road. One of the men reached up to open the doors again.

Simon took a deep breath and opened his mouth.

'HIPPOPOTAMUS!' he shouted.

Stephanie Baudet

Elizabeth

'What do you want for Christmas?' asked Kate's mother.

'I want a red ball,' said Kate, 'and a new dress and a book and a doll. I want a doll with golden curls who walks and talks and turns somersaults.'

'Well,' said Kate's mother, 'we shall see what surprises Christmas brings.'

It seemed as though Christmas would never come, but of course Christmas came. Kate opened her presents under the tree. There was a red ball and a new dress and a book and other gifts. And underneath them all, in a long white box, there was a doll. It was a soft cloth doll with warm brown eyes and thick brown plaits like Kate's.

'What does it do?' asked Kate.

'Everything a doll's supposed to do,' her mother said.

Kate picked the doll up from its box. Its arms hung limply at its sides. Its weak legs flopped, and they couldn't hold it up. 'What's its name?' asked Kate.

'She doesn't have a name,' Kate's mother said. 'No one has a name until somebody loves her.'

Kate set the doll back in the box. 'Thank you,' she said to her mother politely. 'It's an ugly doll,' she said to herself inside. 'It's an ugly doll, and I hate it very much.'

There were no more presents under the tree.

Kate's cousin Agnes came for Christmas dinner. Agnes had a new doll whose name was Charlotte Louise. Charlotte Louise could walk and talk. 'Where is your Christmas doll?' asked Agnes.

Kate showed her the cloth doll lying in the box.

'What does it do?' asked Agnes.

'It doesn't do anything,' Kate replied.

'What is its name?' asked Agnes.

'It doesn't have a name,' said Kate.

'It certainly is an ugly doll,' said Agnes. She set Charlotte Louise down on the floor, and Charlotte Louise turned a somersault.

'I hate you, Agnes,' Kate said, 'and I hate your ugly doll!'

Kate was sent upstairs to bed without any Christmas cake.

The next day was the day after Christmas. Kate's mother asked her to put away her presents. Kate put away her red ball and her new dress and her book and all her other gifts except the doll.

'I don't want this ugly doll,' she said to James the collie. 'You may have it if you like.'

James wagged his tail. He took the cloth doll in his mouth and carried it out to the snowy garden.

By lunchtime James hadn't come home, and Kate was sorry she had given her doll to him. She couldn't eat her sandwich or her cake. 'James will chew up that doll,' she said to herself. 'He'll chew and chew until there's nothing left but stuffing and some rags. He'll bury her somewhere in the snow.'

She put on her coat and mittens and boots and went out into the garden. James was nowhere to be seen. 'I'm sorry,' said Kate inside herself. 'I'm very, very sorry, and I want to find my doll.'

Kate looked all over the garden before she found her. The doll was lying under the cherry tree, half-buried in the snow, but except for being wet and cold, she seemed as good as new. Kate brushed her clean and cradled her in her arms. 'It's all right now, Elizabeth,' she said, 'because I love you after all.'

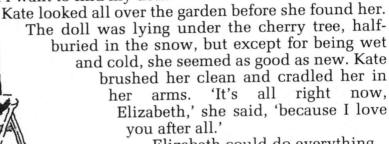

Elizabeth could do everything.

When Kate was happy, Elizabeth was happy.

When Kate was sad, Elizabeth understood.

When Kate was naughty and had to go upstairs, Elizabeth went with her.

Elizabeth didn't care for baths. 'She doesn't like water,' Kate explained, 'because of being buried in the snow.' Elizabeth sat on the edge of the bath and kept Kate company while she scrubbed.

Elizabeth loved to swing and slide and go round and round on the merry-go-round.

When Kate wanted to be the mother, Elizabeth was the baby.

When Kate wanted to be Cinderella, Elizabeth was a wicked stepsister and the fairy godmother too.

Sometimes Kate forgot about Elizabeth because she was playing with other friends.

Elizabeth waited patiently. When Kate came back, Elizabeth was always glad to see her.

In the spring, Elizabeth and Kate picked violets for Kate's mother's birthday and helped Kate's father fly a kite.

In the summer, everyone went to the seaside. Agnes was there too, but Agnes's doll, Charlotte Louise, was not.

'Where is Charlotte Louise?' Kate asked, holding Elizabeth in her arms.

'Charlotte Louise is broken,' Agnes said. 'We threw her in the dustbin. I shall have a new doll for Christmas.'

Agnes wouldn't go into the water. She was afraid. But Kate went in for a dip. She set Elizabeth on a towel to sleep safely in the sun. When she came out of the water, Elizabeth was gone.

'Help,' cried Kate, 'please, somebody help! Elizabeth is drowning!'

Everyone heard the word 'drowning', but nobody quite heard who. Grown-ups shouted and ran around pointing their fingers towards the sea.

Then out of nowhere
Like a streak,
Galloping, galloping,
James the collie came.

Out into the sea and back to shore he swam, Elizabeth hanging limply from his mouth.

After an hour in the sun, Elizabeth was as good as new.

Everyone except Agnes said that James was brave and good and a hero.

Kate didn't say that Agnes had thrown Elizabeth into the sea, but inside herself she thought that Agnes had.

In the autumn, Elizabeth helped Kate gather berries in the meadow for jams and jellies and berry pies.

Then Christmas came again. Of course there were presents under the tree. For Kate, there was a new sledge and a new dress and a book and other gifts. For Elizabeth, there was a woollen coat and hat, and two dresses, one of them velvet.

Agnes came for Christmas dinner. Agnes had a new doll whose name was Tina Marie.

'Tina Marie can sing songs,' said Agnes. 'She can blow bubbles too, and crawl along the floor.'

Kate held Elizabeth tightly in her arms. 'Well,' said Kate in a whisper, 'Tina Marie is the ugliest doll I ever saw. She is almost as ugly as you.'

Agnes kicked Kate sharply on the leg and said the most dreadful things to Elizabeth, who was looking particularly nice in her velvet dress.

Agnes's mother was very cross with Agnes.

Agnes spent the rest of the day in disgrace and wasn't permitted any Christmas cake.

'Merry Christmas, Elizabeth,' said Kate as she tucked her into bed, 'and Happy Birthday too! You are the best and most beautiful doll in the world, and I wouldn't swop you for anyone else.'

Liesel Moak Skorpen

Springtime

On that first morning when the sky was blue again, Mary wakened very early. The sun was pouring in slanting rays through the blinds and there was something so joyous in the sight of it that she jumped out of bed and ran to the window. She drew up the blinds and opened the window itself, and a great waft of fresh, scented air blew in upon her. The moor was blue and the whole world looked as if something Magic had happened to it. There were tender little fluting sounds here and there and everywhere, as if scores of birds were beginning to tune up for a concert. Mary put her hand out of the window and held it in the sun.

'It's warm – warm!' she said. 'It will make the green points push up and up and up, and it will make the bulbs and roots work and struggle with all their might under the earth.'

She kneeled down and leaned out of the window as far as she could, breathing big breaths and sniffing the air until she laughed because she remembered what Dickon's mother had said about the end of his nose quivering like a rabbit's.

'It must be very early,' she said. 'The little clouds are all pink and I've never seen the sky look like this. No one is up. I don't even hear the stable-boys.'

A sudden thought made her scramble to her feet.

'I can't wait! I am going to see the garden!'

She had learnt to dress herself by this time, and she put on her clothes in five minutes. She knew a small side door which she could unbolt herself, and she flew downstairs in her stocking feet and put on her shoes in the hall. She unchained and unbolted and unlocked, and when the door was open she sprang across the step with one bound, and there she was standing on the grass, which seemed to have turned green, and with the sun pouring down on her and warm, sweet wafts about her and the fluting and twittering and singing coming from every bush and tree. She clasped her hands for pure joy and looked up in the sky, and it was so blue and pink and pearly and white and flooded with springtime light that she felt as if she must flute and sing aloud herself, and knew that thrushes and robins and skylarks could not possibly help it. She ran around the shrubs and paths towards the secret garden.

'It is all different already,' she said. 'The grass is greener and things are sticking up everywhere and things are uncurling and green buds of leaves are showing. This afternoon I am sure Dickon will come.'

The long warm rain had done strange things to the herbaceous beds which bordered the walk by the lower wall. There were things sprouting and pushing out from the roots of clumps of plants and there were actually here and there glimpses of royal purple and yellow unfurling among the stems of crocuses. Six months before Mistress Mary would not have seen how the world was waking up, but now she missed nothing.

When she had reached the place where the door hid itself under the ivy, she was startled by a curious loud sound. It was the caw-caw of a crow, and it came from the top of the wall, and when she looked up, there sat a big, glossy-plumaged, blue-black bird, looking down at her very wisely indeed. She had never seen a crow so close before, and he made her a little nervous, but the next moment he spread his wings and flapped away across the garden. She hoped he was not going to stay inside, and she pushed the door open wondering if he would. When she got fairly into the garden she saw that he probably did intend to stay, because he had alighted on a dwarf apple-tree, and under the apple-tree was lying a little reddish animal with a bushy tail, and both of them were watching the stooping body and rust-red head of Dickon, who was kneeling on the grass working hard.

Mary flew across the grass to him.

'Oh, Dickon! Dickon!' she cried out. 'How could you get here so early! How could you! The sun has only just got up!'

He got up himself, laughing and glowing, and tousled; his eyes like a bit of the sky.

'Eh!' he said. 'I was up long before him. How could I have stayed abed! Th' world's all fair begun again this mornin', it has, an' it's workin' an' hummin' an' scratchin' an pipin' an' nest-buildin' an' breathin' out scents, till you've got to be out on it 'stead o' lyin' on your back. When th' sun did jump up, th' moor went mad for joy, an' I was in the midst of th' heather, an' I run like mad myself, shoutin' an' singin'. An' I come straight here. I couldn't have stayed away. Why, th' garden was lyin' here waitin'!'

Mary put her hands on her chest, panting, as if she had been running herself.

'Oh, Dickon! Dickon!' she said. 'I'm so happy I can scarcely breathe!'

Seeing him talking to a stranger, the little bushy-tailed animal rose from its place under the tree and came to him, and the rook, cawing once, flew down from its branch and settled quietly on his shoulder.

'This is th' little fox cub,' he said, rubbing the little reddish animal's head. 'It's named Captain. An' this here's Soot. Soot, he flew across th' moor with me, an' Captain he run same as if th' hounds had been after him. They both felt same as I did.'

Neither of the creatures looked as if they were the least afraid of Mary. When Dickon began to walk about, Soot stayed on his shoulder and Captain trotted quietly close to his side.

'See here!' said Dickon. 'See how these has pushed up, an' these an' these! An' eh! look at these here!'

He threw himself upon his knees and Mary went down beside him. They had come upon a whole clump of crocuses burst into purple and orange and gold. Mary bent her face down and kissed and kissed them.

From *The Secret Garden* by Frances Hodgson Burnett

Goat comes to the Christmas party

'Hurry! Hurry! Hurry!' said Gran'ma to Araminta. 'It's time to go to the party.'

'Hurry! Hurry! Hurry! said Araminta to Jerome Anthony. 'It's time to go to the party.'

Christmas had come to the country, and there was going to be a party at the schoolhouse. Everybody was going, so Araminta and Jerome Anthony and Gran'ma had to hurry, else they'd be late and miss something.

'I wish Goat could go to the party,' said Araminta, shaking her head sadly. 'It seems a shame that Goat can't have any Christmas at all.'

'Goats don't have Christmas,' laughed Jerome Anthony. 'What ever would Goat do at a party?'

'Hurry! Hurry! Hurry!' said Gran'ma, looking at her watch.

So they put on their hats and coats and mittens. They tied their scarves under their chins, and they started out. It was cold, so they walked fast and it didn't take any time to get to the schoolhouse. If they hadn't hurried they might have been late, for the party was just about to begin.

Everyone was there sitting on the school benches that were pushed back against the wall of the room. The beautiful paper chains and popcorn strings were there on the Christmas tree just where they belonged. And over in one corner was a table filled with cakes and lemonade and candy, for of course a party isn't a party without good things to eat.

'Where is Gran'pa?' asked Jerome Anthony, turning around in his seat. 'I'm afraid Gran'pa is going to be late.'

'Don't you worry,' said Gran'ma, smiling. 'Gran'pa will get here. He has a surprise for you.'

'Surprise!' whispered Araminta, very excited. Then her face was sad. 'Oh dear, I do wish Goat could be here for the surprise.'

Just then there was a little noise at the back door and everyone turned around. Well, you can't imagine what they saw! Santa Claus! There he was in a red suit with white trimmings, and a red cap with a white tassel. And he had the reddest face you've ever seen, with a long white beard at the bottom of it.

'Oh! Oh!' yelled everybody.

'Shh-h-h!' whispered everybody.

For Santa Claus had somebody with him. This somebody was black and white with long floppy ears and a short stumpy tail. This somebody had long curly horns that looked very much like the branches of a tree. This somebody was hitched to a new green wagon. Yes, you've guessed it, Santa Claus had a reindeer with him, and this reindeer was pulling a wagon full of toys!

'Oh! Oh! Oh!' yelled everybody.

'Shh-h-h-h!' whispered everybody.

For Santa Claus and the reindeer were starting up the aisle towards the Christmas tree. They walked along steadily until they came to a bench where Jerome Anthony and Araminta were sitting, and then something very queer happened. That reindeer lifted his stumpy tail; he shook his head and his ears went flip-flop.

'GOAT!' yelled Araminta, jumping up and down. 'Goat has come to the party!'

We can't be sure whether it was Araminta yelling or the sight of the Christmas tree, but anyway, just then Santa Claus's reindeer stopped acting like a reindeer and began acting like a goat instead. He butted Santa Claus out of the way. He broke loose from his wagon. He began *eating* the Christmas tree!

'Hey! Watch out!' said Santa Claus, falling against one of the benches. When he got up, that red face with the long white beard had fallen off.

'Gran'pa!' yelled Jerome Anthony. 'Gran'pa got here after all!'

We can't be sure whether it was Jerome Anthony yelling or the sight of that goat eating the Christmas tree, but anyway, Santa Claus stopped acting like Santa Claus and began to act like Gran'pa instead. He grabbed hold of Goat. But every time he tried to stop Goat eating the popcorn off the tree, Goat reared up and butted him against the benches again.

'Let me help,' said Araminta, jumping up. 'I can manage that Goat.'

She grabbed Goat by his bridle and started to lead him away before he ruined the tree. But just then Goat caught sight of the table full of cakes and candy and lemonade, and he pulled towards that.

Now when goats see something that they want to eat, you know how hard it is to keep them away from it. Araminta pulled and pulled, but it didn't do any good. Goat kept on getting closer and closer to that table of good food.

'Oh! Oh! Oh!' everybody yelled. They didn't want all their party refreshments to be eaten up.

'Shh-h-h!' everybody whispered, because it looked as if Jerome Anthony was going to do something about it.

He took two pieces of chocolate cake from the table and he held them out to Goat.

'Here, Goat!' he said.

Goat looked at the cake held out for him to eat; he reared up on his hind legs and shook those pretend reindeer horns off his short horns; then he ran after Jerome Anthony! Jerome Anthony ran down the middle of the schoolhouse, holding that cake so Goat could see it. Goat ran after him.

'Humph!' said Araminta, taking a deep breath, 'I shouldn't have worried about Goat not having any Christmas. He had more than anybody else.'

Gran'pa put on his red face with the white whiskers and there he was – a Santa Claus again. 'Merry Christmas!' he laughed as he began to give out the toys. 'Merry Christmas!' yelled everybody.

'Maa-aa! Maa-a-a!' came Goat's voice from the schoolhouse yard.

But nobody opened the door to let him in.

Eva Knox Evans

The autograph

One Saturday afternoon Mark was sitting back in an armchair feeling really upset. One leg was in plaster and it was resting on a cushion on a stool in front of him.

'I'm fed up,' he said to his mother.

'Never mind,' she said. 'Broken legs get better, you know. Now why don't you watch the football on television, while I go in the kitchen and make a cake for tea? Shall I switch on for you?'

'No,' frowned Mark. He was still upset. Fancy falling off his bike and breaking his leg. And it would have to happen just when his Dad and his big brother, Steve, had promised to take him to a real football match. His first real football match, in the stadium, and with Vince Oliver playing. Dad's sports paper called Vince Oliver 'the fastest thing on two legs' – and the match was today, and he was going to have to miss it, because of his broken leg.

'I'm fed up,' said Mark again.

'Never mind,' said his Dad, 'I'll bring you my programme back, and I bet they'll be showing the match on telly later this evening. I'll ask Mum to let you stay up to see it.'

'I'm still fed up,' said Mark.

Steve came in with an ice-cream.

'Here you are,' he said. 'I've just bought it for you off Sam's van. He asked how you were, and I said you were fed up because you were missing the match. So he put an extra sprinkle of nuts on top and stuck an extra chocolate flake in – said it was Sam's Special and it would cheer you up.'

Now Mark had to smile and began to lick the ice-cream.

'We'll have to go now, son,' said his Dad, coming in with his red and white scarf around his neck. 'I won't forget your programme.'

'And I tell you what,' said Steve, 'I'll try to get Vince Oliver's autograph for you. His very own name, written by himself in his very own handwriting – how about that?'

Mark felt really cheerful now, and waved goodbye to them and let his mother switch on the television for him, while he enjoyed his Sam's Special. He watched television most of that Saturday afternoon. Then his leg began to itch, and because there was plaster on it, he couldn't get at it to scratch it. Then he began to get stiff sitting in the same position in the same chair for hours on end.

'I hate this plaster,' he said to his mother when she came in to see how he was.

'Never mind,' she said.

Everybody seems to be saying that to me today, thought Mark. But I *do* mind. I don't want a rotten plaster on my leg. I want to be at the match with Steve and Dad. I want to see Vince Oliver play.

'Will you come in the kitchen and ice the top of the cake for me, Mark?' asked his mother. 'I'll let you use the icer to make squiggly patterns, if you like.'

Mark sniffed, then cheered up and hopped into the kitchen on his good leg. He had to hold on to chairs and doorposts to help him. Then his mother helped him up on to a high stool to do the icing.

When his Dad and Steve got in, he could see that their team had won. They both looked pleased. Dad was smiling and Steve was chanting:

'Up the Reds! Up the R-e-ds!'

'Here's the programme,' said Dad, handing it to Mark. 'We won: three-nil.'

'Did you see Vince Oliver?' asked Mark.

'Course,' said Steve. 'He got two of the goals. Guess what, though – near the end of the match he was tackled and he fell against one of the goal posts. They had to help him off.'

'Hey, I hope he's not badly hurt,' said Mark. 'So you didn't get his autograph?'

'No, sorry, I'll try next time he's playing.'

But they found out later that Vince Oliver was to be out of football for some time; he had broken his arm.

Two weeks later Mark had to go back to the hospital. The doctor wanted to see his leg and put on a new plaster. He sat with his Mum in the waiting room. A nurse came in.

'Mark Foster, your turn, please.'

Mark and his Mum went into a little room where another nurse cut down the side of his plaster with a pair of specially strong scissors. After that a doctor examined his leg and said it was mending beautifully. Then the nurse put fresh plaster round his leg. His Mum pushed him back to the waiting room in a wheel-chair and they sat and waited for the plaster to dry.

'Two more weeks, Mark, and you should be playing football again,' smiled the nurse.

His Mum went over to her to make the next appointment for him. The man in the chair next to Mark's had his arm in plaster. He had been listening.

'Do you like football, then?' he asked.

'Oh yes,' said Mark. He told the man about how he'd been going to see his first real football match when he fell off his bike and couldn't go. 'And I specially wanted to see Vince Oliver play,' said Mark, 'so when I had to stay at home, my brother said he'd get his autograph, but he couldn't, because Vince broke his arm.'

'Yes,' said the man with the arm in plaster. 'Yes, I did.'

'*You* did?' said Mark. He stared. 'You? Are you Vince Oliver? But you're not like my pictures of you. You're not in your football things.'

'No, I only wear them for training and for matches,' laughed Vince. 'Usually I wear ordinary clothes. That's why you didn't recognise me. You're used to seeing pictures of me in red and white.'

Mark was so amazed, he couldn't speak. He just stared and stared. Vince Oliver, *the* Vince Oliver, was sitting on the chair next to him. He couldn't believe it.

'Tell you what,' said Vince. 'I can still write with my left hand. Would you like my autograph now – or is it too late?'

Mark could only shake his head. Vince took a pen from his pocket and bent down over Mark's leg. Mark squinted sideways to watch. Vince was writing:

'From one footballer to another. All the best, Vince Oliver.'

The plaster was taken off two weeks later. When the nurse had removed it, Mark said: 'I want to keep that, please. It's my autograph from Vince.'

The nurse looked very surprised, but she gave it back to him. Now it's hanging on Mark's bedroom wall for everyone to see. A little label is pinned next to it. It reads:

'The fastest thing on two legs autographed this for the slowest thing on one leg.'

Margaret Joy

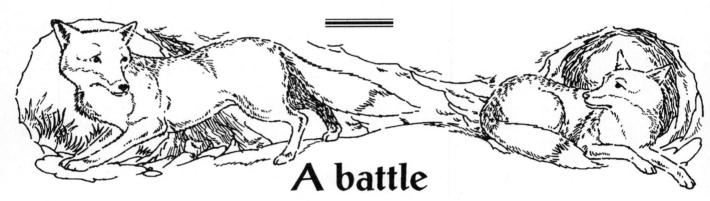

A battle

Fox and Scarface are the leaders of the two groups in the forest. Rather than risk the large scale destruction that a war between the two would bring, Fox decides that he must challenge Scarface alone.

There was an excited buzz of conversation in the set as Fox crept into the tunnel and vigorously shook himself in preparation. Vixen followed him worriedly.

'Must you do this, dearest?' she asked him.

'It's our only hope,' answered her mate. 'If we stay here we shall all be slaughtered or starved to death.'

'But Scarface is treachery itself,' Vixen urged. 'You can't trust him. Even if he should accept your challenge, he might set the others on you if you showed signs of winning.'

Fox smiled gently at her. 'I know you are concerned for me and, were it just you and me, things might be different. But I must take this risk for the others' sake.'

'Oh, why must they always depend on *you*?' she whispered fiercely. But she knew Fox would not be budged.

He answered: 'It was my quarrel in the first place. I'm doing no more than my duty.'

Then she watched him go out into the sunlight.

At Fox's appearance Scarface yapped in triumph. But there was no movement towards him as yet. Only Tawny Owl and Whistler flew to a closer perch, while Kestrel hovered low in the air, ready to swoop down if necessary.

Fox looked at Scarface steadily and then his glance turned to the other assembled throng, who were fidgeting nervously. He noticed Ranger had placed himself well back in the rear.

'You have come in strength, I see,' said Fox coolly. 'Do you need all these to overcome me?'

'You have your followers, also,' Scarface growled.

'No.' Fox shook his head. 'No followers – only friends.'

'Oh yes – your precious friends. Well, today they are going to regret they were ever your friends.'

'You have no dispute with them,' Fox said. 'It is me you fear.'

Scarface's eyes blazed. 'Fear?' he barked. 'You talk to me of fear? I didn't acquire these scars by being afraid. I fear nothing!'

'An idle boast,' Fox answered provokingly. 'I say you fear me; and I believe your fear has governed all your actions since I first came to the Park.'

Scarface tensed himself and seemed about to spring on the taunting Fox, who watched him through narrowing eyes. But then his body relaxed again. 'You are clever,' he said. 'I see what game you're playing.'

'Game?' Fox queried. 'I haven't come to play, but to fight.'

The tribe of foxes began to mill about, murmuring to each other. It was clear their confidence did not match their leader's.

'You are an arrogant creature.' Scarface replied with a cynical grin. 'You would set yourself against the whole pack?'

'Not I,' said Fox. 'Why would I wish to fight them? Only *you* have made yourself my enemy.'

'Oh, so you wish to fight *me*?' Scarface chuckled.

'To settle this issue once and for all – yes.'

'You're a cool customer, I'll give you that. But, you see, the odds are against you.'

'I believe we have an even chance,' Fox replied, 'in a fair fight.'

Scarface fell silent. He seemed to have fallen into a trap. If he should refuse the fight, he would be taken for a coward. He looked up with a grim smile. 'Why do you offer yourself as a sacrifice?' he asked with a grudging respect.

'Because I fight on one condition,' answered Fox. 'If I prove victorious, my friends are to go unharmed.'

Scarface broke into a harsh laugh. 'And all this for a collection of mice and hedgehogs,' he rasped. His face became as hard as stone. 'All right, you have your wish,' he growled. 'And when I've killed you, I'll fight your cubs, one by one, and destroy them all.'

Fox was quite aware of the seriousness of his situation. He had laid his challenge at the feet of an animal more hardened and experienced in battle than any in the whole Reserve. The only advantage on his side was his comparative youth, for he had no illusions about the other's strength and cunning.

The two animals faced each other as if assessing the opponent's qualities. Fox decided to take a defensive stance and so, at Scarface's first rush, he had ample time to swing aside. Then Scarface again rushed headlong at him but Fox dropped flat on his belly, and Scarface's jaws snapped at the air. But the old warrior turned quickly and bit savagely at Fox's scruff. Fox broke free, leaving Scarface with a good mouthful of his fur. The other foxes watched in silence as their leader paused before his next move, while his adversary backed steadily away.

Scarface raced forward again and, with a leap, crashed right on top of Fox, bowling him over and driving all the breath from his body. As Fox lay, gasping painfully, Scarface barked in triumph and, teeth bared, lunged for his throat. But Fox scrambled clear in the nick of time and stood with heaving sides, his lungs labouring with difficulty. From the corner of his eye, he saw the heads of Vixen, Badger and Bold at the entrance to the set, watching in dismay. With a supreme effort he gulped down more air and held himself ready again. Now Scarface came in close,

snapping left and right with his awful jaws, while Fox stepped further and further back at his advance. He felt his enemy's teeth and knew that Scarface had tasted blood. They reached a patch of uneven ground and Fox stumbled, his back legs stepping into a dip of the land. Scarface got a grip on his muzzle and held on, biting deep. But Fox kicked out fiercely with his front legs, knocking him back on to his haunches, and then followed up with a lightning thrust at his front legs.

Scarface yelped with pain as Fox's teeth sank into his lower leg and he tried desperately to shake him off. But Fox held fast, pinioning him to the ground and, as Scarface fell on his back trying to wrestle free, Fox transferred his grip to the other animal's throat. To kill was not in Fox's mind but he resolved to weaken Scarface so much so that he would be in no mood for fighting for long days to come. Even as Scarface struggled at his mercy, Kestrel zoomed down with a message: 'The Warden is coming this way.'

Fox maintained his advantage for a few moments longer and then loosened his grip. Scarface lay still, his breath whistling agonisingly through his open jaws. Fox saw the approaching human figure and then ran for Badger's set. Ranger and the rest of the band had already dispersed. The Warden came up to the injured Scarface and bent to help him. As he did so, the animal made a feeble snap at his extended hand, rolled over on to his feet and limped away, his brush hanging in a dejected manner between his legs.

In the set Fox was greeted as a hero again. Most of the animals thought Scarface was dead.

'I didn't kill him,' Fox said as he sat heavily down by Badger while Vixen carefully and soothingly licked his wounds.

'Why not? Why not?' cried Vole. 'Let us finish him off now!'

'The Warden came,' Vixen explained quietly, pausing for a moment in her work. 'But Scarface is defeated. He won't be back.'

From *Fox's Feud* by Colin Dann

The borrower

There were five children in the family, Mary, Kate, Maurice, Michael and James, and of the five Kate felt sure that she was the most unfortunate. Why was she the one her mother had chosen to run an errand for Mrs Dignam, *again*? Kate must have run hundreds of errands for Mrs Dignam. Hundreds and hundreds, and without so much as an apple, let alone a few sweets, by way of thanks. Not that Kate was a greedy child. True, she had a liking for sweets, but she wasn't mad for them. No, it was just that, like most children, she had a well-developed sense of fair play. And it simply wasn't fair to keep sending her great long errands to the Creamery – three miles, there and back! – with no reward at all.

She laced her boots with a sulky look on her face – this was in the days when children wore boots, and their mothers wore long awkward skirts of serge that swept the floor, and the girls had white pinafores, and hair in plaits, which in the case of Kate's twisted when they should have hung straight. She muttered as she bent down, 'I'm sick of going her errands.'

'What's that?' Her mother was inclined to be severe, and Kate could be defiant.

'Nothing, mother.' What was the use? When you were always told to be polite to the neighbours. In a small farming community such as theirs that was one of the most important rules, and Mrs Dignam – and her easy-going husband – were their next neighbours along the lane.

Mrs Dignam had married late in life and had no children of her own. That was why she was forever borrowing Kate. It wasn't all she borrowed. She was a mean woman and she borrowed in a mean way. It was almost an art with her. She would come in the evening – when it was too late to buy anything – and then ask, with apologies and smiles, for the tiniest little loans possible: 'just half a cup of sugar, Ellen' – this was the children's mother – or 'a few spoonfuls of tea', or 'a wee bit of black thread to sew a button on', all such small items she surely could not be expected to return them – though she easily could have.

'What have I to get this time?' Kate asked.

'A three-pound bag of cooking salt and a pair of mended shoes.'

Oh *no*. Why was it always something heavy and awkward to carry?

'Can Mary come with me?'

'No. She has the geese to bring in.'

They all had jobs to do. It was only a small farm, but fertile, and if everyone worked who could work, they could manage. Kate knew that really, and plodded off alone, burdened with her colossal sense of injustice; wishing too that she had blue eyes like her sister's china doll, and dark hair like Michael's, instead of her own carroty red – because if you were going to be fed up you might as well be fed up about everything.

'Did she give you the money?'

She had reached the Creamery, or rather the fine general store attached to it. Here farmers could buy what they wanted and either pay or have it balanced against the milk they brought in.

Kate handed the manager the Creamery book. 'She said to put it down.'

He was a cheerful young man in a blue striped shirt, and he whistled as he fetched the mended shoes and made them into a parcel with the salt, and jotted down the cost. All this time Kate was gazing at the shelf behind his head – crammed with sweet jars from one end to the other.

'Is that all, the salt and the shoes?'

'Oh, and twopence worth of sweets.'

He looked up at her, surprised.

She had very nearly surprised herself. This was no calculated crime; it was the prompting of the moment. Good or bad? She hadn't time to sort it out – he was speaking again.

'Are these for Mrs Dignam?'

'No, they're for me – for going on so many errands.' Her voice sounded peculiar, and she could feel a blush rising – from her ankles, as it seemed to Kate. He must know she was lying. The manager himself looked like a figure in a distorting mirror, the kind she had seen, once, at the seaside. Very strangely, he winked. He didn't say anything but he winked – and filled in the tuppence. At least, she thought he winked; and in any case she chose gloriously – humbugs, pear drops, treacle toffee and fruit bon bons – you got a lot for tuppence in those days.

Kate could hardly wait to get away with her prize. She hurried gleefully up the lane, telling herself how glad she was and how clever she'd been. Then she stopped and opened the bag. Oh what joy, what satisfaction there would be in that first sweet! And indeed the first one did taste truly delicious. She had chosen a humbug; she was saving the pear drops for Maurice, her friend. And some for Mary? No – Mary would give her away. So would the little ones, without meaning to. She munched her way through a few more. She had really more than, in the circumstances, she could manage. She thought of throwing them away then, but her pride wouldn't let her. She trudged on. She was on the last stretch now, and her mind began flinging up daft, hopeful images of the outcome. Mrs Dignam wouldn't check the book. She would check it, but she wouldn't mind. Transfer of parcel from right arm to left arm. She'd always *meant* for Kate to have a few sweets. Of course, that was it! Nearer home now. She ate a treacle toffee, thoughtfully. She would have liked to save something for her mother – her mother liked fruit bon bons. Was she *mad*? If her mother ever found out – she would *kill* her! She ate another humbug. Trudge trudge, munch munch. Strangely cloying and unattractive that humbug became. Queer hot and cold feelings ran all over her and her heart thumped in a sickly fashion. And here was the Dignams' farm.

There was no one about, only the old dog and he knew her. She crept quietly into the kitchen, put the parcel on the table and made off.

Maybe nothing would happen at all.

The evening passed. The jobs were done, the little ones were in bed and the lamp was lit. Their father was out, somewhere. Their mother was sewing, making, or rather re-making, clothes. Mary was mending socks. They sat in the kitchen by the range, Kate pretending to read and listening to the slow tick-tock of the clock. 'You're safe. You're safe. You're safe,' said the clock. But oh, thought Kate, would bedtime never come?

A hand tapped at the window.

'Can I come in?' A head appeared around the kitchen door.

'Come in, Janet, come in.'

Mrs Dignam came fully into view; in her hand she had the Creamery book. 'There's a little mistake here, Ellen. Look, look, you can see: twopence, and against it, in this column, he's written "sweets"!' Her glance slid from the page, towards Kate. Kate trembled.

'I see,' said her mother, with amazing calmness. 'Come here, Kate. Was this your idea?'

Kate nodded, speechless with fright.

But in the same calm tone her mother continued: 'I think, Janet, you've rather made use of the child – and her shoe leather – but she has done wrong. Hand me my purse, child. You shall have the twopence back.'

From Kate's point of view, there could have been no better answer. But Mrs Dignam took it as a rebuke, which indeed it was. She took it well.

'Oh no, no,' she cried. 'She's a good child. I wouldn't think of it.' Her hand made a small move forward to take the coppers, then drew back. She smiled apologetically and turned to go. Then, as she reached the door – 'I wonder, Ellen,' she said – 'I'm very low for washing soda; could you spare me a small handful?'

Their mother didn't hesitate for a second. 'Well, Janet,' she said. 'It just so happens I can let you have a whole new packet – you can give me one back when you're ready. Run and get it for me, Kate.' And Kate did.

Patricia Miles

The fish angel

Noreen Callahan was convinced that her father's fish store on Second Avenue was, without a doubt, the ugliest fish store on the East Side. The sawdust on the floor was always slimy with fish drippings; the fish were piled in random heaps on the ice; the paint on the walls was peeling off in layers; even the cat sleeping in the window was filthy. Mr Callahan's apron was always dirty, and he wore an old battered hat that was in worse shape than the cat, if such a thing were possible. Often, fish heads would drop on the floor right under the customers' feet, and Mr Callahan wouldn't bother to sweep them up. And as time passed, most of his customers went elsewhere for their fish.

Mr Callahan had never wanted to sell fish in a fish store. He had wanted to be an actor, to do great, heroic, marvellous things on the stage. He tried, but was unsuccessful, and had to come back to work in his father's fish store, the store which was now his. But he took no pride in it; for what beauty was possible, what marvellous, heroic things could be done in a fish store?

Noreen's mother helped in the store most of the week, but Saturday was Noreen's day to help while her mother cleaned the house. To Noreen, it was the worst day of the week. She was ashamed to be seen in the store by any of her friends and classmates, ashamed of the smells, ashamed of the fish heads and fish tails, ashamed of the scruffy cat, and of her father's dirty apron. To Noreen, the fish store seemed a scar across her face, a scar she'd been born with.

And like a scar, Noreen carried the fish store with her everywhere, even into the schoolroom. *Fish Girl! Fish Girl! Dirty Fish Girl!* some of the girls would call her. When they did, Noreen wished she could run into the dark clothes closet at the back of the room and cry. And once or twice, she did.

But pleasant things also happened to Noreen. A few weeks before Christmas, Noreen was chosen to play an angel in the church pageant, an angel who would hover high, high up on a platform above everyone's head. And best of all, she would get to wear a beautiful, beautiful angel's gown. As beautiful as her mother could make it.

Mrs Callahan worked on the angel's gown every night, sewing on silver spangles that would shine a thousand different ways in the light. And to go with the gown, she made a sparkling crown, a tiara, out of cloth and cardboard and gold paint and bits of clear glass.

On the day of the pageant, Noreen shone almost like a real angel, and she felt so happy and light that with just a little effort she might have flown like a real angel, too. And after the pageant, Noreen's mother and father had a little party for her in their living room. Mr Callahan had borrowed a camera to take pictures of Noreen in her angel's gown. 'To last me at least a year of looking,' he said.

For though Mr Callahan hated his fish store, he loved Noreen with a gigantic love. He often told Noreen that some children were the apple of their father's eye, but she was not only the apple of his eye, but the peach, pear, plum and apricot, too.

And Noreen would ask, 'And strawberry?'

'Yes, b'God,' her father would say. 'You're the fruit salad of m' eye, that's what you are. Smothered in whipped cream.'

And so he took picture after picture with the big old camera that slid in and out on a wooden frame. Noreen had a wonderful time posing with her friend Cathy, who had also been an angel in the pageant. But the party came to an end as all parties must, and it was time to take off the angel's gown and the tiara, and become Noreen Callahan again. How heavy Noreen felt after so much lightness and shining. Into the drawer, neatly folded, went the heavenly angel. 'Perhaps next year,' her mother said, 'we'll have it out again.'

That night, Noreen dreamed that she was dancing at a splendid ball in her dress of silver and her crown of gold. Round and round the ballroom she went, as silver spangles fluttered down like snow, turning everything into a shimmering fairy's web of light. And then she was up on her toes in a graceful pirouette. Everyone watched; everyone applauded. As she whirled, her dress opened out like a great white flower around her and... suddenly she felt herself sliding and skidding helplessly. She looked down; the silver spangles had changed to fish scales. The floor was covered with fish heads and fish tails and slimy, slippery sawdust. And everyone was calling: *Fish Girl! Fish Girl! Fish Girl!*

Noreen awoke, not knowing quite where she was for a moment. Then she turned over in the bed and cried and cried, till she finally fell asleep again.

The next week passed in a blur of rain and snow that instantly turned to slush. Every day, when she came home from school, Noreen looked at the dress lying in the drawer. *Wear me, wear me,* it seemed to say. But Noreen just sighed and shut the drawer, only to open it and look again an hour later.

And then, all too soon, it was Saturday. The day Noreen dreaded. Fish store day. How she wished she could turn into a real angel and just fly away.

Suddenly Noreen sat down on her bed. She knew it was decided before she could actually think. The angel gown! How could anyone wait a year to have it out again? She would wear it now. Now! In her father's store. And then people would know that she had nothing to do with that dirty apron and filthy floor. And perhaps those children would stop calling her Fish Girl. She would be a Fish Angel now.

Mrs Callahan saw the gown under Noreen's coat, as Noreen was about to leave the house. She rarely scolded Noreen, but this was too much! It was completely daft! That gown would be ruined; her father would be very angry. Everyone would laugh at her; everyone would think she was crazy! But Mrs Callahan saw that nothing, absolutely nothing, could stop Noreen. And she finally gave in, but not before warning Noreen that next year she would have to make her own dress. An angel's gown in a fish store! Why it was almost a sin!

When Noreen arrived at the fish store and took off her coat, Mr Callahan was busy filleting a flounder. But when he saw Noreen he gasped and nicked himself with the knife.

'*Aggh!*' he called out, and it was a cry of surprise at the gown, and anger at Noreen, and pain from the cut, all in one. He nursed his finger, not knowing what to say to Noreen in front of all those customers.

'What a lovely gown,' said a woman.

'What happened?' asked another. 'Is it a special occasion?'

'His daughter,' whispered a third. 'His daughter. Isn't she gorgeous?'

And Mr Callahan simply couldn't be angry any more. As the customers complimented him on how absolutely beautiful his daughter looked, he felt something he hadn't felt for a long, long time. He felt a flush of pride. Perhaps marvellous things, even heroic things *could* be done in a fish store.

Mr Callahan watched Noreen as she weighed and wrapped the fish, very, very carefully so as not to get a single spot on her dress. Wherever she moved, his eyes followed, as one follows the light of a candle in a dark passage.

And towards the end of the day, Mr Callahan took off his filthy apron and his battered hat. He went to the little room in the back of the store, and returned wearing a clean, white apron.

Christmas came and passed, and New Year, and Noreen wore her gown and tiara every Saturday. And more and more customers came to see the girl in the angel gown. Mr Callahan put down fresh sawdust twice a day, and laid the fish out neatly in rows, and washed and cleaned the floors and window. He even cleaned the cat, and one night in January he painted the walls white as chalk. And his business began to prosper.

The children who had called Noreen *Fish Girl,* called her nothing at all for a while. But they finally found something which they seemed to think was even worse. *Fish Angel,* they called her. *Fish Angel.* But Noreen just smiled when she heard them, for she had chosen that very name for herself, a secret name, many weeks before.

And Saturday soon became Noreen's favourite day of the week, for that was the day she could work side by side with her father in what was, without a doubt, the neatest, cleanest fish store on the East Side of New York.

Myron Levy

Uncle Podger

You never saw such a commotion up and down a house in all your life, as when my Uncle Podger undertook to do a job. A picture would be standing in the dining-room, waiting to be put up, and Aunt Podger would ask what was to be done with it, and Uncle Podger would say,

'Oh, you leave that to *me*. Don't you, any of you, worry yourselves about that. *I'll* do all that.'

And then he would take off his coat and begin. He would send the girl out for nails, and then one of the boys after her to tell her what size to get, and from that, he would gradually work down, and start the whole house.

'Now you go and get me my hammer, Will,' he would shout, 'and you bring me the rule, Tom; and I shall want the step-ladder and I had better have a kitchen chair, too; and Jim! You run round to Mr Goggles, and tell him, "Pa's kind regards and hopes his leg's better and will he lend his spirit-level?" And don't you go, Maria, because I shall want somebody to hold the light; and when the girl comes back she must go out again for a bit of picture-cord; and Tom! – where's Tom? – you come here. I shall want you to hand me up the picture.'

And then he would lift up the picture, and drop it, and it would come out of the frame, and he would try to save the glass, and cut himself; and then he would spring round the room, looking for his handkerchief. He could not find his handkerchief because it was in the pocket of the coat he had taken off and he did not know where he had put his coat, and all the house had to leave off looking for his tools and start looking for his coat while he would dance round and hinder them.

'Doesn't anybody in the whole house know where my coat is? I never came across such a set in all my life. Six of you! – and you can't find a coat that I put down not five minutes ago! Well, of all the –'

Then he'd get up and find out that he had been sitting on it.

And when half an hour had been spent in tying up his finger, and a new glass had been got, and the tools, and the ladder, and the chair, and the candle had been brought, he would have another go, the whole family standing round in a semicircle, ready to help. Two people would have to hold the chair, a third would help him up on it, and hold him there, and a fourth would hand him a nail, and a fifth would pass him up the hammer, and he would take hold of the nail, and drop it.

'There!' he would say in an injured tone, 'now the nail's gone.'

The nail would be found at last, but by that time he would have lost the hammer.

'Where's the hammer? What did I do with the hammer? Great heavens! Seven of you, gaping round there, and you don't know what I did with the hammer!'

We would find the hammer for him, and then he would have lost sight of the mark he had made on the wall, where the nail was to go in, and each of us had to get up on the chair beside him, and see if we could find it; and we would each discover it in a different place, and he would call us all fools, one after another, and tell us to get down.

Then he would use a bit of string and at the critical moment, when the old fool was leaning over the chair at an angle and trying to reach a point three inches beyond what was possible for him to reach, the string would slip, and down he would slide on to the piano, a really fine musical effect being produced by the suddenness with which his head and body struck all the notes at the same time.

And Aunt Maria would say that she would not allow the children to stand round and hear such language.

At last, Uncle Podger would get the spot fixed again, and put the point of the nail on it with his left hand, and take the hammer in his right hand. And with the first blow, he would smash his thumb and drop the hammer, with a yell, on somebody's toes.

Aunt Maria would mildly observe that, next time Uncle Podger was going to hammer a nail into the wall, she hoped he'd let her know in time so that she could make arrangements to go and spend a week with her mother while it was being done.

'Oh, you women, you make such a fuss over everything,' Uncle Podger would reply, picking himself up. 'Why, I *like* doing a little job of this sort.'

And then he would have another try, and, at the second blow, the nail would go clean through the plaster, and half the hammer after it, and Uncle Podger be precipitated against the wall with force nearly sufficient to flatten his nose.

Then we had to find the rule and the string again, and a new hole was made; and, about midnight, the picture would be up – very crooked and insecure, the wall for yards round looking as if it had been smoothed down with a rake, and everybody dead beat and wretched – except Uncle Podger.

'There you are,' he would say, stepping heavily off the chair on to somebody's corns, and surveying the mess he had made with evident pride.

'Why, some people would have had a man in to do a little thing like that!'

Jerome K. Jerome

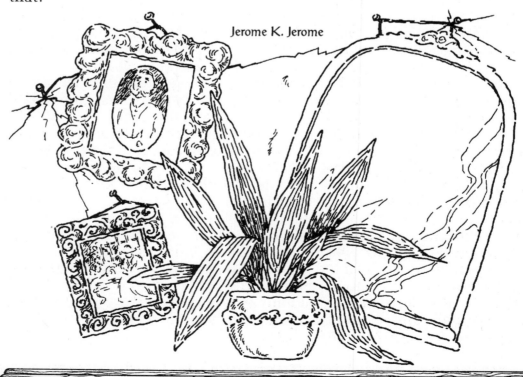

WONDERFUL TO BEHOLD

The magic egg

A long time ago there lived a very poor old couple. The only thing they owned was a hen. One single hen. And even the hen wasn't much use to them, for every time she laid an egg – the egg disappeared. By the time the old woman went to put the egg in her apron and carry it still warm to the cottage, there was no egg. Just like that.

This went on day after day, week after week. The old couple of course grieved at such misfortune.

'How long will the bad luck last?' the old woman wailed as she wrung her hands. The old man shrugged his shoulders and shook his head.

Then the old man had an idea. He would watch the hen very closely. That way he might see what happened to the eggs, or at least get some clues.

As he was watching the hen very quietly, the old man saw her sitting on the nest laying an egg. Now he would know what had been happening! He stayed patiently nearby where the hen couldn't see him. As she jumped off the nest with a flutter and a clucking, the egg slipped out of the nest and rolled onto the road. It kept rolling faster and faster. The man ran after the egg as fast as he could and at last caught up with it. You might think that this is the end of the story – but far from it. The egg turned out to be magic.

As soon as the old man took it in his hands it spoke to him: 'Let me go!'

'No, I need you,' the old man replied.

'Do let me go, Grandpa,' Egg insisted, 'or you'll regret it later.'

These words worried the old man. Who knows what might happen if he didn't obey Egg's command. So he let Egg go.

Now Egg went forth on its own journey. He rolled along, rolled along... and suddenly – stop! He met Lobster.

'Where are you going, Egg?'

'On important business, you shall see; why don't you come along with me?'

'I'll come,' said Lobster, and he followed Egg.

The two set off together. On they went till they met Small Mouse.

'Where are you going, Egg?' Small Mouse asked.

'On important business, you shall see; why don't you come along with me?'

'I'll come,' said Small Mouse. And so the three of them went farther. They travelled until they met Cat.

'Egg! Where are you going with your friends?' Cat wanted to know.

'On important business, you shall see; why don't you come along with me?'

'I'll come.'

And all of them went on together.

After a while they met Rooster-with-spurs.

'Good day, little Egg. Where are you going?'

'On important business, you shall see; why don't you come along with me?'

'Yes I will!' Rooster was happy to follow Egg. And all five of them went towards the woods. But Rooster wasn't the last to join them. At the edge of the woods they met Goat.

'Where are you rushing, Egg, with all your brave companions?' asked Goat, looking down on everybody.

'On important business, you shall see; why don't you come along with me?'

'I'll come along!' Goat agreed, joining the procession.

Egg led them to the heart of the forest, where they soon saw a big house. Now this house happened to belong to foxes. Foxes? Yes, twelve robber foxes. Egg told his companions about this and asked them to wait while he rolled around the house to see what he could see. Then he asked them to follow him inside. There was no one in the house. The foxes were out on a robbing job, Egg said, and he told his companions what to do:

'I am going to lie in the ashes in the bottom of the oven. You, Small Mouse, crawl into that hole in the corner. You, Lobster, get into the kettle of water. You, Cat, lie down on top of the oven. Rooster will get into the attic and you, Goat, hide behind the door.'

Since Egg was their leader, they all did what he advised. Late at night the robber foxes returned. One fox started to make a fire in the oven, but as soon as she came to the hearth – pfft! Egg sprayed ashes into the fox's eyes. Another fox ran to fetch water so as to wash the eyes of the first one. As soon as she came to the kettle, Lobster grabbed her by the paw and pinched it with all his might.

Now Small Mouse squeaked from the hole in the corner, while from the top of the oven Cat made fierce growling noises.

The foxes all became very frightened and jumped out of the door. As soon as they were out of the house, Rooster yelled: 'Koo-ka-re-koo!' And Goat began butting them with his horns.

So what did the foxes do? Of course they abandoned their house and ran so fast the wind couldn't catch them!

This was just what Egg was waiting for. He wanted to find something to take home to the poor old couple. He rolled over to the barn and opened the door. What a surprise! The barn was full of geese and ducks – so many you couldn't count them. And there were also bags of feed. So Egg and his friends loaded themselves up with geese and ducks and bags of grain and corncobs – to take to the old man and his wife.

The old couple welcomed Egg and his companions, and treated them with great respect!

'Lobster – what a marvellous creature,' they said. 'How nice – Small Mouse. Oh, it's good to have a cat. What a handsome rooster! And welcome to you, Goat!' The old couple knew there was plenty of food for everyone. They were no longer poor.

Then they all had a fine feast and ate as much as they wanted.

Retold by Marguerita Rudolph

Stone soup

Once there was a man who spent his days walking about the countryside. Here and there, and now and again, he took a job if he felt like working. He was strolling along a clay road one day, when he saw a stone. It was as big as his fist, as round as the sun, as flat as a chopping-board and as white as the inside of an onion. He picked it up.

Later on, feeling hungry, he called at a cottage and asked for something to eat. The stone was still in his hand. 'What's that you have there?' asked the woman who came to the door.

'Just my soup stone, that's all,' said the man.

'A soup stone! A *soup* stone? I've never heard of such a thing!' said the woman. 'What do you use it for?'

'To make soup. And many a good bowl of soup it's made, although it's years old.'

'Well, *that* is something I'd like to see,' said the woman. 'I've never heard such a yarn before. Soup, indeed!' she laughed. 'Nonsense, nonsense!'

'And nonsense to you!' snorted the man. 'If you let me use your fire and a big pot, I'll soon show you how my stone can make soup.'

'All right, come in. I don't believe it, but I'll get you a pot right away,' said the woman, bustling into her pantry to bring out a pot.

The man dropped the stone into it and partly filled the pot with water, then hung it over the fire. When the pot began to boil he took off its lid, stirred and stirred it, sniffed the steam and then peered into it. 'Mmmmm, it's coming along nicely,' he said.

'How long before it's ready?' asked the woman.

'Not long! And it smells good already,' the man sniffed. 'It'd be even better if it had an onion or two in it.'

'Oh, I can let you have a couple of onions,' said the woman, going to a basket and bringing back some onions.

The man put them in the soup.

After a while he took off the lid again, stirred and stirred the water and onions, sniffed the steam and peered into the pot. 'Mmmmmmmmm! It's going to be good soup from the smell of it,' he said.

'Ah! Is it ready, then?'

'Not quite! But it'll be very good when it is. It'd be even better if I had a spoonful of salt and a few vegetables.'

'I can let you have a carrot or two. And I'll give you some salt,' said the woman, going to a cupboard to bring back her salt-pot and a bunch of carrots, three sticks of celery and a handful of parsley. Into the pot they went.

After a while the man took the lid off the pot again. He stirred it round and round. He sniffed up the steam and was about to speak when the woman said, 'Mmmm! I can smell it now. It's good soup, as you say. Is it ready?'

'Won't be long now! And it's going to be really good soup,' said the man. 'It only needs a little bit of meat and a few potatoes in it to make it the best soup ever to be cooked in this pot.'

'I can easily fix that,' said the woman, hurrying to the cool room to bring back a slab of meat and some potatoes, *and* a chicken and a piece of bacon. 'These will help to make it even more tasty,' she said. They went into the pot. Then the woman said, 'Odds and ends always help to make good, wholesome soup.' And this time, she dropped in the pot a handful of pearl barley, four tomatoes and a piece of parsnip.

When the man took off the lid again he sniffed the steam and rolled his eyes up to the ceiling. 'Perfect soup, just perfect!' he drooled. 'All we need now are two plates and some bread.'

'I'll get those, and some spoons,' said the woman. And within minutes they were eating the good soup. Oh, it was as good as the man had promised. It was so good the woman said wistfully, 'I wish I had a little stone to make soup like this.'

'They aren't easy to come by,' said the man.

'No, I didn't think a soup stone would be,' said the woman. 'Still, there's no harm in wishing for one, I suppose.'

'And your wish will be granted,' said the man. 'You've been good to me, letting me use your pot and fire, so I'll give you my stone.'

'You are kind, but whatever will you do without it?'

'I'll go back to where I found this one,' the man told her. 'I'm sure to pick up another if I look hard enough.'

The woman was so delighted to keep the stone she gave the man a bundle of bread and cheese and apples.

She's still making stone soup, you know, but she always adds some carrots and onions, salt and celery, meat and chicken and bacon and tomatoes, and a handful of barley. It always tastes as good as the soup the man made, which I don't suppose surprises you at all.

Jean Chapman

Why the Manx cat has no tail

On the Isle of Man there live hundreds of cats that have no tails – no, nothing at all where a tail ought to be. And if you asked one of those Manx cats why he had no tail, he would tell you that it was because of a certain stubborn cat who was his mother's, grandmother's, grandmother's, grandmother's... and so on and on... way back to the time of Noah.

And here is how it happened.

Years and years ago Noah built an Ark. He built it large and he built it strong, because Noah knew that one day the rains would fall and the whole world would be flooded. When the Ark was finished, he called to the animals; and, two by two, they came. Day after day, week after week, Noah called. And still they came: large animals and small animals, fat animals and thin animals. And Noah and his wife and his sons found room for them all.

Now Noah himself had a cat that was a family pet. She was a sort of coppery colour, with big, round eyes, a very soft coat and a long and lovely tail. She was an affectionate cat, but she was stubborn, as stubborn as – well, as stubborn as only some cats can be.

The very morning the rains began to fall that cat decided to go out a-mousing. Other cats might hate the rain, but she did not care about a few drops of water. She wanted to go mousing and go mousing she would, even if it were the last thing she did. And it very nearly was!

The rains fell and they fell. It was the kind of morning that no self-respecting mouse would think to venture abroad. So though that copper-coloured cat was a fine mouser, she had no luck at all. But she went on trying.

Still the rains fell and they fell; and then, suddenly, the skies opened and it simply torrented down.

Noah looked out and saw the rains torrenting down, and he began to think that it was time he closed the door of the Ark. And then he saw that copper-coloured cat, the family pet, creeping about outside.

'Puss! Puss! Puss!' he called. 'Come, puss!'

And she heard all right. But what did she do? She waved her tail, careless like, and said to herself, 'I'll catch a mouse this day if it's the last thing I do.'

'Puss! Puss! Puss!' he called again. 'Come now, puss!'

And again she waved her tail, careless like.

'Time to close the door,' said Noah, shaking his head. And then in a loud voice, he cried out, 'Who's out is out and who's in is in!'

This time that cat turned and looked. Oh dear! – there was water lapping up against the foot of the Ark. And oh dear! – there was Noah, closing the huge, heavy door.

Then she was up and off, bounding towards the Ark, running for her life. But that door was slowly, slowly swinging shut... almost... almost...

almost... Then – *whoosh!* – she squeezed herself through the merest crack.

Just in time? No, not quite. For as she came in Noah slammed the door shut, and oh! but it cut off her long and lovely tail.

But she *was* in. So she counted her blessings and sat down, wet through, quite bedraggled and all sore where her tail had been. And there and then she vowed that she would never, never go out in the rain again if she could help it.

Well, the rains fell for forty days and forty nights, and the whole world was flooded. But the Ark floated on the water; and Noah and his family and the animals and the copper-coloured cat were safe inside the Ark. And as time passed, her sore place healed.

After many months the flood subsided and the Ark settled on dry ground. And still the cat counted her blessings. But, there was no denying it, she *did* miss her tail.

Now how she had heard of the Isle of Man, I do not know. But as soon as the Ark had settled on dry ground that stubborn, copper-coloured cat said:

'Bee bo bend it,
My tail's ended;
But I'll go to Man,
As fast as I can,
And get copper nails
And mend it.'

And away she went and travelled the world until she came to the Isle of Man.

But she never did find copper nails nor her lost tail, so she never did mend it. And that is why, to this day, Manx cats have no tails and, of course, like every other cat, they truly hate the rain.

Sophia Morison

The Greenwood

Twelve miles from Nottingham, in the heart of Sherwood Forest, a young man with keen grey eyes sat beside a roaring fire. Robert Locksley was very much alive. The robbers had untied his hands as soon as they had reached their camp, and given him a fine supper. Now they wanted to know all about the young man who had dared to defy their leader – the tall man they called Will Scarlet.

'There is little to tell,' said Robert. 'Locksley Farm came to me from my father, and his father before him. Now it is in the hands of Sir Guy of Gisborne; and I am an outlaw, like yourselves.'

'We are proud to call ourselves outlaws,' Will said quietly, 'for much wickedness is done in the name of the law these days.'

'Death to Prince John!' shouted a black-bearded man from the circle round the fire.

'Death to the Sheriff!' roared someone else. Then everyone began shouting together until the tall man held up his hand. He turned to Robert. 'We are for the King,' he said.

'And I,' said Robert simply. 'May he soon return.'

The tall man again held up his hand. 'We men of Sherwood have been forced to leave our homes and families, to choose a new way of life here in the forest –'

'And kill innocent travellers for gold?' interrupted Robert.

Will tried to explain. 'We take only from those who have stolen from others,' he said.

'And end up thieves and murderers,' Robert added.

'They are all brave men,' said Will. But the outlaws were silent. The young man made them feel uncomfortable.

Robert broke the silence. 'I have seen the faces of the poor,' he said. 'They are not free like you. They are tied forever to cruel masters like Sir Guy of Gisborne. The little they have is taken from them by the men of power.'

'By the Sheriff, more like,' someone said.

'Aye, and that fat Abbot at St Mary's,' added the little man.

'Quiet, Much,' said Will. He was listening intently.

'Steal from the rich, by all means,' continued Robert, 'they have more than enough. But why not give back to the poor what has been taken from them?'

'Rob the rich to feed the poor,' said the black-bearded man, 'is that what you mean?'

'I think so,' said Robert in some confusion. He had not meant to give a speech.

'Will you join us here in the forest?' asked Will suddenly.

Robert laughed. 'I think I have no choice,' he answered. 'But I have much to learn.'

'First you should have a new name,' said Will. Then he smiled. 'You must forgive the rough treatment in the forest: with any luck the Sheriff thinks you dead by now. He must not hear the name of Locksley again.' He looked down at his suit of faded russet, and added, 'I was not born to the name of Will Scarlet.'

'Nor I Jack Smithy,' said the man with the beard.

'They call me Much the Miller,' said the little man.

Will looked at Robert. 'What do you say to Robin O' Greenwood?' he asked.

'Too long,' muttered Jack Smithy.

'Robin Wood?' suggested Robert.

'We have a Wood already,' a new voice said. 'Thomas Wood of Dale.'

Robert pulled his cloak over his head and grinned. 'Shall it be Robin Hood, then?'

'Aye,' said Will, 'Robin Hood will do.'

'Robin Hood is good,' said Jack Smithy, who was somewhat too fond of the sound of his own voice. 'But what can Robin Hood give us in return for his new name? He looks hardly more than a boy.'

'I can plough a straight furrow,' said Robin.

'In the forest!' said Jack in disgust.

'I can tell a good cow.'

'Deer are the only beasts in Sherwood,' Jack growled.

'I can use a bow,' said Robin. 'My father taught me.'

'Not so well as Will, I'll bet,' said someone.

The tall man stepped into the firelight. 'I am glad to meet a fellow archer,' he said. 'Tomorrow we shall test your skill.'

The robbers were impatient. 'The wand, the wand,' they shouted. 'Let us have the contest now.' Robin's father had told him about the wand. It was a whippy length of peeled willow nailed to a tree, almost impossible to hit in broad daylight. Now night was falling fast.

'Jack found your bow in the forest,' said Will, and the black-bearded man handed Robin his beloved silver-tipped bow. Robin peered into the gloom. The wand was barely visible. He took aim and shot. His arrow landed a finger's breadth from the wand. Will's arrow landed quivering between Robin's and the wand. The robbers roared their approval. Robin took a deep breath and shot again. This time the arrow flew straight to the wand and split it clean in two. The robbers gasped.

'Not bad for a farmer's boy,' said Jack.

Will bowed. 'I have never split the wand,' he said.

'Nor had I before this moment,' said Robin. He had surprised himself.

In the months that followed, the outlaws taught Robin everything they knew. He learned how to walk silently in the forest paths, how to hoot like an owl and how to wait for hours in the rain wedged in the fork of a tree. He learned how to fight with knives, how to wrestle, and how to tell a good story.

Robin felt that he had little to offer in return: a keen eye and a sure aim, that was all. But he was wrong. The outlaws found in Robin something that had been missing from their lives. The young man's enthusiasm, his sense of fun and his gentle ways reminded them of the homes and families they had lost. Soon Robin became the undisputed leader of the band.

Within a year over a hundred men had come to Sherwood. They were no longer a dirty, dishevelled band of robbers but a highly trained army, dressed in Lincoln green and dedicated to Robin's rallying call – rob the rich to feed the poor. Many a starving peasant had his grain sack mysteriously filled, and hungry families found food waiting on their doorsteps. People began to talk with awe about Robin Hood and the men of Sherwood. But while the poor folk rejoiced, the rich grew angry. Two men in particular feared and hated the name of Robin Hood – a cold-voiced knight and a little fat man with a gold chain – Sir Guy of Gisborne and the Sheriff of Nottingham.

Sarah Hayes

Hare the Hero

Once upon a time there was a little hare who was afraid of everything. He spent most of his time trembling. The sound of the wind, even a leaf falling, could make him jump. And being a hare, of course, when he jumped, he *jumped!* He was laughed at by all the other hares in the forest. *They* were afraid of the wolf, and the fox, and the bear, as any sensible animal would be. But they weren't afraid of the snow falling, or a bird suddenly taking off from the branch of a tree, as he was.

They called him Trembler.

And then one day, the little hare said to himself, 'Now look here, you're not a little hare any longer! In fact, you're a big hare! *In fact,* you're one of the biggest hares in the forest. IN FACT, it's time you stopped trembling!' Another hare who happened to be going by asked, 'Why are you talking to yourself, Trembler?' 'Don't you call me Trembler!' said the little hare who'd become a big hare. 'I'm tired of being frightened! I'm not going to be frightened any more, by anything! I've done with trembling!'

And he went through the forest telling all the hares the same story. He had simply decided to be brave, that was it! Indeed, he meant to be *very* brave! 'But what about the bear?' they asked. 'The bear! I wouldn't give a couple of acorns for the bear!' 'But what about the fox?' 'The fox! I wouldn't give one of last year's beech nuts for the fox!' 'But what about the wolf?' 'The wolf had better look out, that's all I can say!' And the hare beat the ground with his feet as if it had been a drum.

Now, by chance, a wolf was prowling very near at hand. To tell the truth, he was hoping to catch a hare or two. He could hardly believe his luck when he heard the sounds of a hare or three talking – a hare or four – perhaps a hare or five. Because they'd gathered to hear Trembler beating his feet on the ground and boasting about what he'd do if he caught sight of a wolf. 'And you can stop calling me Trembler!' he was yelling. 'In future I would like to be called... Hare the Hero! When I've eaten up the first wolf to get in my way, I want everyone to call me HARE THE HERO!'

'Ho ho!' thought the wolf. 'So he's going to eat me up, is he? I wonder how he's going to do that? Well, if he manages it, they can call me Wolf the Weakling!' And he crept closer, and made ready to spring.

At which moment Hare the Hero caught sight of him, and was *terrified!* He wasn't just frightened, he was horribly scared! He didn't just tremble: he shook from head to foot. And without thinking, he leapt high into the air, and came down on the wolf's back. He rolled down it, gave another tremendous leap, and made off as fast as he could – actually, even faster than that. He imagined he could feel the wolf's hot breath on his tail. And surely that was the sound of the wolf's teeth snapping together, no more than an inch behind him! He ran until he could run no more. He ran until all the green trees in the forest became one huge hot green blur. Then he fell exhausted under the biggest and thickest bush he could see.

But where was the wolf?

Well, the wolf was running twice as fast in the other direction. When the hare gave his great leap and fell onto the wolf's back, he thought it was a gun being fired. A hunter! It must be a hunter! And while the hare was fleeing one way through the forest, believing the wolf's teeth were snapping together an inch behind his tail, the wolf was fleeing through the forest the other way, believing he could hear only an inch behind *his* tail the bang, bang, bang of shots from the hunter's gun.

It was a long time before the wolf slowed up, and a very long time before he thought it safe to stop running.

As for all the other hares, who'd dived into the nearest bushes, they took longer still to show their noses. And when they did, they talked about nothing but Trembler's bravery. Well, no – it certainly wasn't right to call him Trembler any more. Hare the Hero, that was his name! 'Did you see how he scared the life out of the wolf!' they asked one another. 'He went for him without thinking twice about it!' And some said they'd seen Hare the Hero's teeth closing on the wolf's tail.

But where *was* Hare the Hero? Had he pursued the wolf? Might he even now be making a meal of him? They went searching through the forest. And at last they found him, lying panting under the biggest and thickest bush of all. 'Hare the Hero!' they cried. 'Oh, there you are, Hare the Hero! And we thought you were boasting! Oh, Hare the Hero, how brave you are!'

'Brave?' said the hare. He stopped trembling and came out from under the bush. 'Brave? Oh – why yes, of course. You're right! I *am* brave!' And he beat with his feet on the ground as if it had been a drum. 'And you're all... tremblers!' he cried.

And from that time on, even he believed that he was the bravest hare alive.

A Russian fairy tale retold by Edward Blishen

How Ganesh got his elephant head

Shiva, most powerful god of the Hindus, was married to a goddess called Parvati.

Parvati always kept a guard at the entrance to her palace, so she could be sure of privacy and not be disturbed, especially at bathtime.

'Prepare my bath,' Parvati would say, 'Don't forget to put in milk, honey and almond oil, and make sure it's just the right temperature.' She then would check that the guard was at the door, before stepping into her bathing area. 'Make sure no one enters,' she would say.

Now it so happened, that, one day, Shiva had been out hunting for deer and was on his way home. He arrived at the door to his palace. The guard wasn't sure as to what he should do.

'If I let him in, she'll get annoyed; if I keep him out, he'll get annoyed. I can't win!' the poor guard thought. Eventually he decided to step aside for the Master of the House and Shiva entered.

Parvati was furious and, that evening, summoned all her girlfriends to her.

'What can I do?' she asked. 'The guards will always obey Shiva before me.'

'Why don't you make your own guard who will just do what you say. You are a goddess and have the gift of life, after all,' said one of the girls.

'Great idea! I'll do it right now!' smiled Parvati. She said a prayer, some magic words, and a cloud of sparkle dust exploded in front of her. When it cleared, there stood the most exquisitely beautiful little boy, strong, handsome with cherry brown eyes, long eyelashes, black hair with golden-brown hints in it, a perfect mouth and a small straight nose. He was dressed in green, with gold jewellery.

'My son!' exclaimed Parvati, 'you will be my special protector.'

'What do you want of me, Mother?' asked the boy, turning his face up towards her. He spoke in a clear, sweet voice, and his laugh was like a tinkling bell.

'Stand guard at my door, and let no one enter,' said Parvati, as she went inside, feeling happy and secure at last.

Soon Shiva arrived back at the Palace from his day's hunting. He was surprised to see the boy, and said, 'Stand aside!'

'No! Halt there!' replied the child.

'How dare you! Move out of the way!'

He raised his hand to hit the boy, who managed to duck and level a good karate kick at Lord Shiva.

Thwack!

'Foolish! Don't you know who I am?' the God asked.

'No. And you don't know either!' shouted the boy, who jumped and aimed another careful kick.

Thwack!

Shiva was so cross at this outrage, that he used his laser vision to stare at the boy who had dared to oppose him. He stared and he stared. He stared so hard that the laser beams from his eyes caused the boy's head to fall off his neck.

'Thud,' it went, as it fell on the ground and rolled away. The boy fell down, unconscious.

'What's happened to my son?' cried Parvati, who appeared just at that point, having completed her bath.

'Your son? I didn't have a clue! I'm so sorry,' said Shiva, his face going white as he realised the awfulness of what he'd done. Parvati was in deep distress. She fell back, her eyes closed, into the arms of her servant-girls. She whispered quietly, 'I will wreak death and destruction upon the whole Kingdom if my son is not brought back to life at once,' her eyes still closed.

'Oh dear,' said Shiva. He had to think fast. He summoned his soldiers.

'Go, go to all four corners of the Earth. Search fast, high and low. Bring me back the head of the first creature that you come across.' Shiva turned to his wife.

'It'll be all right, dear,' he tried to soothe her. 'I know some magic whereby the boy will be made well again.' Parvati lay silent, still, and angry. The girls fanned her from head to toe, running around, trying to keep her cool.

Eventually a soldier returned – with the head of an elephant.

Shiva looked at the head, then at the boy.

'You fool – it's not,' he began, but then he looked at Parvati.

'Oh well, it's better than nothing, I suppose,' he said, placing the creature's head on the boy's body. The child sat up and looked around, feeling his head with his hands. He looked questioningly at his mother.

Parvati opened her eyes. Everyone held their breath and waited. She looked at the child. Slowly, she smiled.

'My son, I am glad and grateful that you are alive. To me, you look even more beautiful with your elephant head, for you are still mine. I will give you magic, god-like powers and you will be worshipped and praised throughout the world. You will be called Ganesh.'

And so it came to pass. From that day on, before anyone began a new business, took an exam or built a house, it was Ganesh they prayed to for good luck. The boy with the elephant head became one of the most popular gods of the Hindus.

Indian tale retold by Rani Singh

The girl who loved wild horses

The people were always moving from place to place following the herds of buffalo. They had many horses to carry the tipis and all their belongings. They trained their fastest horses to hunt the buffalo.

There was a girl in the village who loved horses. She would often get up at daybreak when the birds were singing about the rising sun. She led the horses to drink at the river. She spoke softly and they followed.

People noted that she understood horses in a special way. She knew which grass they liked best and where to find them shelter from the winter blizzards. If a horse was hurt she looked after it.

Every day when she had helped her mother carry water and collect firewood, she would run off to be with the horses. She stayed with them in the meadows, but was careful never to go beyond sight of home.

One hot day when the sun was overhead she felt sleepy. She spread her blanket and lay down. It was nice to hear the horses eating and moving slowly among the flowers. Soon she fell asleep.

A faint rumble of distant thunder did not waken her. Angry clouds began to roll out across the sky with lightning flashing in the darkness beneath. But the fresh breeze and scent of rain made her sleep soundly.

Suddenly there was a flash of lightning, a crash and rumbling which shook the earth. The girl leapt to her feet in fright. Everything was awake. Horses were rearing up on their hind legs and snorting in terror. She grabbed a horse's mane and jumped on his back.

In an instant, the herd was galloping away like the wind. She called to the horses to stop, but her voice was lost in the thunder. Nothing could stop them. She hugged her horse's neck with her fingers twisted into his mane. She clung on, afraid of falling under the drumming hooves.

The horses galloped faster and faster, pursued by the thunder and lightning. They swept like a brown flood across hills and through valleys. Fear drove them on and on, leaving their familiar grazing grounds far behind.

At last the storm disappeared over the horizon. The tired horses slowed and then stopped and rested. Stars came out and the moon shone over hills the girl had never seen before. She knew they were lost.

Next morning she was wakened by a loud neighing. A beautiful spotted stallion was prancing to and fro in front of her, stamping his hooves and shaking his mane. He was strong and proud and more handsome than any horse she had ever dreamed of. He told her that he was the leader of all the wild horses who roamed the hills. He welcomed her to live with them. She was glad, and all her horses lifted their heads and neighed joyfully, happy to be free with the wild horses.

The people searched everywhere for the girl and the vanished horses.

They were nowhere to be found.

But a year later two hunters rode into the hills where the wild horses lived. When they climbed a hill and looked over the top they saw the wild horses led by the beautiful spotted stallion. Beside him rode the girl leading a colt. They called out to her. She waved back, but the stallion quickly drove her away with all his horses.

The hunters galloped home and told what they had seen. The men mounted their fastest horses and set out at once.

It was a long chase. The stallion defended the girl and the colt. He circled round and round them so that the riders could not get near. They tried to catch him with ropes but he dodged them. He had no fear. His eyes shone like old stars. He snorted and his hooves struck as fast as lightning.

The riders admired his courage. They might never have caught the girl except her horse stumbled and she fell.

She was glad to see her parents and they thought she would be happy to be home again. But they soon saw she was sad and missed the colt and the wild horses.

Each evening as the sun went down people would hear the stallion neighing sadly from the hilltop above the village, calling for her to come back.

The days passed. Her parents knew the girl was lonely. She became ill and the doctors could do nothing to help her. They asked what would make her well again. 'I love to run with the wild horses,' she answered. 'They are my relatives. If you let me go back to them I shall be happy for ever more.'

Her parents loved her and agreed that she should go back to live with the wild horses. They gave her a beautiful dress and the best horse in the village to ride.

The spotted stallion led his wild horses down from the hills. The people gave them fine things to wear: colourful blankets and decorated saddles. They painted designs on their bodies and tied eagle feathers and ribbons in their manes and tails.

In return, the girl gave the colt to her parents. Everyone was joyful.

Once again the girl rode beside the spotted stallion. They were proud and happy together.

But she did not forget her people. Each year she would come back, and she always brought her parents a colt.

And then one year she did not return and was never seen again. But when hunters next saw the wild horses there galloped beside the mighty stallion a beautiful mare with a mane and tail floating like wispy clouds about her. They said the girl had surely become one of the wild horses at last.

Today we are still glad to remember that we have relatives among the Horse People. And it gives us joy to see the wild horses running free. Our thoughts fly with them.

Paul Goble

The ghost who came out of the book

There was once a very small ghost who lived in a book – a book of ghost stories, of course. Sometimes people caught a glimpse of it and thought it was some sort of bookmark, but mostly people did not see it at all. When anybody opened the book to read it the ghost slipped out from between the pages and flew around the room, looking at the people and the people's things. Then, when the ghost saw that the person reading the book was growing sleepy or was finishing the story, it slid back into the book and hid between the pages again. There was one page it especially liked with a picture of a haunted house on it.

One evening a child was reading the ghost stories and the ghost slipped out of the book as usual. It flew around the top of the room and looked at spiders' webs in the corners of the ceiling. It tugged at the webs and the spiders came out, thinking they'd caught something. Then the very small ghost shouted 'Boo!' at them, frightening them so that they ran back into their cracks and corners to hide. While the ghost was doing this, the child's mother came in, shut the book, kissed the child and put the light out, all in a second or two. The ghost was shut out of the book and left outside in the world of the house.

'Oh well,' said the ghost, quite pleased, 'a good chance to try some haunting on a larger scale. I'm getting a bit sick of spiders anyway.'

The door was shut with an iron catch so the ghost couldn't get into the rest of the house. It just flew around the bedroom a few times and went to sleep at last in the folds of the curtains, hanging upside-down like a bat.

'What a day to look forward to tomorrow!' it thought happily just before it went to sleep. 'I'll scare everyone in the place. I might not bother to go back to the book again.'

But alas, the next morning the ghost slept in.

The mother of the house came in briskly and flicked the curtain wide. The ghost, taken by surprise, broke into two or three pieces and had to join up again.

'There's a cobweb up there,' the mother of the house said, and before the ghost was properly joined up again she vacuumed it into her vacuum cleaner. Of course, a vacuum cleaner was nothing to a ghost. This ghost just drifted straight out again, but it certainly felt shaken and there was dust all the way through it.

'Now I am getting very angry,' the ghost said to itself, and it followed the mother of the house into the kitchen and hissed a small buzzing hiss into her ear.

'Goodness, there's a fly in the kitchen,' said the mother, and she took out the fly spray and squirted it in the direction of the hiss.

Being a ghost, the ghost didn't breathe, but the fly spray made it get pins and needles all over and it went zigging and zagging about the kitchen, looking like a piece of cobweb blown about the kitchen by a playful breeze. At last it settled on the refrigerator.

'I'll just take things quietly for a bit,' the ghost whispered to itself. 'Things are getting too much for me.' It watched the mother dust the window ledges.

'Why does she do that?' the ghost wondered, for the dust looked like speckles of gold and silver and freckles of rainbow. Some dots of dust were like tiny glass wheels with even tinier glass wheels spinning inside them. Some specks were whole worlds with strange islands and mysterious oceans on them, but all too small, too small for anyone but a very small ghost to see.

But when the mother began to make a cake the ghost gasped, for she poured in a measure of sugar that looked like thousands of ice diamonds all spangled and sparkling with white and blue and green. 'Let me have a closer look at them,' the ghost murmured to itself, and it flew down into the sugar. At that moment the mother of the house began to beat the cake mixture with her electric egg beater.

'Help!' screamed the ghost as it was whirled into the sugar and butter and got runny egg all over it.

The cake mixture was so sticky that the ghost got rather glued up in it, and before it knew what was happening it was poured into a greased tin and put into the oven. Being a ghost, nothing dangerous could happen to it. In fact the warmth of the oven was soothing and the ghost yawned and decided, as things were so unexpected and alarming outside, to stay where it was. It curled up in the centre of the cake and went to sleep.

It did not wake up until tea time. Then it heard voices.

'Oh boy – cake!' it heard the voices say.

'Yes,' said the mother of the house. 'I made it this morning.' And in the next moment a knife came down and cut the ghost in two. It joined up again at once, and when the slice was lifted out of the cake the ghost leaped out too, waving in the air like a cobweb and shouting, 'Boo!'

'Oh!' cried the children. 'A ghost! A ghost! The cake's haunted.'

'Nonsense – just a bit of steam,' said the mother firmly, touching the cake with the back of her hand. 'Funny thing though – it's quite cool.'

'Perhaps it's a sort of volcano cake,' the father suggested. 'Never mind! It tastes lovely.'

'It tastes haunted!' the children told each other, for they were clever enough to taste the ghost taste in between the raisins, a little bit sharp and sour like lemon juice.

The ghost meanwhile flew back to the bedroom where the book lived.

'First the whirlwind and then the desert,' it said to itself, thinking of the vacuum cleaner and the vacuum cleaner's dust bag. 'Then the ray gun and after that the treasure,' (thinking of the fly spray and the sunlit dust). 'Then the moon-mad-merry-go-round and the warm sleeping place,' (that was the electric egg beater and the oven). 'And then the sword!' (that was the knife).

'But I did some real haunting at last – oh yes – real haunting and scared them all. "Boo!" I cried, and *they* all cried, "A ghost! A ghost!"'

That night someone picked up the book of ghost stories and opened it at the very page the ghost loved best – the one with a picture of a haunted house on it. The ghost flew in at the door of the haunted house and looked out from behind the curtain of the haunted window. 'Home again!' it said. 'That's the best place for a small ghost. Small but dangerous,' it added. 'Quite capable of doing a bit of haunting when it wants to.'

Then the book was closed and the very small ghost went to sleep.

Margaret Mahy

The dragon and Saint George

There are no dragons today – mainly thanks to the knights and heroes who so thoughtlessly rode about the place killing them off. This is a pity, for dragons must have been astonishing creatures; part snake and part crocodile, with bits of lion, eagle and hawk thrown in for good measure. Not only could they leap into the air and fly (a tremendous feat when you think how heavy their scales must have been) but they could also run at great speed. Not that a dragon would ever run away. Dragons were generally very brave creatures. When they were angry or frightened, smoke would come hissing out of their nostrils. When things got really rough, flames would rush out of their mouths. But there was no such thing as a cowardly dragon.

Only the Chinese understood and admired the dragon. It was often said that some of the greatest Chinese emperors had been born the sons of dragons. Dragon bones and teeth were used as medicine. A dragon guarded the houses of the Chinese gods and brought rain to the earth when the crops needed it. That is why the Chinese still fly dragon kites and honour the dragon by including paper models of it in their New Year celebrations. The Chinese really did like the dragon.

But in fourth century Palestine – when Saint George was born –

dragons were more feared than admired. It is true that they did have some unsettling habits. They tended to live in rather dank and nasty caves, for example, often guarding huge piles of treasure which had almost certainly been stolen from somebody else. They also had an unhealthy appetite for human flesh, their favourite food being princesses – although any young woman would do. But they were not the only man-eating animal on the globe. It was just that they got all the bad publicity.

Anyway, Saint George was the most famous dragon-killer of all – which is strange because he never actually killed a dragon. The other strange thing is that he really was born in Palestine, even though he later became the patron saint of England.

His father was a high-ranking officer in the Roman army and for a time George too served as a soldier, under the Emperor Diocletian. He was converted to Christianity at a time when the Christians were suffering their worst persecution and travelled the world spreading the gospel and doing good.

His encounter with the dragon happened at a small town called Silne. Today Silne has become known as the city of Beirut. And this is where the story begins.

The people of Silne had lived in fear of the dragon for many years. It lived in a cave on the edge of a stagnant lagoon a few miles from the town. Now the vapours from this lagoon would often be carried by the wind into the town and the people came to believe that the dragon was responsible for the rotten smell that seeped through their streets. So they began to feed the dragon two sheep every day in the hope that it would go away. Of course, once the dragon got used to a free luncheon at twelve o'clock regularly, it decided to settle down and stay. Perhaps it even decided that the townspeople must be genuinely fond of it because they treated it so well.

Certainly it had no idea that they were afraid.

Eventually the townspeople – who really were rather daft – began to run out of sheep. So a council was called at which all the most important people and the king himself met to decide what they were to do.

'We have given the dragon one thousand of our sheep,' the minister for external affairs said. 'But still it won't go away.'

'Perhaps it won't go away,' the minister for internal affairs said, 'because it does not like sheep.'

'I agree,' the minister for ministerial affairs said. 'But what are we to give it instead?'

Then the king spoke and his face was grim.

'It is well known,' he said, 'that dragons like the taste of children. We must give him our children. Once a week we will feed the dragon with our sons and daughters.'

The result of this edict was a frightful commotion which took several minutes to quieten down. Then the king spoke again.

'We will have a lottery,' he continued. 'Every child in the town will be given a number. Once a week a number will be drawn out of a hat. The child that has that number will be given to the dragon in order to save the town.' He rose to his feet. 'That is my law,' he concluded. 'There are to be no exceptions.'

Three months passed during which time no fewer than a dozen children were torn from their weeping parents, tied up and left outside the dragon's cave. Seven boys and five girls met this terrible end, the flesh picked so cleanly from their bones that the little skeletons gleamed pure white in the morning sunlight. As for the dragon, it noticed the change in its feeding. It was even a trifle puzzled. But the king had been quite right to say that it would like the taste. In fact it found children delicious. And so it stayed.

By the time George arrived, an atmosphere had descended on Silne more poisonous than any mist that had been blown in from the lagoon. Every Tuesday, the day of the lottery, the streets were so silent that if the town had become a cemetery you wouldn't have noticed the difference. Few people left their homes and those that did went about their business with a pale face, their mouths stretched in a grimace of fear, each avoiding the other's eyes. Then at midday a bell would ring. Soldiers would knock on the door of a house somewhere in the town. A great cry

would break the silence. And everywhere parents would hug their children and thank the gods that their number had not been chosen.

Saint George came on a Tuesday afternoon, a few hours after one of the lotteries had ended. It didn't take him long to find out what was happening in Silne and when he did find out he shook his head, half in astonishment, half in despair. Straight away he went to the palace to find the king, and as he walked into the throne-room he heard the following conversation.

'You can't!' the king was saying. 'I forbid it!'

'But you told us to,' one minister replied.

'You made the law,' a second said.

'And you said no exceptions,' a third added.

'But she is a princess... my daughter.' Tears ran down the king's cheeks. 'She didn't even tell me that she had been given a number. When I find the idiot who gave her a number, I'll...'

'The princess was not given a number,' the first minister interrupted. 'She took one. She wanted to be like all the other children.'

'My only child!' the king wept. 'You can't do it!'

'It is too late, your majesty,' the second minister said. 'It is already done.'

Saint George realised that there was no time to waste. He left the palace without even introducing himself, leapt onto his horse and rode out of the town in the direction of the lagoon. It wasn't difficult to find. The stench from the stagnant water was so strong that he could literally follow his nose.

The sound of weeping told him that he had found the cave and that, contrary to what the minister had said, he was not too late. The dragon had overslept that day and the princess was still alive, sitting on the ground with her hands tied behind her back. Saint George got off his horse and walked over to her, and at that precise moment there was a sudden rumble from inside the cave and the dragon appeared.

The dragon was far smaller than Saint George had expected – not a lot larger than his horse. It was bright green in colour with a peculiar, misshapen body. Its wings, for example, were far too small to enable it to fly. On one wing there was a pink ring and on the other a red one. It had two rather squat legs and claws and a long, serpent-like neck. But the only really menacing thing about it was its teeth which were white and very sharp. (The most accurate picture of the dragon was painted in the fifteenth century by an Italian called Uccello. You can see it hanging in the National Gallery in London.)

When the princess saw the dragon, she closed her eyes and waited for the end. But Saint George wasn't afraid.

'Naughty dragon!' he exclaimed. 'Do you really mean to eat this young girl?'

The dragon growled uncertainly. The girl opened her eyes.

'Do you not know that eating people is wrong?' Saint George continued. 'It's bad for dragons. And it's even worse for people!'

Smoke trickled out of the dragon's nostrils and formed a question mark over its head.

'Enough of this foolishness!' Saint George untied the girl and helped her to her feet. Then he took a ribbon from her dress and tied it round the dragon's neck. 'Let us go back to Silne and talk this over.' He bowed to the princess. 'I must say, lady,' he said, 'you will make a wiser and kinder ruler than your father. That much your actions have shown.'

You can imagine the uproar in Silne when Saint George and the princess returned, leading the dragon on a ribbon. Suffice it to say that once they understood what had happened, the entire town converted to Christianity.

And so, in fact, did the dragon.

A short while later the king retired from the throne and his daughter, who had in the meantime married a neighbouring prince, became queen. The two of them ruled well and wisely for many years and it would be nice to think that the dragon ended its days in the palace gardens, a friend and playmate of the queen's children, and even – although perhaps this is asking too much – a vegetarian.

Anthony Horowitz

Football on a lake

The two Chans, father and son, were wealthy landowners who lived near a great lake. More than anything, they enjoyed boating; but they were also known throughout the country as famous footballers. Even up to the time that he was forty, father Chan went on with the game; and he might have been playing until he was sixty, if he hadn't come to a sad end, being lost in a boating accident on the lake. Nobody knew just what happened on that evening; but next day the boat was found drifting bottom upward, and of old Chan there was no trace.

For a long time after that had happened, young Chan wouldn't go near the lake; he left it to his serving boys to keep the boat in repair, and do his fishing for him. And then one moonlit evening, as he was taking a solitary walk, thinking melancholy thoughts and not heeding where he was going, he absent-mindedly wandered down to the lake close to the place where the boat was moored.

The moonlight lay along the water in a broad glittering path. Young Chan, still almost absent-mindedly, unmoored the boat, edged it into the water, jumped in, took up the oars, and rowed out along the glittering trackway of the moon.

Now all around him was silence, except for the swish, swish of the oars as they dipped and rose. And then suddenly young Chan heard a very strange flurry of noise and saw a very strange sight. Up out of the lake rose five men carrying a huge mat. They spread the mat upon the surface of the water, and then they dived down again, and came up again bringing food in silver dishes, and wine in wonderful glass goblets that shone and twinkled in the moon's rays. And when all was ready, three of the men sat down to dine, whilst the other two, an active man and a lad, waited on them.

Not one of those people took any notice of Chan, or of his boat. But Chan took notice of them; in fact he couldn't take his eyes off those three who were dining. Strangely enough, he couldn't see their faces, though of course they must have had faces! What he did see, and wonder at, was the magnificence of their clothes. One was dressed in a blue robe, two were dressed in white robes. The blue robe was sparkling with sapphires, the white robes sparkled with diamonds. All three wore big turbans on their heads, and the turbans also sparkled with jewels. And if the rainbow has seven colours, those turbans had more, and the colours kept shifting and changing so that it made young Chan feel giddy to look at them. So he turned his attention to the two servants: the active man and the lad. The lad had goggle eyes and a pouting mouth; he reminded young Chan of a carp. But when young Chan looked at the man, his heart seemed like to jump clean out of his body, for surely, surely that serving man was his father! But no, no, it couldn't be; for when the serving man spoke to the boy, giving him some sharp directions, that serving man's voice was shrill as the wind whistling through rushes, and never in his life had young Chan heard his father speak like that!

Well, by and by, when the three who were feasting had eaten and drunk their fill, one of them said, 'Now we will have a game of football! You, boy, bring up the ball.'

The boy dived down under the water, and the next moment came up again carrying a monstrous ball. It was so large that he could scarcely get his arms round it to carry it; it was transparent, but it seemed to be made of silver, glittering both inside and out. Young Chan's eyes were so dazzled that it was all he could do to look at it.

The three men got up from the table. The table, with its silver dishes, glass goblets and all, together with the mat, sank gently down under the water, and was lost to sight. The man in the blue robe turned to the serving man and said, 'Now, famous footballer, show us one of your kicks!'

The serving man took a run at the ball and gave a kick. Up went the ball twenty feet into the air, sparkling and shining. Down it came again, up it went again, the three lake men taking sides, one with the serving man, two against. Chan couldn't see any goals, and the game seemed to have no rules. It was just a scuffle, two against two, the glittering ball whirling up, bouncing down, faster, and faster, and *faster*.

Now young Chan was standing up in the boat. He was so excited that he began to shout. But nobody took any notice of him, until – well, what do you think? The ball, after an extra vigorous kick from the serving man, which seemed to send it flying up almost as high as heaven, came flying down again, and landed in the boat right at young Chan's feet. That was more than young Chan could bear: join in the game he must and would! And with a loud shout he kicked the ball as hard as he could.

But the ball was as light as a feather, and as soft as rice paper. Young Chan's foot went right through it. Still, up it went: up and up and up,

with its many coloured lights streaming from the hole that Chan had made in it. And then, as swiftly as it had flown up, down it came again, until it touched the water, when it fizzed and went out.

'Well kicked, well kicked indeed!' shrilled the serving man who was so like Chan's father, yet whose voice was so different. 'Why, I remember in the old days when I was at home, and my son, young Chan, and I were famed throughout the country for – well, there, I gave such kicks as that... But –'

'Father, Father,' cried young Chan, 'don't you know me? Look at me, I *am* young Chan – I *am* your son.'

The serving man gave a shout of joy. He came rushing over the surface of the water towards the boat. But the three men of the lake, the men with the big turbans and the sparkling robes, were screaming with rage. Now from under those sparkling robes they drew sharp swords. They rushed across the water, waving those swords, and shrieking, 'Kill the scoundrel! Kill the scoundrel who has spoiled our game!'

Young Chan could never clearly remember what happened after that. He had drawn his own sword, he was fighting for his life, hacking away at the turbaned heads and the long white arms of the lake men. And Chan's father was catching hold of the lake men's legs, and was dragging them away from the boat, until first one, and then another, and then the third of the lake men fell back under the water. Old Chan scrambled into the boat, plumped down in the stern and took the tiller, young Chan took the oars... And the next moment there they were, old Chan and young Chan, making for land.

But they were not safe yet. Suddenly a huge mouth yawned open in the lake. And out of that huge mouth came a roaring wind which lashed the water into monstrous waves. On came the huge mouth, nearer and nearer: in another moment the Chans' boat would have been swallowed, had not father Chan seized one of two great flat stones, which were kept in the boat to use as anchors, and thrown it bang into the gaping mouth. The gaping mouth, sucking on the stone as if it had been a lollipop, disappeared under the water. Then the lake became calm again, and the two Chans got safe to shore.

And if, that evening, there were any two men in this world happier than old Chan and young Chan, all I can say is that you would have to go a very long way to find them. But I doubt if they ever went boating on that lake again.

Ruth Manning-Sanders

A visit from St Nicholas

'Twas the night before Christmas, when all through the house
Not a creature was stirring, not even a mouse;
The stockings were hung by the chimney with care,
In hopes that St. Nicholas soon would be there;
The children were nestled all snug in their beds,
While visions of sugar-plums danced in their heads;
And mamma in her kerchief, and I in my cap,
Had just settled our brains for a long winter nap –
When out on the lawn there arose such a clatter,
I sprang from my bed to see what was the matter.
Away to the window I flew like a flash,
Tore open the shutters and threw up the sash.
The moon, on the breast of the new-fallen snow,
Gave a lustre of midday to objects below;
When what to my wondering eyes should appear
But a miniature sleigh and eight tiny reindeer,
With a little old driver, so lively and quick,
I knew in a moment it must be St. Nick.
More rapid than eagles his coursers they came,
And he whistled, and shouted, and called them by name:
'Now, Dasher! now, Dancer! now, Prancer and Vixen!
On, Comet! on, Cupid! on, Donner and Blitzen!
To the top of the porch, to the top of the wall!
Now, dash away, dash away, dash away all!'
As dry leaves that before the wild hurricane fly,
When they meet with an obstacle, mount to the sky,
So up to the house-top the coursers they flew,
With the sleigh full of toys – and St. Nicholas too.
And then in a twinkling I heard on the roof
The prancing and pawing of each little hoof.
As I drew in my head, and was turning around,
Down the chimney St. Nicholas came with a bound.
He was dressed all in fur from his head to his foot,
And his clothes were all tarnished with ashes and soot;
A bundle of toys he had flung on his back,
And he looked like a peddler just opening his pack.

His eyes how they twinkled! his dimples how merry!
His cheeks were like roses, his nose like a cherry;
His droll little mouth was drawn up like a bow,
And the beard on his chin was as white as the snow.
The stump of a pipe he held tight in his teeth,
And the smoke it encircled his head like a wreath.
He had a broad face and a little round belly
That shook, when he laughed, like a bowl full of jelly.
He was chubby and plump, – a right jolly old elf,
And I laughed, when I saw him, in spite of myself.
A wink of his eye and a twist of his head
Soon gave me to know I had nothing to dread.
He spoke not a word, but went straight to his work,
And filled all the stockings; then turned with a jerk,
And laying his finger aside of his nose,
And giving a nod, up the chimney he rose.
He sprang to his sleigh, to his team gave a whistle,
And away they all flew like the down of a thistle;
But I heard him exclaim, ere he drove out of sight,
'Happy Christmas to all, and to all a good night!'

Clement Clarke Moore

On Christmas Eve

On Christmas Eve at half-past two
Sleep tight for Santa Claus is due.
In your garden, by the hedge,
Stand his reindeer and his sledge.
Down your chimney he will squeeze
With soot and birds' nests on his knees;
Using language rather shocking,
Stuffing toys into your stocking.
Oh! what joy when day is dawning
To see your toys on Christmas morning.

Geoffrey R. Clarke

The legend of Ra and Isis* of Ancient Egypt

Isis wished to become great and powerful,
a maker of things, a goddess of the earth
'Can I not become like Ra?' she asked
And so it was that Isis went to Ra
where he grew old and dribbled and slobbered
and Isis took that spit where it fell to the earth
and kneaded it and shaped it in her hands
till it became the snake.
And it came about that the snake bit Ra
and Ra came to Isis and spoke like this:
'As I went through the Two Lands of Egypt
looking over the world I have created,
something stung me
something, I know not what

is it fire?
is it water?
I am colder than water
I am hotter than fire
my flesh sweats
I shake
what I see, fades in front of me
I can no longer see the sky itself
sweat rushes to my face
as if it were a summer's day.'

Then Isis spoke to Ra:
'It is a snake that has bitten you:
a thing, that you, yourself, have created
has reared up its head against you?
I say to you,
it is my power, my words
that will drive out the poison of the snake
I will drive it from your sight

*Ra is the most important god of Ancient Egypt. Isis is the mother of the gods.

I will put it beyond the reach of the rays of the sun
So, godly father,
tell unto me, your secret name,
for if you want to live
it is your secret name that will save you.'

and Ra said
'I have made the skies and the earth
I have made the mountains
I have made all that is above them
I have made the great and wide sea
I have made the joys of love
I have stretched out the two horizons
like a curtain
and I have placed the gods there

when I open my eyes
I make light
when I close them
darkness comes.
The waters of the River Nile rise
when I say so
yet the gods themselves do not know
my secret name
I have made the hours
I have made the days
I have made the festivals of the year
I have made the floods of the River Nile
I have made fire
I provide food for the people in their houses

I am called Khepera in the morning
I am called Ra at Midday
I am called Tmu in the evening'

But the poison did not leave the body of Ra
and poison bit into him deeper and deeper

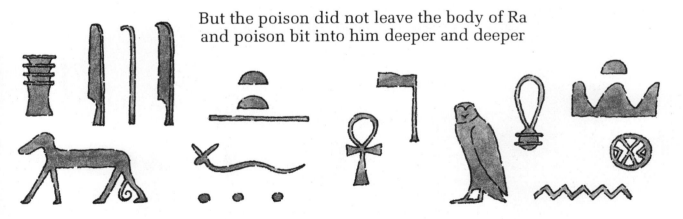

and the great god could walk no more.
Then Isis said to Ra
'But you have not said your secret name
Tell it me now
and the poison will flow from your body
for he who tells his secret name
will live.'

Now the poison burned like fire
fiercer even than a flame
fiercer even than a furnace
and so the great god said
'I will allow you, Isis
to search into me
so that my secret name can pass from me to you.'

Then the great god hid himself
from the other gods
and his place in the Boat of a Million Years was empty

The secret name of the great god, Ra
was taken from him
and Isis the maker of magic
said,
'Poison go!
Flow from Ra now!
It is my magic that moves
It is I
who can make the poison surrender
and flow out on to the earth

Ra live!
Poison die!
Poison die!
Ra live!
These are my words, I am
Isis, the great goddess
the queen of the gods
the one and only
who knows Ra by his secret name.'

From *The Papyrus of Turin* adapted and retold by Michael Rosen

PAST AND PRESENT

Daedalus and Icarus

Of all the Greeks, Daedalus, an Athenian, was most widely known, throughout the ancient world, as a cunning craftsman, artist and inventor. He it was who perfected the art of sculpture. There had been statues before his time, but none had ever been so lifelike as those of Daedalus. They were famous not only in Greece but over the sea in Egypt and other parts of Africa. In Egypt he was worshipped as a god. But he was not simply a sculptor, he was also an inventor and an improver of all works useful to man. He built baths in Greece and a great reservoir in sun-baked Sicily. He constructed the masts and yards of ships, while his son Icarus was thought to have been the inventor of sails.

One of the principal crafts invented by Daedalus was that of carpentry. He was said by ancient writers to have invented glue, the plumb-line, the gimlet, the axe and the saw. But some say it was his pupil Perdix who invented the saw, making the first examples from the backbones of big fish.

Daedalus had become very proud of his world-wide reputation as a sculptor and inventor, and he was glad to take as a pupil his sister's son, Perdix. But Perdix became so quick and clever a pupil that people began to say he was a better craftsman than his master. This made Daedalus jealous. One day, in rage and envy, he took the young man to the top of a high tower he had built in order, as he said, to show him the wonders of Athens. Then, when Perdix was gazing out towards the sea, Daedalus pushed him from the top of the tower, intending to kill him. But the young man was protected by the goddess Athene, who turned him into a partridge before he hit the ground. So by becoming a bird, Perdix narrowly escaped death, and from that time to this the partridge has always flown low.

For his attempted murder Daedalus was condemned to death by the Athenian court of justice. No sooner had he heard his sentence than the famous craftsman fled the city and took refuge in the island of Crete. King Minos had already heard of Daedalus's great skill as an inventor, so he welcomed him into his service and made him construct many ingenious things at his palace of Cnossos.

Now the god Poseidon had sent a beautiful white bull to Crete with orders that it should be sacrificed to him there. But Minos's wife Pasiphae fell in love with the bull, and persuaded her husband not to sacrifice it. In revenge Poseidon caused Pasiphae to give birth to a monster with the head of a bull and the body of a man. This was the famous Minotaur, and it was such a cause of shame to King Minos that he determined to hide it. Accordingly he sent for Daedalus and made him construct a hiding-place in which the monster might live without being seen. Daedalus built a maze or labyrinth, in which a series of cunning passages led to the centre. So intricate was the labyrinth that Daedalus himself could scarcely find his way out to the entrance. Here the Minotaur was able to stamp about and charge angrily back and forth amidst the maze of alleyways unseen by anyone.

'This is indeed a marvellous construction,' said Minos, 'and it is easy to see that you are the cleverest designer the world has ever seen.'

So Minos kept Daedalus in Crete, making him construct other marvels of ingenuity – baths and fountains, temples and statues, paved floors and splendid flights of stairs.

Then at last Daedalus grew tired of the service of King Minos and longed to return to Athens, where he felt that his crime might have been forgotten or at least forgiven. He had brought with him to Crete his young son Icarus, and the boy too, now grown to manhood, wished to see his native land. But the craftsman could at first think of no way of escape. Crete was an island far distant from Athens, and Daedalus and his son could not build a ship in secrecy and man it for the voyage home. But his cunning brain was hard at work. At last he hit on the most daring invention of his life. Many an hour he had spent looking thoughtfully at the sea-birds as they wheeled and circled about the rocky coast. 'Ah,' said he, 'if only I could fly like them! But why not? The gods have not given men wings, but they have given them a brain and hands to fashion wings for themselves.'

So in a secret place, hidden from idle curiosity, he collected together all the feathers of birds he could find, great and small. He sent his son Icarus about the island to bring back as many as he could. Then he laid them out on the ground in order – first the big feathers, then the small. When he decided he had enough, he fastened them together with wax, curving the wings like those of a bird. Icarus watched his father intently. At last the wings were finished, and Daedalus strapped them to his shoulders and went up to a piece of rising ground. Turning into the wind, he ran forward and was delighted to find himself airborne. Day after day he practised on higher and higher slopes until he reckoned the time had come to make the flight to Greece. He constructed a second pair of wings for Icarus, and together the young man and his father mastered the art of flying.

At last the day of departure came. The sun was high in the unclouded heavens, and the wind was favourable. Daedalus and Icarus carried their wings to a lofty cliff looking towards Greece and prepared for flight. When the wings were strapped firmly on their backs, Daedalus said to his son:

'Follow me. Do as I do. Don't fly too low or your wings will be weighed down with spray from the sea. Don't fly too near the sun either, or its heat will melt the wax that holds the feathers in place. Either way you will be destroyed. Do as I say, and may the gods go with you. Now let us be off.'

So saying, he ran towards the edge of the cliff and launched himself

into the air. Borne up by the wind, he journeyed straight towards his native shore.

Icarus did just as his father had done. But he was so happy to find himself aloft in the pure blue sky that he soon forgot the good advice he had been given. He wheeled and dipped like a great sea-bird, and then he soared upwards till the land and even the sea were almost out of sight. How brilliant the blazing sun appeared! Icarus was fascinated by it and could not withstand the temptation to see how high he could fly. Hotter and hotter it blazed down upon him. Too late he felt the wax on his wings begin to melt. He could not descend fast enough for the wax to cool. The wings that had borne him aloft now began to break up, and soon the ill-fated young man plunged helplessly into the sea, like a falling star. Icarus was drowned.

Daedalus had crossed the Aegean Sea and was almost home to Athens before he turned to catch sight of his son. Icarus was not to be seen. In alarm Daedalus turned and flew back to the south. It was not long before he saw, as he swooped down towards the blue waves, a pair of damaged wings floating uselessly on the sea. In sorrow Daedalus returned to Athens alone. The sea where his son had met his death was named the Icarian Sea.

From *Heroes and Monsters: Legends of Ancient Rome* by James Reeves

The day of Trafalgar

This excerpt from *England Expects* recalls the events of the Battle of Trafalgar on 21 October 1805.

'As the day began to dawn, a man at the topmost head called out, "A sail on the starboard bow!" And in two or three minutes more he gave another call, that there was more than one sail... Indeed they looked like a forest

of masts rising from the ocean... As morning got light we could plainly discern them from the deck, and were satisfied it was the enemy, for the Admiral began to telegraph to that effect. They saw us, and would gladly have got away when they discovered we counted 27 sail of the line. But it was too late, and situated as they were, hemmed in by Cape Trafalgar on the one side, and not being able to get back to Cadiz on the other.'

Tense and alert, the British fleet awaited their enemy. Nelson scribbled a note to Lady Hamilton: '...The signal has been made that the enemy's combined fleet are coming out of port. We have very little wind, so that I have no hopes of seeing them before tomorrow. May the God of battle crown my endeavours with success. At all events, I will take care that my name shall ever be most dear to you and Horatia, both of whom I love as much as my own life...'.

He hurriedly wrote another note to Emma next day, Sunday:

'October 20th. In the morning, we were close to the mouth of the Straits [of Gibraltar], but the wind had not come far enough to the westward to allow the combined fleets to weather the shoals off Trafalgar. But they were counted as far as forty sail of ships of war, which I suppose to be thirty-four of the line, and six frigates. A group of them was seen off the lighthouse of Cadiz this morning, but it blows so very fresh and thick weather, that I rather believe they will go into the harbour before night. May God Almighty give us success over these fellows, and enable us to get a peace.'

Anxiously, Nelson repeated to Captain Blackwood of the frigate *Euryalus* to keep the enemy in sight of his frigates until the fleet was in battle formation: 'Captain Blackwood to keep with two frigates in sight of

the Enemy in the night. Two other frigates to be placed between him and the *Defence*, Captain Hope. *Colossus* will take her station between *Defence* and *Mars*. *Mars* to communicate with the *Victory*. Signals by night: If the enemy are standing to the southward, or towards the Straits, burn two blue lights together, every hour, in order to make the greater blaze. If the enemy are standing to the westward three guns, quick, every hour.'

Within minutes of sighting the enemy, the *Victory* made signal No. 72 to the fleet: 'Form the order of sailing in two columns'. Scattered after a night without lights, the fleet began to close up in two lines of battle. The *Victory's* flags were run down, then signal No. 76 went up: 'Bear up and sail in direction shown,' together with E. N. E. flags. Frigates repeated the signals to outlying ships. Slowly, their yards braced to a new set, their sails filled in the breeze, and the great ships, rolling on the swell, headed round to the eastward. The light grew clearer. From the decks the sailors could make out the French and Spanish fleet, scattered for five miles across the horizon, nine or ten miles away.

Throughout the night the French and Spanish Admirals expected an attack. The British flares and gun fire were never far away. As the darkness lifted, the French and Spanish anxiously scanned the horizon for their enemy. At 6.30 a.m. the frigate *Hermione* flew the warning-signal: 'Enemy in sight to windward.' No shred of doubt remained: battle was now certain. Nine miles to the west the *Victory* flew its third signal of the day, No. 13: 'Prepare for battle.'

Frantic preparations were taking place aboard every British ship: Second Lieutenant Ellis of the Marines, aboard the *Ajax* recalled that, shortly before seven o'clock, 'I was sent below with orders, and was much struck with the preparations made by the blue-jackets, most of whom were stripped to the waist. A handkerchief was tightly bound round their heads and over the ears, to deaden the noise of the cannon, many men being deaf for days after an action... Some were sharpening their cutlasses, others polishing the guns... whilst three or four, as if in a mere bravado, were dancing a hornpipe. But all seemed anxious to come to close quarters with the enemy. Occasionally they would look out of the ports, and speculate as to the various ships of the enemy, many of whom had been on former occasions engaged by our vessels.'

'During this time,' recalled Jack Nastyface, 'each ship was making the usual preparations, such as breaking away the captain's and officer's cabins, and sending all the lumber below. The doctors, parson, purser and loblolly men [medical aides] were also busy getting the medicine chests and bandages out, and sails prepared for the wounded to be placed on,

that they might be dressed in rotation as they were taken down to the aft-cockpit.

'In such a bustling and, it may be said, trying as well as serious time, it is curious to notice the different dispositions of the British sailor. Some would be offering a guinea for a glass of grog, whilst others were making a kind of mutual verbal will, such as: "If one of Johnny Crapeau's shots [a term given to the French] knocks my head off, you will take all my effects, and if you are killed and I am not, why, I will have yours" and this is generally agreed to.

'On every ship drummers beat to quarters. In the dim light of the gun-decks, gun-crews of 10, 12 or 15 men each begin work. Port-lids are raised and the iron guns, weighing up to 2½ tons, are run forward on massive wooden carriages to the ports. Tompions are taken from muzzles, and breeching ropes anchored to take the recoil. One gun broken loose in action can kill as many men, as it careers across the deck, as enemy gunfire.

'Tables are stowed, sleeping-hammocks stuffed in the bulwarks for protection against musket-fire. To lessen fire risk, buckets of water are placed ready to wet the canvas screens around hatchways. The decks are sprinkled well with sand to stop them becoming too slippery with blood. Master gunners unlock the powder-magazines and weigh the charge bags. A 32-lb shot takes a third of its weight in powder. Cannon balls are carried to the guns in hammocks. On the forecastles and poops canisters of musket balls and scrap iron stand by the 68-pounder carronades. The slow-match, for lighting a fuse should a flintlock fail, is lit and burns over a water barrel.'

Alone in his cabin, Nelson wrote the last entries in his private diary: 'At daylight saw the enemy's combined fleet from East to E. S. E. Bore away. Made the signal for Order of Sailing, and to Prepare for Battle; the enemy with their heads to the southward; at seven the enemy wearing in succession. May the Great God, whom I worship, grant to my country, and for the benefit of Europe in general, a great and glorious victory; and may no misconduct in any one tarnish it, and my humanity after victory be the predominant feature in the British fleet. For myself, individually, I commit my life to Him, who made me, and may his blessing light upon my endeavours for serving my country faithfully. To him I resign myself and the just cause which is entrusted to me to defend. Amen. Amen. Amen.'

Roger Hart

Thomas Barnardo

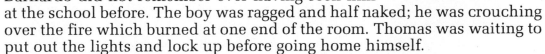

Thomas Barnardo (1845–1905) was an Irish doctor who devoted himself to helping the poor of London's East End. He founded Dr Barnardo's Homes for children suffering poverty, neglect or abuse.

One evening, when all the children had gone home from the school, one boy stayed behind. Thomas Barnardo did not remember ever having seen him at the school before. The boy was ragged and half naked; he was crouching over the fire which burned at one end of the room. Thomas was waiting to put out the lights and lock up before going home himself.

He spoke to the boy: 'Come, my lad, it's time to go now.'

The boy hunched over the fire and lowered his head and pretended for a moment that he had not heard. Then he looked up and said, 'Please, sir, let me stop.'

'Stay here? What for? You ought to go home at once. Your mother will wonder where you are.'

'I ain't got no mother,' said the boy.

Barnardo was silent for a moment and then he said, more kindly, 'But your father, where's he?'

'I ain't got no father.'

Now it had been a long and tiring day and Barnardo was himself very tired, so he spoke a little more sharply, 'Stuff and nonsense, boy! Don't tell me such stories! Where do you live? Who are your friends?'

'Ain't got no friends. Don't live nowhere.' The boy seemed afraid.

'Now, my lad, it's no use your trying to deceive me. Come over here and tell me the truth. What do you mean saying you have no friends? Where do you come from? Where are your friends? Where, in fact, did you sleep last night?'

For some reason Thomas Barnardo did not believe the boy. He looked more closely at him; he saw his weak, shivering and dirty body and the rags in which he was dressed – the boy had no shirt, shoes or stockings. If the boy were telling the truth this was a new sort of child, one far worse off than any that Thomas had tried to help up till then.

'How old are you?' he asked the boy; there was greater kindness in his voice now.

'Ten, sir.' Thomas was shocked; the boy was small and thin and his body was the body of a child much younger – but his face was the face of an old man, pinched with cold, hunger and misery.

Suddenly Thomas felt that the boy was telling the truth and he turned his face away to hide the tears that came to his eyes. He was sorry that he had ever spoken sharply to the boy.

'Do you mean to say, my boy, that you really have no home at all and that you have no father or mother or friends?'

'That's the truth, sir. I ain't telling you no lies.'

'Where did you sleep last night, then?'

'Down in Whitechapel, along of the haymarket, in one of them carts filled with hay.'

'How was it that you came to my school?'

''Cos, sir, I met a chap as I knowed, and he told me that if I come up here to the school I'd get a warm.' Then the boy added wistfully, 'He said perhaps you'd let me lie by the fire all night.'

'But we don't keep open all night,' said Thomas.

'I won't do no harm, sir,' said the boy, 'if only you'll let me stop. Please do, sir.'

It was a raw winter's night and the sharp and bitter east wind whined around the shed; the child heard it and shivered as if it were already cutting him to the bone. He took one last look at the fire and then, hanging his head as if in shame, he began to shuffle slowly towards the door and the cold night air that awaited him outside. As Barnardo watched him he was touched by the complete lack of hope in the child whom he was sending out into the bitter night. Suddenly he called the boy back and the child turned, new hope in his face.

'Yes, sir?' asked the boy eagerly.

'Tell me,' said Barnardo, 'Are there any other poor boys in London like you, boys with no homes and no friends?'

The boy smiled as if he could not believe that a man like Barnardo did not know the answer to this question without asking him. At last, seeing that Barnardo really did not know, he answered, 'Oh! yes, sir, lots. Heaps of them. More than I could count.'

Thomas Barnardo made a bargain with the boy, Jim, that if he gave Jim some food and a warm place to sleep, Jim would show him where these homeless boys could be found.

When Jim Jarvis had drunk the last of the coffee and eaten the last of the bread and butter, he and Thomas Barnardo went out into the streets once more; Jim walked more boldly now and he put his hand in the hand of his new-found friend. They walked through the silent midnight streets towards the old-clothes market of old Petticoat Lane. The houses on either side were silent and still and the only sound was the echo of the footsteps of the man and the boy. Jim Jarvis took Barnardo to a long, low shed which stank of old clothes; they went through the shed together until, at the far end, they were faced by a high wall and could go no further. The wall was the end wall of a warehouse and there was no way round it.

'Well, Jim, where are they?' asked Barnardo.

'Up there, sir,' said Jim. Barnardo looked up to the roof of the warehouse but could see nothing; he did not believe what he had been told.

'Up there? But how do they get up there?'

Jim put his finger to his lips and then took Barnardo nearer to the wall and showed him how little holes had been made in the brickwork – toe-holes – and then made signs to show that this was the way up. Jim, without shoes, went up first and was able to do it easily; Barnardo followed, but it was not so easy for him because he was wearing shoes and he was an older man. Jim helped him up the last bit by holding down a stick he had found at the top; Barnardo held this and Jim helped pull him up to the roof.

When Barnardo had got his breath back he looked round at the cold, bitter sky and then he looked down at the roof. And there he saw a group of boys lying asleep on the tiles. Many of them lay flat on their backs; their heads were near the top of the roof and their feet were in the guttering. Others lay curled up, clutching one another for warmth. They had no covering of any sort; they were in rags and their feet were bare. There was one boy of eighteen, but the rest were under fourteen and some of them were very young, only eight or nine.

Barnardo could hardly believe what he saw. At that moment the moon came out from behind the clouds and its light shone over the sleeping roofs of London and picked out the cold, pinched faces of the sleeping boys. One boy stirred and cried out with cold in his sleep, but none of the boys woke.

At that moment, standing on that roof in the bitter cold of the night, Thomas Barnardo shivered as if with the cold – but the cold he felt was the chill of horror that there should be such children forced to live such wretched lives.

Donald Ford

Florence Nightingale

Throughout the world, Florence Nightingale (1820–1910) is recognised as the founder of modern nursing. This excerpt from her biography describes her campaign to improve the treatment of soldiers injured in the Crimean War.

Florence wanted to lay before the queen the plight of ordinary soldiers, and ask for her support in a campaign to improve their health and conditions. Those endless lines of filthy, blood-stained men, moaning for water, or screaming under the surgeons' knives, must not be forgotten now that the war was over. There might be another war, and the same disasters must not occur again. Florence did not mean to put her case in words alone. Working with feverish urgency, she gathered pages of facts and statistics to back her arguments, and took them to Balmoral with her.

The queen and Prince Albert were impressed by her knowledge and concern for the army. 'I wish we had her at the War Office,' the queen remarked. They were impressed too by her incredible lack of interest in her own achievements. Indeed Florence's strange mixture of characteristics surprised everyone who met her at this time; they discovered that she could be both an iron lady and the lady with the lamp.

Outwardly, she was almost insignificant – slender, dressed in black, with her hair combed back from her thin, pale face. The glow which had attracted admirers in her youth had quite gone. Yet a few minutes' conversation with her revealed a remarkable strength of will. It was a quality the doctors and nurses at Scutari had always recognised. They might object to her orders, but when she said – 'It must be done' – she had a quiet authority which no one could resist.

And, just as with the doctors and nurses, Florence got her way with the queen. She had decided that what was needed was a Royal Commission, a sort of public inquiry, on the health of the army. The queen heartily agreed. But though the wills of the two women were strong, their power was limited. Florence held no official position. The queen could advise, but she could not dictate. Nevertheless, acting together, and using all their powers of persuasion, the manoeuvred the right Cabinet minister round to their viewpoint. A Royal Commission was set up, with Sidney Herbert as chairman.

Things were at last moving in the direction Florence wanted. Now she might have allowed herself a few pleasures, taken a holiday, even returned to her old career of nursing. Instead, with a speed and obsessive determination which swept aside all minor interests, she began collecting all the information she could find which might be useful to the Royal Commission, and arranging it in graphs, tables and pie charts. (Florence invented the pie chart.) She had a small band of genuine helpers, led by Sidney Herbert, who did not mind how much they did for her.

Nothing stopped Florence. Ill though she was, she drove the Royal Commission to its conclusion, and she was rewarded. Everything she wanted was promised, from an army medical school to new drains for barracks. Yet even this did not satisfy her. The promises were merely words on paper. They would have to be put into effect by the War Office, and bitter experience had shown her what the War Office was like. If it had cheated the army in time of war, with its bunglings over shirts and cabbages and medical supplies, it would certainly cheat a Royal Commission. The War Office would have to be reformed.

Meanwhile, Sidney Herbert, as head of the War Office, had the job of reforming it. Ever since he and his wife had encouraged Florence's nursing, she had relied on him more than anyone. They were close friends. His warmth and charm – for he was a delightful man – softened Florence's harshness. Now, as she gathered facts and figures to help his case, he began to falter. He was ill, he told her. He couldn't go on.

Once Florence had been a dedicated nurse. Now she had lost patience with illness. She raged at Sidney, telling him that her health was far worse than his. She was confined to bed almost all the time, but she never stopped working. He was threatening to throw up a great crusade because his head ached. Remorselessly she drove him on.

But even Florence's will power could not halt the kidney disease which Sidney had contracted. Together the two invalids, one fiercely impatient, one meekly resigned, struggled with their impossible task. Florence expected death for herself almost daily, but it was Sidney who finally collapsed. 'Poor Florence,' he murmured as he was dying, 'our joint work unfinished.'

As another man took his place at the War Office, the plans for reform faded away. They had never, in fact, been necessary, for all the Royal Commission's recommendations were carried through. Barracks were drained and ventilated properly; army food improved; the death rate from disease dropped dramatically. The changes were entirely due to Florence's dynamic combination of intelligence and determination; but, as she mourned for Sidney, she could hardly raise her head from her mountains of paper to see what had happened.

Angela Bull

Fifty years in chains

My story is a true one, and I shall tell it in a simple style. It will be merely a recital of my life as a slave in the Southern States of the Union – a description of Negro slavery in the 'model Republic'.

My grandfather was brought from Africa and sold as a slave in Calvert county, in Maryland. I never understood the name of the ship in which he was imported, nor the name of the planter who bought him on his arrival, but at the time I knew him he was a slave in a family called Maud, who resided near Leonardtown.

My father was a slave in a family named Hauty, living near the same place. My mother was the slave of a tobacco planter, who died when I was about four years old. My mother had several children, and they were sold upon master's death to separate purchasers. She was sold, my father told me, to a Georgia trader. I, of all her children, was the only one left in Maryland.

When sold I was naked, never having had on clothes in my life, but my new master gave me a child's frock, belonging to one of his own children. After he had purchased me, he dressed me in this garment, took me before him on his horse, and started home; but my poor mother, when she saw me leaving her for the last time, ran after me, took me down from the horse, clasped me in her arms, and wept loudly and bitterly over me.

My master seemed to pity her, and endeavoured to soothe her distress by telling her that he would be a good master to me, and that I should not want anything. She then, still holding me in her arms, walked along the road beside the horse as he moved slowly, and earnestly and imploringly besought my master to buy her and the rest of her children, and not permit them to be carried away by the Negro buyers. Whilst thus entreating him to save her and her family, the slavedriver, who had first bought her, came running in pursuit of her with a raw-hide in his hand. When he overtook us, he told her he was her master now, and ordered her to give that little Negro to its owner, and come back with him.

My mother then turned to him and cried, 'Oh, master, do not take me from my child!' Without making any reply, he gave her two or three heavy blows on the shoulders with his raw-hide, snatched me from her arms, handed me to my master, and seizing her by one arm, dragged her back towards the place of sale. My master then quickened the pace of his horse; and as we advanced, the cries of my poor parent became more and more indistinct – at length they died away in the distance, and I never again heard the voice of my poor mother.

Young as I was, the horrors of that day sank deeply into my heart, and even at this time, though half a century has elapsed, the terrors of the

scene return with painful vividness upon my memory. Frightened at the sight of the cruelties inflicted upon my poor mother, I forgot my own sorrows at parting from her and clung to my new master, as an angel and a saviour, when compared with the hardened fiend into whose power she had fallen.

She had been a kind and good mother to me; had warmed me in her bosom in the cold nights of winter; and had often divided the scanty pittance of food allowed her by her mistress, between my brothers, and sisters, and me, and gone supperless to bed herself. Whatever victuals she could obtain beyond the coarse food, salt fish and corn bread, allowed to slaves on the Patuxent and Potomac rivers, she carefully distributed among her children, and treated us with all the tenderness which her own miserable condition would permit. I have no doubt that she was chained and driven to Carolina, and toiled out the residue of a forlorn and famished existence in the rice swamps, or indigo fields of the South.

My father never recovered from the effects of the shock, which this sudden and overwhelming ruin of his family gave him. He had formerly been of a gay, social temper, and when he came to see us on a Saturday night, he always brought us some little present, such as the means of a poor slave would allow – apples, melons, sweet potatoes, or, if he could procure nothing else, a little parched corn, which tasted better in our cabin, because he had brought it.

He spent the greater part of the time, which his master permitted him to pass with us, in relating such stories as he had learned from his companions, or in singing the songs common amongst the slaves of Maryland and Virginia. After this time I never heard him laugh heartily, or sing a song. He became gloomy and morose in his temper, to all but me; and spent nearly all his leisure time with my grandfather, who claimed kindred with some royal family in Africa, and had been a great warrior in his native country.

Charles Ball

Black beetles

This excerpt from *Lanhydrock Days* describes a common domestic problem at the turn of the century.

Sarah, the cook at Lanhydrock house, was worried. She had always taken pride in the cleanliness of her kitchens. But now they were infested with beetles, and the day's work was punctuated by the screams of the maids.

'Argh!' shrieked Lizzie, as she went to grind some sugar with the mortar and pestle and there in the bowl was a large black insect, scrabbling around the sides trying to get out but always falling back to the centre.

'Ssh!' hissed Sarah. 'Don't make such a fuss!'

'I can't abide 'em,' said Lizzie. 'They're such creepy-crawly things, they give me the shivers.'

'Be quiet!' snapped the cook. She did not want them talked about, it might be overheard by her employers.

She lived in dread of a beetle being found in the soup served at table to his lordship, or a cockroach crawling out of her ladyship's serviette. Sarah ordered that the tables, walls and floors should be scrubbed with disinfectant every evening after the long day's work, in all the kitchens and store rooms, so that not a speck of food would be left for the cockroaches at night.

Still they multiplied, and Sarah's fear of being found out grew. And then one day she heard that his lordship intended to carry out his annual inspection of the kitchens before the end of the month.

That night she confided her fears to her close friend Véronique, lady's maid to Lady Robartes. The two women had rooms next door to each other, high up in the attic. The rooms were comfortably furnished with brass and iron bedsteads, and had easy chairs in front of the coal fires.

Sarah rested her tired feet on the fender. 'I just don't know what to do,' she said. 'If his lordship finds out, I shall lose my job.'

'What does Mrs Beeton say?'

Véronique went to a shelf and took down the red, gold and green volume of *Mrs Beeton's Book of Household Management*. It was so heavy that she needed two hands to carry it. She rested it on her lap and turned to the index.

'*Voilà!*' she exclaimed. 'Recipe to destroy beetles.'

She turned to the page and read it out. '"Place a fairly deep saucer of stale beer upon the hearth at night time, and rest three or four sticks upon the edge of the saucer for the insects to crawl up." Come on, *ma chérie*, let's do it straight away!'

The two servants crept down the women's staircase and felt their way along dark corridors, not daring to switch on a light. Quietly, they opened the kitchen door. There was a gentle rustling noise coming from the room, the sound of hundreds of insect legs scrabbling over wood and stone.

Véronique switched on the electric light. There were beetles everywhere, crawling over the tables and floor. They froze as the light came on, and then scuttled into dark corners.

Sarah despaired. It was even worse than she had thought. But the two women fetched cooking ale from the larder and set out saucers around the kitchen, filled them to the brim and placed fire-lighting sticks as ladders for the beetles to climb. They put out the light, and went to bed.

Sarah was up at five-thirty the next morning, to get to the kitchens before the maids arrived to start work at six. She could see at a glance that Mrs Beeton's recipe had not worked. The saucers had not been touched, except for one where a single cockroach swam round and round. As she picked it up, some of the beer slopped out, and the cockroach with it. It ran off across the hearth.

That evening Véronique was in her room, reading a ladies' magazine. She leafed idly through the advertisements for mangling machines and kitchen ranges, hand grenade fire extinguishers ('Beware of worthless imitations'), knife polish and soap.

'*Sacré bleu!*' she exclaimed suddenly, and ran next door.

Sarah was already packing her case, sure that she would lose her job at the end of the month.

'Look, Sarah, look!' cried the lady's maid, excitedly brandishing the magazine.

Sarah looked, and there below the advertisement for straw hat polish was an announcement in heavy black print: THOMPSON'S PATENT COCKROACH CATCHER.

The next day, when one of the steward's men was going into Bodmin, Sarah gave him some money for a postal order. She wrote a letter requesting three cockroach catchers, enclosed the order, and popped it into the servant's letter-box.

A few days later a large parcel came for her in the post. She undid the string and unwrapped the brown paper. Inside a cardboard box, protected by more crumpled paper, were three glass flasks. She lifted them out carefully. They had cork stoppers in the top, and there were holes in the bottom of each, where the glass came up the inside of the flask and turned back in a lip.

That evening she set them up, following the instructions that she had found amongst the packing. She filled the glass circle at the bottom of each flask with a sticky mixture of jam and water. She hardly slept that night, so anxious was she to know what would happen.

She held her breath as she neared the kitchen early the next morning. She expected no better results than she had had from Mrs Beeton's advice.

She opened the door a crack, and peeped in. The traps were crammed with cockroaches. The ones at the bottom had already drowned in the sticky liquid, the rest were treading on top of them to try and get out, but could not pass over the inward curve of the glass lip. Sarah rubbed her hands in glee.

'Lizzie!' she called. 'Empty these down the scullery drain.'

'Ooh, ma'am, I couldn't!' said Lizzie, shrinking away.

'Nonsense!' exclaimed Sarah. And she took out the corks, and poured away the sticky, squirming mess.

For a week the cockroach traps were full each morning, and then the numbers decreased. At the end of the month Lord Robartes inspected the kitchens.

'Hygiene is of the utmost importance,' he said, concerned for the health of his ever-increasing family.

'Well done, Sarah,' said his lordship. 'I'll have a word with the steward and see if he can manage to increase your wages. Thanks to you, the kitchens are spotless.

Thanks to THOMPSON'S PATENT COCKROACH CATCHER, thought Sarah, smiling to herself and dropping a curtsey.

John Branfield

Your country needs you

This passage from *Lanhydrock Days* tells of two men's experiences of World War I.

The train steamed through the narrow valley. An officer in a first-class compartment stood up and straightened his khaki uniform. He put on his cap and looked out of the window, waiting for the train to stop at the small country halt.

The train slowed, and the trees that grew close to the line gave way to a long platform. He was the only passenger to get out, and a porter took his luggage. Outside the station a pony and trap waited.

'Good day, sir,' said the young man who was driving.

'Hullo, John,' said Tommy warmly. He was fond of John Kellow, a stable-boy who loved horses and who had a feeling for them.

'Tell me what's been happening on the estate,' Tommy asked. 'How many men have left to join the army?'

There was a footman and an under-gardener, and someone who worked on the home farm.

'Is that all?' exclaimed Tommy. 'The country needs every man it can get. Have you thought of volunteering yet?'

'I've thought of it, sir.'

'Then why haven't you done it?'

John shifted uneasily on his seat, and flicked the whip at the flies above the horse's ears. 'It's my old mother, sir,' he admitted. 'I'd like to go and do my bit, but she's fearful. She has no one else to support her.'

'Your country needs you, John.'

The next day Tommy went to the stables, looking for John Kellow. 'You didn't volunteer John?' he asked, having noticed those who had signed on.

'I promised my mother that I wouldn't, before I went to the meeting,' he said. 'But that doesn't mean that I won't.'

'Do it now!'

'I'll tell her I can't put if off much longer.'

'Good chap!' said Tommy.

Before his leave was over, he heard that John Kellow had gone to the barracks and taken the king's shilling.

After a few days in the base camp, they had orders to move up to the front line. They marched under cover of darkness, though the sky ahead of them was continually lit by flares. The noise of gunfire grew louder.

The road they marched along was full of holes, and the wagons carrying munitions jolted past. The telegraph poles stood at angles, with the wires hanging loose, and the trees were blackened stumps. They passed through a ruined village.

The air became bitter with the smoke from the guns. A shell landed nearby and they all threw themselves to the ground. The flame burst into the air and shrapnel howled over their heads. It was their first experience of enemy fire.

They reached a burnt-out wood on a slight hill, and mist and smoke lay in the fields beyond. They could see other columns moving forward. A file of transport horses waded knee-deep in the mist. After a short rest, they pushed on, past shell-smashed lorries, until they reached the front line. It was lit from end to end, and the explosions made one continuous roar.

The men they were replacing hurried away, gaunt after two weeks in the trenches. There was no time to settle in. They had arrived at the start of a bombardment, and within minutes it began in earnest. A shell landed close by, and mud and fragments shot over them. There were screams further down the line where there had been a direct hit.

They were all terrified. They crouched in the bottom of the trench amongst the mud, and waited for the shell that would fall right on them. Gradually it grew quieter.

'It's over,' called Captain Robartes to his men. 'We've come through all right.'

But now that the thunder of the guns had ceased, they could hear other sounds. The cries of the wounded down the line grew worse.

The noise was terrible. Men could not scream like that, they thought.

'It's the horses!' cried John Kellow. 'It's wounded horses!'

It became louder, from all directions.

'Why don't they shoot them?' he asked desperately.

'They must attend to the men first.'

They stood up to look behind the lines over the top of the trench. They could see the bodies of horses lying on the ground. Others were galloping madly, falling and staggering to their feet.

Their screams were unbearable. John took his rifle and leaped up over the side of the trench.

'Come back!' shouted Captain Robartes. 'Don't be an idiot!'

But John ignored the command. He ran towards a horse writhing on the ground, and raised his rifle. A rattle of machine-gun fire came from the enemy line. He spun round, and fell.

John Branfield

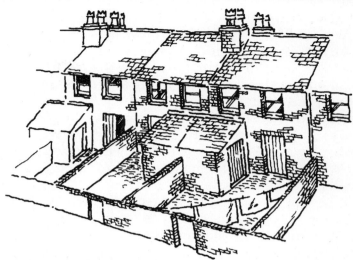

Our house, sixty years ago

It was in the middle of a long street of houses – a terrace. The front door opened out on to the street. At the back, we had a little garden and a back yard.

The coal-house and the lavatory were in the back yard, next to the kitchen door. When my Dad came home from the pit, he took most of his clothes off in the back yard. He hit them against the wall, to get the coal dust out. Then he dropped them into the old tin tub and came into the kitchen to get washed.

The kitchen was long and narrow. There was a deep, white sink, with a wooden draining board next to it. When we were little, we used to sit in the sink to be washed, and then on the draining board to dry off. Dad washed most of the coal dust off himself. The water turned thick and black with shiny white soap bubbles on top. Dad used to blow big soap bubbles up in the air for us.

Across from the sink was a mangle, a wash-tub and a rubbing board. We didn't have a washing machine. Mum filled a big tub full of hot, soapy water. She put all the dirty clothes into it and swooshed them around with a peggy-legs. This was a wooden pole, with five 'legs' at the bottom and two handles at the top. After that, she put the rubbing board into the water and rubbed the washing up and down it, to get it really clean. It was very hard work. But I helped with the next bit: I pushed the handle of the mangle so that the rollers squeezed all the dirty water out. Then my Mum had to rinse the washing in the sink and I mangled the clean water out. Then, at last, it was ready to be hung out on the line in the yard. But if it was raining we had to bring it into the living room and hang it all round the fire place.

The living-room was the most important room in the house. It was so important that we called it 'the House'. Day and night, summer and winter, there was always a big fire burning in the black cooking range. The fire heated the water and the oven. Mum did all the cooking in the oven and we ate our meals in the same room. We kept all our pots and pans in a cupboard next to the fireplace. We kept our toys and books and games in another cupboard. We had to play in 'the house' because it was the only room with a fire. If we were ill, we slept on the settee in front of the fire until we got better. On winter mornings, when it was very cold upstairs, we washed and dressed on the rag-rug by the fire. Then we made toast in front of the fire and warmed milk on the oven top. We sat by the fire to eat our breakfast: toast-and-dripping and milk-and-honey.

The House was like a dark, brown burrow. All the doors, cupboards and floors were brown. The top half of the walls was cream and the bottom half was covered in shiny brown wallpaper. Mum used dark colours because it was so dirty outside. If we opened a window, sooty flakes fell in. When we brought the washing in from the line outside, it was often covered in black smuts.

So Mum often hung the washing in the pantry, where we kept our food. A sack of potatoes was kept close to the door, and cabbages, leeks and sprouts were all laid out on the cool, red-tiled floor. The high shelves were filled with big glass jars of tomatoes, beans, and pears that Mum had preserved. Milk, butter, cheese and fresh meat were kept on a stone slab at the back of the pantry. There was an air-vent there to keep the food cool and fresh. In summer Mum boiled all the milk to stop it turning sour. It also stopped us drinking it – it tasted terrible!

The passage ran from the living-room to the front door and out to the street. On one side of the passage was a row of pegs for our overcoats and mackintoshes. On the other side was the door to the front room – we called it 'the Room'. We never used the Room except at Christmas. We lit a fire, then, and put out all the best chairs for visitors.

Next to the Room were the stairs. They were steep and dark, leading up to the landing. My parents' bedroom was on the right side of the landing, and our bedroom was on the left.

The bathroom was in the middle, between the two bedrooms. When my dad had finished his first wash in the kitchen, he came upstairs to have a real bath. We had a bath every Friday night but he had one every day. The bath was white and very deep. There was a deep, white sink next to it, and the airing cupboard with the hot water tank in it. There wasn't a lavatory inside the house. If we wanted to go to the lavatory in the night, we had to use the pot from under our bed. Then we had to take it downstairs and empty it in the outside lavatory next morning.

The bedrooms were very cold. They had no heating and no carpet, just lino. In winter Mum put flannel sheets on the hot water tank and we wrapped ourselves up in them before we got into bed. Then we kept warm, even under one blanket and an old coat.

We all loved our house. We had lots of happy times there. And, do you know, my mother still lives there! Of course, it has a lavatory in the bathroom now, and another in the shower-room, downstairs. The shower room was made from the old coal house and lavatory. In the kitchen there is a fridge, an electric cooker and a washing machine. The big coal fire in the black cooking range has gone from the 'House'. There is a little gas-fire there now, and central heating in all the other rooms. There are pale carpets on every floor and all the rooms are painted white. The air is cleaner now – and so is the house. But it's still 'our house' where I grew up, sixty years ago.

Bette Paul

Mohandas Gandhi

Gandhi (1869 –1948) led the people of India to independence from Britain. Indians called him the Mahatma, or 'Great Soul'.

When war broke out in Europe in September 1939, the Viceroy of India declared that India too was at war with Germany. India was indignant. It was not that the Indian people supported fascism. It was simply that they had not been consulted about their involvement. Gandhi made it clear that he felt all war to be wrong but that his sympathies were 'wholly with the allies'. For its part the Indian National Congress decided that it would help to fight the Nazis, but only as a free country. The British Government was therefore invited to explain its war aims. But the Viceroy's response was unbending. Britain, he said, was not yet in a position to explain her war aims, and he would only promise future talks about 'dominion status'. As a result, the Indian leaders decided against support of the war effort. Inevitably, the arguments grew more heated as Japanese troops drew near to the Indian border, and as people became more and more restless, Gandhi feared violence in the streets. In an historic decision on 7 August 1942 Gandhi and the All-India Congress Committee asked the British to leave India.

Two days later Gandhi was arrested and imprisoned in the Aga Khan Palace. Gandhi tried writing letters to the Viceroy in an attempt to find a compromise. For six months he waited patiently and then he resolved on a twenty-one day fast. For three weeks he took nothing but water with the juice of citrus fruits. The Mahatma nearly died. In fact the Government went so far as to collect the wood for his cremation and to arrange the route for his funeral procession. It also prepared to suppress the riots that it knew would break out at the news of Gandhi's death.

It took Gandhi some time to recover and while he was still weak another blow struck him. Gandhi and Kasturbai had been married for more than sixty years. Kasturbai did not adjust as readily to being shut away as Gandhi did. She hated the Aga Khan prison and her health began to fail her. She developed a very bad cough and palpitations of the heart. Finally she died in her husband's arms. Gandhi was so broken by his loss that he was released from his imprisonment.

On 15 August 1947 India was finally granted Independence, but for Mahatma Gandhi the achievement of the aim to which he had given so much of his life held little excitement. Independence day was accompanied by the division of the old India into two countries: India for the Hindus and Pakistan for the Muslims. Gandhi's dream of a united India in which Hindus and Muslims lived side by side in brotherhood was shattered. In Calcutta where he spent the eve of Independence there were celebrations in the streets but elsewhere a mass migration had begun as millions of Muslims moved to Pakistan and millions of Hindus processed to India. Almost a million people died in clashes between people of the two different faiths. Eventually the violence reached Calcutta and West Bengal and Gandhi was reduced to fasting to cleanse the hearts of the people. Hindus and Muslims alike were moved by the Mahatma's act of self-sacrifice. Both communities pledged themselves to peace and the fast was described as a miracle because it did what several divisions of troops could not do. Gandhi had brought about peace in West Bengal.

Soon, however, it was Delhi that was paralysed by riots. Again Gandhi fasted and the whole nation came to a standstill. Only when the Hindu community leaders of Delhi had promised to protect the lives and property of Muslims would Gandhi break his fast and drink a glass of juice.

However, there were those who could not share his tolerance. As Gandhi struggled to protect the Muslims of India, there were some extremist Hindus who saw him as an obstacle to the rebirth of ancient Hindu India. On 20 January 1948 a bomb was thrown at Gandhi during the evening prayer meeting. It exploded at some distance from him and he took little notice of it. Instead he begged the police not to press charges against his attacker, and when they tried to increase his security, he would not let them search people coming to prayer meetings. 'If I have to die', he insisted, 'I should die at the prayer meeting. You are wrong in believing that you can protect me from harm. God is my protector.'

Shortly before he died Gandhi told his secretary to bring him all his important letters. 'I must reply to them today, for tomorrow I may not be,' he said. On 30 January 1948 about 500 people had gathered for the evening prayer meeting. Gandhi greeted them all with the palms of his hands pressed together and many of them rose from their seats in response. Suddenly, a Hindu man broke from the crowd and almost knelt before the Mahatma, then fired three shots. Gandhi fell instantly. He died with the words, 'Ram, Ram' (Oh God) on his lips.

It was Nehru, whom Gandhi had helped to become Prime Minister of the new India, who announced the tragic news to the nation. In a famous speech, he said: 'The light has gone out of our lives and there is darkness everywhere and I do not quite know what to tell you and how to say it. Our beloved leader, Bapu as we call him, the father of our nation is no more. Perhaps I am wrong to say that. Nevertheless we will not see him again as we have seen him these many years.' But he added: 'The light has gone out, I said, and yet I was wrong. For the light that shone in this country was no ordinary light.'

Kathryn Spink

Martin Luther King

Martin Luther King (1929 – 68) led the struggle for racial equality in the United States. Like Gandhi, he urged people not to use violence.

One afternoon in 1935 a six-year-old boy came home from school and ran across the road outside his home to play with two of his friends. His family called him 'Mike' or 'M. L.', but he was later to be known as Martin Luther King. He was the son of a minister at the local Baptist church in Atlanta, Georgia, a bustling city in the south-east corner of the United States.

The King family was greatly respected in Atlanta. Martin's grandfather had founded the church, and his father was an important figure in the local community. His friends were the two children of the local grocer, and he had played with them ever since he could remember, flying kites and model planes, riding bicycles or practising baseball and basketball in the back yard. But they and Martin had now started at different schools and Martin was anxious to find out what their school was like compared with his own.

He was surprised when their mother told him that the boys could not play with him any more. He asked her why, but at first she just made excuses, saying the boys were too busy. Martin was puzzled and asked her again for the reason. Finally, she told him. They were white, and he was black, and now that the children had all reached school age, they must go their separate ways. They would never be allowed to play with Martin again.

'None of us had seriously thought anything about white children being different,' Martin recalled later. Hurt and confused, he had run home to his mother and asked her to explain. 'Don't let this thing worry you,' she told him. 'Don't let it make you feel you are not as good as white people. You are as good as anyone else, and don't you forget it.' But from that day onwards, Martin gradually learned how differently black and white people were treated.

Two years later, when he was eight, his father took him out one day to buy a pair of shoes. They sat down near the front of the shop. A white assistant came over to them and said, 'I'll be happy to serve you if you'll just come to those seats at the back.' 'Why?' asked Martin's father. 'There's nothing wrong with these seats.' 'Sorry,' said the assistant, 'but you'll have to go back there. These seats are for whites only.' 'We'll either buy shoes sitting here,' replied Daddy King, 'or we won't buy shoes at all.' Both father and son walked out of the shop. 'It was probably the first time I had seen Daddy so furious,' remembered Martin later. 'I remembered him muttering "I don't care how long I have to live with this system, I am never going to accept it. I'll oppose it until the day I die".'

As he got older Martin gradually learned more about the differences between black and white. Policemen would always refer scornfully to a young negro as 'boy' or an elderly one as 'uncle'. Once, when a traffic policeman yelled at his father, 'Boy, what d'you mean running across the road against that Stop sign?' Daddy King replied politely, 'I'm a man. That's a boy there,' and he pointed to Martin beside him. 'I'm Reverend King,' he said proudly. Daddy King insisted on being treated politely by whites, but he knew that black people less well-known than he could command no respect at all.

Martin also noticed how bus drivers yelled 'Nigger' at local black students. It was a way of being rude to them. When he was eleven, a white woman walked up to him in a department store and slapped his face. He had never seen her before. 'The little nigger stepped on my foot,' she explained. No-one criticised her. Martin learned that black children not only had to go to separate schools, but that their parents were expected to move back from the best seats at the front of local buses if white people got on. His father refused to ride on them as a result. It also became clear to Martin that many of the top jobs in the city could be held only by whites.

Martin was learning the bitter lesson that all black people of his age then had to learn — that negroes in the South were treated as second-class citizens just because of the colour of their skin. It was a lesson that was to shape the whole course of his future life.

Nigel Richardson

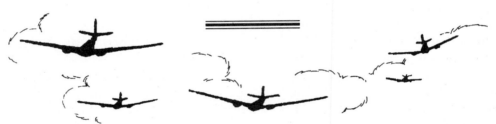

Leaving London

This excerpt from *Carrie's War* is about children who were evacuated to Wales when bombs were falling on London during World War II. First there was the train journey and then the children were allocated to their host families.

He threw up all over Miss Fazackerly's skirt. He had been feeling sick ever since they left the main junction and climbed into the joggling, jolting little train for the last lap of their journey, but the sudden whistle had finished him.

Such a noise — it seemed to split the sky open. 'Enough to frighten the dead,' Miss Fazackerly said, mopping her skirt and Nick's face with her handkerchief. He lay back limp as a rag and let her do it, the way he always let people do things for him, not lifting a finger. 'Poor lamb,' Miss Fazackerly said, but Carrie looked stern.

'It's all his own fault. He's been stuffing his face ever since we left London. Greedy pig. *Dustbin*.'

He had not only eaten his own packed lunch — sandwiches and cold sausages and bananas — but most of Carrie's as well. She had let him have it to comfort him because he minded leaving home and their mother more than she did. Or had looked as if he minded more. She thought now that it was just one of his acts, put on to get sympathy. Sympathy and chocolate! He had had all her chocolate, too! 'I knew he'd be sick,' she said smugly.

'Might have warned me then, mightn't you?' Miss Fazackerly said. Not unkindly, she was one of the kindest teachers in the school, but Carrie wanted to cry suddenly. If she had been Nick she would have cried, or at least put on a hurt face. Being Carrie she stared crossly out of the carriage window at the big mountain on the far side of the valley. It was brown and purple on the top and green lower down; streaked with silver trickles of water and dotted with sheep.

Sheep and mountains. 'Oh it'll be such fun,' their mother had said when she kissed them good-bye at the station. 'Living in the country instead of the stuffy old city. You'll love it, you see if you don't!' As if Hitler had arranged this old war for their benefit, just so that Carrie and Nick could be sent away in a train with gas masks slung over their shoulders and their names on cards round their necks. Labelled like parcels – Caroline Wendy Willow and Nicholas Peter Willow – only with no address to be sent to. None of them, not even the teachers, knew where they were going. 'That's part of the adventure,' Carrie's mother had said, and not just to cheer them up: it was her nature to look on the bright side. If she found herself if Hell, Carrie thought now, she'd just say, 'Well, at least we'll be *warm*.'

Thinking of her mother, always making the best of things (or pretending to: when the train began to move she had stopped smiling) Carrie nearly did cry. There was a lump like a pill stuck in her throat. She swallowed hard and pulled faces.

The train was slowing. 'Here we are,' Miss Fazackerly said. 'Collect your things, don't leave anything. Take care of Nick, Carrie.'

Carrie scowled. She loved Nick, loved him so much sometimes that it gave her a pain, but she hated to be told to do something she was going to do anyway. And she was bored with Nick at the moment. The dying-duck look as he struggled to get his case down from the rack! 'Leave it to me, silly baby,' she said, jumping up on the seat. Dust flew and he screwed up his face. 'You're making me sneeze,' he complained. 'Don't *bounce*, Carrie.'

They all seemed to have more luggage than when they had started. Suitcases that had once been quite light now felt as if they were weighed down with stones. And got heavier as they left the small station and straggled down a steep, cinder path. Carrie had Nick's case as well as her own and a carrier bag with a broken string handle. She tucked it under one arm, but it kept slipping backwards and her gas mask banged her knee as she walked.

'Someone help Caroline, please,' Miss Fazackerly cried, rushing up and down the line of children like a sheep dog. Someone did – Carrie felt the carrier bag go from under her arm, then one suitcase.

It was a bigger boy. Carrie blushed, but he wasn't a Senior: he wore a cap like all the boys under sixteen, and although he was tall, he didn't

look very much older than she was. She glanced sideways and said, 'Thank you *so* much,' in a grown-up voice like her mother's.

He grinned shyly back. He had steel-rimmed spectacles, a few spots on his chin. He said, 'Well, I suppose this is what they call our ultimate destination. Not much of a place, is it?'

They were off the cinder track now, walking down a hilly street where small, dark houses opened straight on to the pavement. There was sun on the mountain above them, but the town was in shadow; the air struck chill on their cheeks and smelled dusty.

'Bound to be dirty,' Carrie said. 'A coal-mining town'.

'I didn't mean dirt. Just that it's not big enough to have a good public library.'

It seemed a funny thing to bother about at the moment. Carrie said, 'The first place was bigger. Where we stopped at the junction,' She peered at his label and read his name. Albert Sandwich. She said, 'If you came earlier on in the alphabet you could have stayed there. You only just missed it, they divided us after the R's. Do your friends call you Ally, or Bert?'

'I don't care for my name to be abbreviated,' he said. 'Nor do I like being called Jam, or Jelly, or even Peanut Butter.'

He spoke firmly but Carrie thought he looked anxious.

'I hadn't thought of sandwiches,' she said. 'Only of the town Sandwich in Kent, because my granny lives there. Though my dad says she'll have to move now in case the Germans land on the coast.' She thought of the Germans landing and her grandmother running away with her things on a cart like a refugee in a newspaper picture. She gave a loud, silly laugh and said, 'If they did, my grand 'ud give them What For. She's not frightened of anyone, I bet she could even stop Hitler. Go up on her roof and pour boiling oil down!'

Albert looked at her, frowning. 'I doubt if that would be very helpful. Old people aren't much use in a war. Like kids – best out of the way.'

His grave tone made Carrie feel foolish. She wanted to say it was only a joke, about boiling oil, but they had arrived at a building with several steps leading up and told to get into single file so that their names could be checked at the door. Nick was waiting there, holding Miss Fazackerly's hand. She said, 'There you are, darling. There she is, didn't I tell you?' And to Carrie, 'Don't lose him again!'

She ticked them off on her list, saying aloud, 'Two Willows, One Sandwich.'

Nick clung to Carrie's sleeve as they went through the door into a long, dark room with pointed windows. It was crowded and noisy. Someone said to Carrie, 'Would you like a cup of tea, bach? And a bit of cake, now?' She was a cheerful, plump woman with a sing-song Welsh voice. Carrie shook her head; she felt cake would choke her. 'Stand by there, then,' the woman said. 'There by the wall with the others, and someone will choose you.'

Carrie looked round, bewildered, and saw Albert Sandwich. She whispered, 'What's happening?' and he said, 'A kind of cattle auction, it seems.'

Nina Bawden

Bedd Gelert

In a remote little village in North Wales, a long, long time ago, there lived a prince named Llewellyn and his beautiful infant son. The mother had died in childbirth and so the prince lavished all his love and care on his only child. Prince Llewellyn also had a trusted faithful hound, named Gelert, who could sense the prince's devotion to the child and so was as protective of him as his master was, or even more so.

One morning, as the child was sleeping peacefully in its cradle, Prince Llewellyn heard the sound of a hunting horn and the barking of hunting dogs nearby.

'A share of that hunt must be mine,' he thought, 'for I am the owner of this land.' So, calling Gelert and pointing to the cradle, he simply said, 'Look after my son, while I am away,' and left. The dog obediently lay down next to the sleeping child.

Before very long the hound's fine nostrils quivered. He could scent an enemy. And indeed there was a wolf nosing in at the doorway. Gelert, quick as lightning, leaped at the beast and the next moment the two were locked in a life and death struggle. The baby went on sleeping peacefully, unaware of any danger, but the two creatures fought savagely, Gelert to protect the infant and the wolf to devour it, for it was ravenously hungry after days of futile roaming the hills and forests.

As they fought, blood splattered all over the walls and floor, and the wolf, getting nearer the scent of its intended prey, pushed the brave dog closer to the cradle. Panting furiously, the wolf thrust Gelert right at its base and overturned it, bespattering the coverlets with blood. Miraculously, the baby continued to sleep soundly, ignorant of the mortal danger it was in and undisturbed by the ferocious growling and snarling of the two combatants. But Gelert, now sensing the imminent danger to his ward, fought back, drove his opponent to the opposite corner and sank his teeth into the wolf's throat. With a last dying snarl the wolf fell back and drew its last breath.

The faithful Gelert lay down, triumphant but exhausted, next to the sleeping child, now untidily covered by blood-stained blankets and coverlets.

About half an hour later Prince Llewellyn returned from his hunt and Gelert dragged himself to his feet and went to meet him. The prince was horrified at the sight that met his eyes, but most of all by the blood on Gelert's mouth and feet. He did not see the wolf's body in the far corner and he could only think that Gelert had killed the child.

He drew his sword and in a movement of blind fury he plunged it into the heart of his faithful hound. The dog gave a piteous and puzzled look up at his beloved master and sank back dead with a final wailing breath.

And then the prince heard a lusty cry from the direction of the cradle. He picked up the child and found it safe and sound, and then his eye fell on the torn and bloody carcass of the wolf in the corner. In a flash everything became clear.

The prince's grief was beyond control and for many years he could not erase the memory of that awful day from his guilty mind.

But if today you are on a visit to Colwyn Bay in North Wales, you can visit the village of Bedd Gelert and see the reputed grave of that famous dog, the actual spot where Prince Llewellyn is supposed to have buried his faithful companion. There is a tombstone there which tells the whole story and is headed:

TO THE MEMORY OF A BRAVE DOG.

Retold by Stephen Corrin

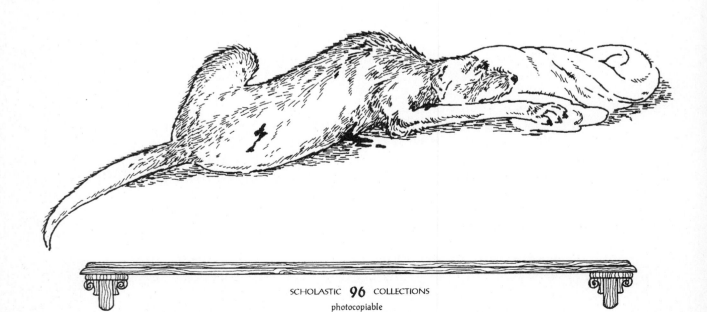

WINNERS AND LOSERS

When Pig got smart

When Pig's slippery slide went out of business (parents had not been amused with their kids coming home covered in mud from head to toe), Pig went out to look for other employment.

'I have lots of bills,' Pig said to the barber.

'Have you had any nibbles for a job?' asked the barber.

'I saw a sign in the window of the candy shop for a salesperson,' said Pig.

'Most unsuitable, Pig,' said the baker, who was having his ears combed out. 'You mustn't be around anything too tempting.'

'You're right,' said Pig.

'I've got it!' said the pharmacist. 'It says here in the paper that the Board of Education is advertising for a truant officer. Seems that kids aren't showing up for school in record numbers.'

'What's a truant officer?' said Pig.

'Someone who tracks down kids who are playing hooky,' said the barber.

'It will just be like hide-and-seek,' said Pig. 'I'm sure I'd be good at it. I'll apply right away.'

He hurried out of the barbershop and went off to be interviewed at the Board of Ed.

'No one else wants the job,' whispered the Head of the Board to the other members. 'We might as well give it to Pig.'

The others agreed.

'The job is yours, Pig. Good luck.'

Pig was overjoyed. It hadn't taken him long to find a job.

I just have the knack, he thought.

'Then it's all settled,' said the Head of the Board. 'You'll begin first thing tomorrow. Report to the Watson School at eight o'clock sharp.'

'Beg pardon?' said Pig. 'Do you mean eight a.m.? I'm a late sleeper. Eleven would suit me much better.'

'Eight A. M.,' said the Head, removing his glasses. 'Of course if you don't *want* the job...'

'I'll be there at eight,' said Pig.

That night Pig set his alarm for seven forty-five the next morning.

'I'll have to rush,' said Pig. 'But I'll get a bit more sleep.'

At eight o'clock the next morning he appeared at the Watson School. He'd slept in his clothes, and they were all rumpled.

'The principal will see you now,' said Miss Gomez, the secretary.

Pig knocked on the principal's door.

'Enter,' said the principal. 'Ah, Pig, your first day on the job. It's going to be a tough one.'

'May I take two hours off for lunch?' said Pig.

'No,' said the principal.

Gosh, thought Pig, this *is* going to be a tough job.

For several days Pig looked for kids playing hooky, but he couldn't find any. Then one day in the park he saw a young dog sitting on a bench, reading a book.

'Shouldn't you be in school?' said Pig.

'Nope,' said the young dog, completely absorbed in his book.

'And why not?' said Pig.

'I know everything already,' said the young dog, turning the page of his book.

'I see,' said Pig.

He decided to be clever.

'Oh, yeah, Mr Smarty?' he said. 'So what is the capital of Miami?'

The young dog put down his book.

'Miami is a city,' he said. 'It is in the state of Florida. And the capital of Florida is Tallahassee.'

'Oh,' said Pig. 'I knew that.'

The young dog went back to his reading. But Pig had not given up.

'If you're so smart,' he said, 'what's seventy-two times twelve?'

'Eight hundred and sixty-four,' said the young dog.

'How did you do that so quickly?' said Pig.

'Brains,' said the young dog.

'Well, you can always learn something in school,' said Pig. 'You might become even smarter.'

'Not today,' said the young dog.

'And just why not?' said Pig.

'Because it's Saturday!' cried the young dog.

And he ran off howling with laughter.

'Have you heard about Pig?' asked the barber.

'Oh no, he got fired again?' said the pharmacist.

'Not exactly,' said the barber. 'Pig was so ashamed by all the things he didn't know that he's gone back to school.'

'Well, maybe Pig is smarter than we thought,' said the pharmacist.

James Marshall

Slowly does it

Something had invaded the forest; something strange and worrying. The Howler Monkey heard it. The Jaguar smelled it. The Macaws saw something moving in the bushes. But no one could tell what it was.

The Something had a strange smell; it left strange tracks; and it made noises that the forest had never heard before. The animals didn't like it at all.

At last, the Jaguar, who was bigger and stronger than the rest, called a meeting to decide what to do. Everyone gathered round nervously. Everyone except the Sloth, that is. He was asleep, as usual, in his tree.

'Well!' growled the Jaguar in his deep fierce voice. 'Does anyone know what this Something is?'

'It's much taller than a monkey,' said the Howler Monkey.

'It has a shiny yellow head,' said a Macaw.

'It makes a terrible snarling noise,' said a Marmoset.

'But sometimes it whistles like a bird.'

'It smells bad, like fire,' said a Snake.

Then the Jaguar asked the question they were most worried about. 'What does it *eat*?'

The animals looked at each other in silence. No one knew what it ate. They just hoped it ate nothing but fruit. The fact was that no one had seen it properly at all.

Then the Jaguar had an idea.

'What about that good-for-nothing Sloth?' he growled. 'He's been hanging about for weeks. He must have seen it. Go and call the Sloth.'

Everyone looked up, and there, high above them in the tallest tree, was a dirty-looking bundle of hair hanging from a branch. The Howler Monkey went tearing up.

'Hey, you! Slowcoach!' he yelled, shaking the Sloth's branch. 'Shift your bulk. Jaguar wants a word with you.'

The Sloth was hanging peacefully by his long shaggy arms and legs, with his head resting on his shaggy chest. Sometimes he ate the leaves he could reach. Mostly he just hung there fast asleep. He had hung so still for so long that green mould was growing in this hair. He took no notice whatever of the Howler Monkey.

The Howler Monkey shouted and bounced till fruit rained down on the animals below, but the Sloth slept on.

Then all the little Marmosets went scampering up to try waking him. 'Quick, quick, quick!' they chattered, jumping from twig to twig like grasshoppers.

The Sloth opened his short-sighted eyes. Then he shut them again.

The Tree Snake went next, coiling and twisting up the tree, and out along the branch.

'I sshould sstop thiss ssnoozing,' he whispered in the Sloth's ear. 'Better ssafe than ssorry.'

The Sloth just opened his mouth in a long, slow-motion yawn.

Then the Macaws had a go. They flew round and round the Sloth, flashing their bright wings and squawking fit to choke.

'Wake up, Slug-a-bed, WAKE UP! Jaguar wants to talk.'

The Sloth unhooked one arm and scratched his tummy drowsily. Then the Jaguar lost his temper. He leapt and clawed his way up the tree, lashing his tail with rage.

'Look here, you mouldy old hammock,' he roared. 'Are you going to talk, or do I have to make you?'

The Sloth peered at his visitor. 'Good...morning,' he said slowly (although it was afternoon by now). 'What...seems...to...be...the...trouble?'

All the animals burst out talking at once: growling, yelling, hissing, chattering and squawking about the Something. The Sloth just hung there smiling, and slowing blinking his eyes.

The rumpus went on for some time, for the Sloth wasn't very bright. It took a while to get a new idea into his shaggy head.

'A...Something?' he said at last. 'What...sort...of...'

'Stop!' interrupted the Howler Monkey. 'Listen!'

Everyone went quiet. Up from the ground far beneath them came a noise more terrifying than anything they had ever heard before. An ugly, ear-splitting snarling roar it was, and it filled them with fear. Then there was a loud crack, a huge crash, and one of the nearby trees just...fell down. The animals could not believe their eyes.

'The Something,' whispered the Jaguar, with his fur standing on end. 'It's eating the trees.'

At that, they all fled in panic, tumbling helter-skelter through the branches to get away. In a moment they were all gone. All except the Sloth, of course. He was left hanging there alone, with his mouth open, and his question unanswered.

'Nobody...tells...me...anything,' he sighed. 'I...s'pose...I'd...better...go... and...see...'

Then, at last, he started to move. Inch by inch he crept along his branch until he reached the main trunk. The awful noise went on and on, but he took no notice. He wrapped his shaggy arms around the tree and began to climb down. Slowly – oh so slowly – he groped his way down, and down...and down. It was growing dark under the trees, and the noise had stopped, but still he toiled on. He was nearly there, and feeling so tired, when into the clearing came...the Something. They stared at each other.

What the Sloth saw was a man. A man with a chainsaw for cutting down trees. But the Sloth didn't know it was a man. He'd never met one before. He peered at it doubtfully. Then he did what sloths always do to stay out of trouble: he kept quite still and smiled.

But what the man saw, however, in that shadowy forest, far from home, was a horrible hairy hobgoblin leering at him with a spooky grin on its face. It made his blood run cold. He let out a strangled cry, and ran for his life.

Next morning the other animals came anxiously creeping back. They sniffed the air for that frightening smell. They listened for the frightening noise. But all they smelled were sweet forest scents; and all they heard were the friendly forest calls. The Something had gone. And there was the Sloth dangling from his branch in the sunshine, and slowly stuffing leaves into his smile.

Robin Ravilious

Mouse party

Miss Mouse was tidying up in the kitchen when her friend the tomcat came in from a stroll.

'See anything interesting today?' said Miss Mouse.

'Maybe,' said the tomcat, who loved to tease.

'What? What?' said Miss Mouse, who *hated* being teased. 'What did you see?'

The tomcat sat down in his favourite easy chair, unfolded the newspaper, and pretended to read.

'If you don't tell me what you saw, you won't get a story,' said Miss Mouse, who knew when to get tough.

'Well,' said the tomcat. 'It seems that a large family of mice has moved in several blocks away. I saw them carrying in furniture and boxes. And one of them was painting a name on the mailbox.

'Oh?' said Miss Mouse. 'Perhaps I know them.'

'They're called the Johnsons,' said the tomcat. 'A common enough name.'

Miss Mouse decided she did not know any mice by the name of Johnson.

'I shall invite them to tea for tomorrow afternoon,' said Miss Mouse, sitting down at her writing desk and scribbling a quick note.

'Hmm,' said the tomcat.

He did not especially relish the idea of having a house full of mice — especially as he'd given up mouse meat. But he didn't want to spoil Miss Mouse's fun.

'Do as you like,' he said.

'You'll join us of course,' said Miss Mouse.

Maybe they won't miss one or two, thought the tomcat, who was feeling a relapse coming on.

'Not so fast,' said Miss Mouse. '*I* know what you're thinking. You must promise to behave, Or else.'

'Oh very well,' grumbled the tomcat.

'What is the address?' said Miss Mouse, licking closed the envelope.

'Two hundred Hollow Road,' said the tomcat.

Miss Mouse wrote the address on the envelope and handed it to the tomcat.

'Be so kind as to drop this off in the Johnson's box,' she said.

The tomcat took the envelope and sauntered out the door.

'I'm trusting you to behave,' said Miss Mouse.

The next afternoon at five minutes to four Miss Mouse surveyed her tea table, which was piled high with cucumber and watercress sandwiches, scones, butter, and various jams. She had laid out her best china and silver and had put some roses from the backyard into a vase.

'Now go put on a tie,' she said to the tomcat.

'Aww,' said the tomcat.

'It's proper,' said Miss Mouse.

And the tomcat obeyed.

At four on the dot a hot rod pulled up in front of the tomcat and Miss Mouse's house. There was a lot of shrieking and laughing and carrying on.

Miss Mouse ran to the window.

'Oh no!' she cried.

'Let the good times roll!' someone yelled.

And everyone got out of the hot rod.

'Oh my stars!' cried Miss Mouse, peeking through the curtain.

'What seems to be the trouble?' said the tomcat coming into the room and adjusting his tie.

'They're coming *here*!' cried Miss Mouse. 'It's the Johnsons and – gulp – they're *rats*! Great big ugly rats!!'

'They did seem on the large side,' said the tomcat.

The Johnsons came to the door, rang the bell, and yelled, 'Open up! We're hungry!'

'Are they wearing ties?' said the tomcat.

'No,' answered Miss Mouse. 'They're shabbily dressed.'

'I'll go change,' said the tomcat.

The Johnsons rang the bell again and again.

It would be rude not to let them in, thought Miss Mouse. After all, I *did* invite them.

And she opened the door.

'Hi, honey!' said Mr Johnson. 'What took ya so long? Nice place ya got here. Let's eat.'

Without bothering to introduce his wife and kids – and there were a lot of them – Mr Johnson plopped down on the sofa and began helping himself to the sandwiches. Right away he broke one of Miss Mouse's china plates.

'Save some for me, ya big lug!' yelled Mrs Johnson. 'Don't make a rat of yourself!'

And finding that terribly amusing, they all laughed loudly. Little bits of cucumber and watercress sandwiches were spewed about the room. And one of the kids broke a teacup.

'What is this stuff?' he said, peering into the teapot. 'Yucko.'

Miss Mouse was outraged.

'I think you'd better leave,' she said.

'Leave?' cried Mrs Johnson. 'We're gonna stay for dinner!'

Suddenly the tomcat stepped into the room.

The Johnsons' beady little red eyes nearly popped out of their heads.

'Holy cow!' they cried. 'She's got a bodyguard!'

And stumbling all over themselves they raced for the door, down the sidewalk, and into the hot rod. And they tore off.

Miss Mouse looked at the mess and sighed.

'I hope you've learned something,' she said to the tomcat. 'That was not a large family of mice, but a family of large *rats*. There *is* a difference!'

'So I see,' said the tomcat.

And just to be sweet he made dinner that night and brought it to Miss Mouse in bed.

James Marshall

Hare and Tortoise

When Tortoise was very little, his mother said to him, 'You will never be able to go very fast. We Tortoises are a slow-moving family, but we get there in the end. Don't try to run. Remember, 'steady and slow' does it.' Tortoise remembered these words.

One day when he was grown-up, he was walking quietly round in a field minding his own business; and Hare thought he would have some fun, so he ran round Tortoise in quick circles, just to annoy him. Hare was proud of himself because everyone knew he was one of the swiftest animals. But Tortoise took no notice, so Hare stopped in front of him and laughed.

'Can't you move faster than *that*? said Hare. 'You'll *never* get anywhere at that rate! You should take a few lessons from *me*.'

Tortoise lifted his head slowly and said:

'I don't want to get anywhere, thank you. I've no need to go dashing about all over the place. You see, my thick shell protects me from my enemies.'

'But how *dull* life must be for you.' Hare went on. 'Why it takes you half an hour to cross one field, while I can be away out of sight in half a minute. Besides, you really do look silly, you know! You ought to be ashamed of yourself.'

Well, at this Tortoise was rather annoyed. Hare was really very provoking.

'Look here' said Tortoise, 'if you want a race I'll give you one; and I don't need any start either.'

Hare laughed till the tears ran down his furry face, and his sides shook so much that he rolled over backwards. Tortoise just waited till Hare had finished, then he said:

'Well what about it? I'm not joking.'

Several other animals had gathered round, and they all said: 'Go on Hare. It's a challenge. You'll have to race him.'

'Certainly,' said Hare, 'if you want to make a fool of yourself. Where shall we race to?

Tortoise shaded his eyes with one foot and said:

'See that old windmill on the top of the hill yonder? We'll race to that. We can start from this tree-stump here. Come on, and may the best animal win!'

So as soon as they were both standing beside the tree-stump, Chanticleer the Cock shouted, 'Ready – steady – go!' and Tortoise began to crawl towards the far-off windmill. The other animals had hurried on ahead so as to see the finish.

Hare stood beside the tree-stump watching Tortoise waddle away across the field. The day was hot, and just beside the tree-stump was a pleasant, shady place, so he sat down and waited. He guessed it would take him about two and a half minutes to reach the windmill, even without trying very hard, so there was no hurry – no hurry at all. Presently he began to drop off to sleep. Two or three minutes passed, and Hare opened one eye lazily. Tortoise had scarcely crossed the first field. 'Steady and slow,' he said to himself under his breath. 'Steady and slow. That's what mother said.' And he kept on towards the far-off windmill.

'At that rate,' said Hare to himself sleepily, 'it'll take him just about two hours to get there – if he doesn't drop dead on the way.'

He closed his eye again and fell into a deep sleep.

After a while Tortoise had crossed the first field and was making his way slowly over the second.

'Steady and slow does it,' he muttered to himself.

The sun began to go down, and at last Hare woke up, feeling chilly.

'Where am I?' he thought. 'What's happened? Oh yes, I remember.'

He got to his feet and looked towards the windmill. But where was Tortoise? He was nowhere to be seen. Hare jumped on to the tree-stump and strained his eyes to gaze into the distance. There, half-way across the very last field before the windmill, was a tiny black dot. Tortoise!

'This won't do,' said Hare. 'I must have overslept. I'd better be moving.'

So he sprang from the stump and darted across the first field, then the second, then the third. It was really much farther than he had thought.

At the windmill the other animals were waiting to see the finish. At last Tortoise arrived, rather out of breath and wobbling a little on his legs.

'Come on, Tortoise!' they shouted.

Then Hare appeared at the far side of the last field, streaking along like the wind. How he ran! Not even Stag, when he was being hunted, could go faster. Even Swallow could scarcely fly faster through the blue sky.

'Steady and slow,' said Tortoise to himself, but no one could hear him, for he had very, very little breath left to walk with.

'Come on, Tortoise!' cried some animals, and a few cried, 'Come on, Hare! He's beating you!'

Hare put on extra speed and ran faster than he had ever run before. But it was no good. He had given Tortoise too much start, and he was still twenty yards behind when Tortoise crawled over the last foot of ground and tumbled up against the windmill. He had won the race!

All the animals cheered, and after that Hare never laughed at Tortoise again.

Æsop, adapted by James Reeves

The adventures of the Little Field Mouse

Once upon a time, there was a little brown Field Mouse; and one day he was out in the fields to see what he could find. He was running along in the grass, poking his nose into everything and looking with his two eyes all about, when he saw a smooth, shiny acorn lying in the grass. It was such a fine shiny little acorn that he thought he would take it home with him; so he put out his paw to touch it, but the little acorn rolled away from him. He ran after it, but it kept rolling on just ahead of him, till it came to a place where a big oak tree and its roots spread all over the ground. Then it rolled under a big, round root.

Little Mr Field Mouse ran to the root and poked his nose under after the acorn, and there he saw a small round hole in the ground. He slipped through and saw some stairs going down into the earth. The acorn was rolling down, with a soft tapping sound, ahead of him, so down he went too. Down, down, down, rolled the acorn, and down, down, down, went the Field Mouse, until suddenly he saw a tiny door at the foot of the stairs.

The shiny acorn rolled to the door and struck against it with a tap. Quickly the little door opened and the acorn rolled inside. The Field Mouse hurried as fast as he could down the last stairs, and pushed through just as the door was closing. It shut behind him and was in a little room. And there, before him, stood a queer little Red Man! He had a little red cap, and a little red jacket, and odd little red shoes with points at the toes.

'You are my prisoner,' he said to the Field Mouse.

'What for?' said the Field Mouse.

'Because you tried to steal my acorn,' said the little Red Man.

'It is my acorn,' said the Field Mouse; 'I found it.'

'No, it isn't,' said the little Red Man. 'I have it; you will never see it again.'

The little Field Mouse looked all about the room as fast as he could, but he could not see any acorn. Then he thought he would go back up the tiny stairs to his own home. But the little door was locked and the little Red Man had the key. And he said to the poor Mouse, 'You shall be my servant; you shall make my bed and sweep my room and cook my broth.'

So the little brown Mouse was the little Red Man's servant, and every day he made the little Red Man's bed and swept the little Red Man's room and cooked the little Red Man's broth. And every day the little Red Man went away through the tiny door and did not come back till afternoon. But he always locked the door after him, and carried away the key.

At last, one day he was in such a hurry that he turned the key before the door was quite latched, which, of course, didn't lock it at all. He went away without noticing – he was in such a hurry.

The little Field Mouse knew that his chance had come to run away home. But he didn't want to go without the pretty, shiny acorn. Where it was he didn't know, so he looked everywhere. He opened every little drawer and looked in, but it wasn't in any of the drawers; he peeped on every shelf, but it wasn't on a shelf; he hunted in every closet, but it wasn't in there. Finally, he climbed up on a chair and opened a wee, wee door in the chimney piece – and there it was!

He took it quickly in his forepaws, and then he took it in his mouth, and then he ran away. He pushed open the little door; he climbed out up the little stairs; he came through the hole under the root; he ran and ran through the fields; and at last he came to his own house.

When he was in his own house he set the shiny acorn on the table. I expect he set it down hard, for all at once, with a little snap, it opened! – exactly like a little box.

And what do you think! There was a tiny necklace inside! It was a most beautiful tiny necklace, all made of jewels, and it was just big enough for a lady mouse. So the little Field Mouse gave the tiny necklace to his little Mouse-sister. She thought it was perfectly lovely. And when she wasn't wearing it she kept it in the shiny acorn box.

And the little Red Man never knew what had become of it, because he didn't know where the little Field Mouse lived.

Sara Cone Bryant

Cat and Mouse

One summer's day, a young mouse set out looking for adventure.

'Be very careful!' said his mother. It's a dangerous world for mice. Watch out for traps, and watch out for the sharp claws of the cat, and above all, don't be too sure of anything.'

As the mouse ran in and out of the stems of the sunflowers a cat saw him and called out in a sweet voice, 'Hello there, Mouse!'

The mouse stopped, hearing his name called, and looked out nervously.

'Come on out, Mouse, and talk to me,' the cat said. 'I'm rather lonely, and I'd love a bit of company.'

'But aren't you a cat?' asked the young and innocent mouse.

'A cat? Perish the thought!' cried the cat piously. 'I am none other than Santa Claus. Look at my white whiskers and white eyebrows if you don't believe me.'

'Are you absolutely *sure* you're Santa Claus?' he asked, because there was still something about the cat that made him very suspicious.

'Of course I am,' said the cat. 'Look! Here are my claws to prove it. That's why I'm called Santa Claus. Come on out. I have presents and things for you just down the path.'

The mouse had heard that Santa Claus had white whiskers and white eyebrows, and also that he gave people presents.

As the mouse came out from among the sunflower stems, the cat pounced on him, catching him straight away.

'You should never believe everything you hear,' the cat said, 'because now I am going to eat you up.'

'You said we'd talk together,' cried the terrified mouse, realising he had been tricked.

'Well, we'll talk a bit first if you like,' said the cat. 'And then I'll eat you up afterwards. I have plenty of time, and I'm not terribly hungry. I just liked the thought of catching a mouse.'

The mouse thought very quickly.

'What makes you so sure I am a mouse?' he asked. 'You're not very clever for a cat.'

'Well, you *are* a mouse,' said the cat.

The mouse made himself laugh very hard. He didn't feel much like laughing. He just made himself laugh through sheer willpower.

'I'm not a mouse,' he said, when he had finished laughing, 'I'm a dog.'

It was the cat's turn to laugh, but it was a very surprised laugh. He had never caught a mouse like this one before.

'I know a mouse when I see one.'

'No – I'm definitely a dog!' declared the mouse, still laughing, 'and when I get my breath back, I'm going to bark at you and chase you up a tree.'

Inside his mouse-mind he was telling himself: I'm not a mouse... I'm a dog. I'm *not* a mouse. I'm a *dog*. He made himself think dog thoughts.

'Just imagine you thinking that I am a mouse!' he cried.

'Well you look *quite* like a mouse,' the cat said, sounding rather less sure of himself. The mouse was looking a lot more like a dog than the cat had thought at first.

'Let me hear you bark!' the cat commanded.

'Wait a moment...' In his mouse-mind he was telling himself: Think *dog*! Bark *dog*! Be *dog*! 'Well, are you ready?'

'Yes!' said the cat.

'Then stand back a bit because I don't want to deafen you with my barking,' the mouse said, and the cat actually did stand back a bit, though he kept one paw firmly on the mouse's tail. The mouse barked as well as he could, but it came out very like a mouse's squeak.

'There!' said the cat triumphantly, 'and I'm going to eat you straight away because I can see you're a very tricky mouse.'

The mouse did not lose his head, even though he thought the cat might take it off with a single bite.

'You really do have mice on the brain. It'll serve you right when I chase you up a tree.'

'Think *dog*! Be *dog*!' he muttered under his whiskers. He made himself laugh in an easy-going fashion.

As he spoke a strange thing happened to the mouse. By now he believed he actually *was* a dog. The cat, which had looked so terrible a moment ago, began to look small and silly. Cowardly, too! He felt *dogness* swell up inside him. He thought he could remember burying bones, fighting other dogs, and, of course, chasing many, many cats. He felt a bark swelling in his throat. He barked again.

My goodness! the cat thought. He really *is* a dog, and here I am with my paw on his tail. The cat looked nervous and the mouse felt very strong. He opened his mouth and barked for the third time. This time there was no doubt about it: it was a really wonderful bark. The cat took his paw off the mouse's tail and ran for the trees with the mouse chasing him, barking furiously. The cat shot up the tree like a furry rocket and hid among the leaves.

Whew! That was a narrow escape, thought the cat, cowering at the top of the tree.

Whew! That was a narrow escape, thought the mouse at the bottom of the tree. 'I'm off home to Mother!'

As he reached the mousehole he saw his mother, nervously collecting sunflower seeds outside.

'Mother!' called the mouse. 'Here I am, home again.'

'Ahhhh! A dog!' screamed his mother and popped down into the mousehole.

The mouse lay outside in the sun with his paws stretched in front of him and his tongue hanging out.

'Think *mouse*,' he panted. 'Think *mouse*!'

So he thought *mouse*, and, as he thought *mouse*, the *dogness* died away.

'What am I doing sitting out here in broad daylight with my tongue hanging out?' he squeaked to himself. 'I must be mad. That cat could come back at any moment.'

Then he scuttled into the mousehole where his mother met him with great delight.

'I'm glad you're back,' she said. 'It's dangerous out there. A big dog ran at me, barking.'

'A cat caught me,' the mouse said, 'but I escaped.'

'Escaped? Oh, my son! How did you manage that?'

'Cleverness,' said the mouse modestly. 'Cleverness and courage. I chased the cat up the tree.'

Exaggerating again, thought his mother, fondly.

Then the mouse and his mother had a delicious dinner of sunflower seeds.

As for the cat, he stayed up in the tree all day for fear of the savage dog that was waiting somewhere below in the summer garden.

Margaret Mahy

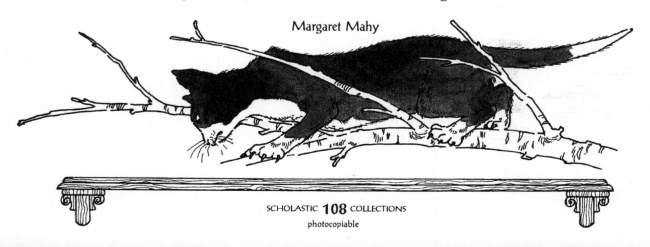

Clever Polly and the stupid wolf

Did I say that the wolf never came back? I'm wrong, he did come back a year or two later. This time Polly was sitting at the window of the drawing-room and she saw the wolf open the garden gate and glance anxiously around. He looked up and saw Polly.

'Good morning, Polly,' said the wolf.

'Good morning, Wolf,' said Polly. 'What have you come here for?'

'I have come to eat you up,' replied the wolf. 'And this time I'm going to get you.'

Polly smiled. She knew that last time she had been cleverer than the wolf and she was not really frightened.

'I'm not going to eat you up this morning,' said the wolf. 'I'm going to come back in the middle of the night and climb in at your bedroom window and gobble you up. By the way,' said the wolf, 'which is your bedroom window?'

'That one,' said Polly, pointing upwards. 'Right at the top of the house. You'll find it rather difficult, won't you, to get right up there?'

Then the wolf smiled. 'I'm cleverer than you think,' he said. 'I thought it would probably mean climbing and I have come prepared.'

Polly saw him go to a flower bed and make a little hole in the earth. Into the hole he dropped something, she couldn't see what, and covered it carefully up again.

'Wolf,' said Polly, 'what were you doing then?'

'Oh' said the wolf, 'this is my great cleverness. I have planted a pip of a grape. This pip will grow into a vine and the vine will climb up the house and I shall climb up the vine. I shall pop in through your bedroom window and then, Polly, I shall get you at last.'

Polly laughed. 'Poor Wolf,' she said. 'Do you know how long it will take for that pip to grow into a vine?'

'No,' said the wolf. 'Two or three days? I'm very hungry.'

'Perhaps,' said Polly, 'in a week or two a little shoot might poke its way above the ground, but it would be months before the vine could start climbing and years and years before it could reach my bedroom window.'

'Oh bother!' said the wolf. 'I can't wait years and years and years to reach your bedroom window. I shall have to have another idea even better than this one. Good-bye, Polly, for the present,' and he trotted off.

About a week later Polly was sitting at the drawing-room window again. She was sewing and did not notice the wolf come into the garden until she heard a sort of scrambling noise outside. Then she looked out of the window and saw the wolf very busy planting something in the earth again.

'Good morning, Wolf,' said Polly. 'What are you planting this time?'

'This time,' said the wolf, 'I've had a Really good idea. I'm planting something which will grow up to your window in a moment.'

'Oh,' said Polly, interested. 'What is that?'

'I have planted the rung of a ladder,' said the wolf. 'By tomorrow morning there'll be a long ladder stretching right up to your bedroom window. I specially chose a rung from the longest ladder I could see. A steeplejack was on the other end of it climbing a church steeple. He will be surprised when he comes down and finds the bottom rung of his ladder has gone. But in a very short time I shall be climbing in at your bedroom window, little Polly, and that will be the end of *you*.'

Polly laughed. 'Oh, poor Wolf, didn't you know that ladders don't grow from rungs or from anything else? They have to be made by men, and however many rungs you plant in this garden, even of steeplejacks' ladders, they won't grow into anything you could climb up. Go away, Wolf, and have a better idea, if you can.'

The wolf looked very sad. He tucked his tail between his legs and trotted off along the road.

A week later Polly, who now knew what to expect, was sitting at the drawing-room window looking up and down the road.

'What are you waiting for?' asked her mother.

'I'm waiting for that stupid wolf,' said Polly. 'He's sure to come today. I wonder what silly idea he'll have got into his big head now?'

Presently the gate squeaked and the wolf came in carrying something very carefully in his mouth. He put it down on the grass and started to dig a deep hole.

Polly watched him drop the thing he had been carrying into the hole, cover it over with earth again, and stand back with a pleased expression.

'Wolf,' called Polly, 'what have you planted this time?'

'This time,' replied the wolf, 'you aren't going to escape. Have you read 'Jack and the Beanstalk', Polly?'

'Well, I haven't exactly read it,' said Polly, 'but I know the story very well indeed.'

'This time,' said the wolf, 'I've planted a bean. Now we know from the story of Jack that beans grow up to the sky in no time at all, and perhaps I shall be in your bedroom before it's light tomorrow morning, crunching up the last of your little bones.'

'A bean!' said Polly, very much interested. 'Where did it come from?'

'I shelled it out of its pod,' said the wolf proudly.

'And the pod?' Polly asked. 'Where did that come from?'

'I bought it in the vegetable shop,' said the wolf, 'with my own money,' he added. 'I bought half a pound, and it cost me a whole sixpence, but I shan't have wasted it because it will bring me a nice, juicy little girl to eat.'

'You bought it?' said Polly. 'Yourself, with your own money?'

'All by myself,' said the wolf grandly.

'No one gave it to you?' Polly insisted.

'No one,' said the wolf. He looked very proud.

'You didn't exchange it for anything?' Polly asked again.

'No,' said the wolf. He was puzzled.

'Oh, poor Wolf,' said Polly pityingly. 'You haven't read 'Jack and the Beanstalk' at all. Don't you know that its only a *magic* bean that grows up to the sky in a night, and you can't buy magic beans. You have to be given them by an old man in exchange for a cow or something like that. It's no good *buying* beans, that won't get you anywhere.'

Two large tears dropped from the wolf's eyes.

'But I haven't *got* a cow,' he cried.

'If you had you wouldn't need to eat me,' Polly pointed out. 'You could eat the cow. It's no good, Wolf, you aren't going to get me this time. Come back in a month or two, and we'll have a bean-feast off the plant you've just planted.'

'I hate beans,' the wolf sighed, 'and I've got nearly a whole half-pound of them at home.' He turned to go. 'But don't be too cock-a-hoop, Miss Polly, for I'll get you yet!'

But clever Polly knew he never would.

Catherine Storr

A desire to serve the people

This passage describes the childhood of Nelson Mandela, leader of South Africa's anti-apartheid movement who was made the country's president in 1994.

When a son was born to Chief Henry Gadla Mandela and his wife, Nonqaphi, on 18 July 1918, they gave him the Xhosa name of Rolihlahla and, because it was the fashion to have a European name, preferably a heroic one, they also called him Nelson.

The boy and his three sisters lived in the family kraal of whitewashed huts not far from Umtata in the Transkei. Although the Mandelas were members of the royal family of the Thembu people, Nelson, like most African children, herded sheep and cattle and helped with the ploughing.

As a young boy he was tall for his age, and was a fast runner. He hunted buck and, when hungry, stole mealie cobs from the maize fields. He loved the countryside with its grassy rolling hills, and the stream which flowed eastward to the Indian ocean.

At night, under Africa's brilliant stars, everyone used to gather around a big open fire to listen to the elders of the tribe. The boy was fascinated by the tales told by these bearded old men. Tales about the 'good old days before the coming of the white man', and tales about the brave acts performed by their ancestors, in defending their country against the European invaders.

Those tales, said Mandela many years later when he was on trial for his life, stirred in him a desire to serve his people in their struggle to be free. A desire which eventually led to his becoming the most famous political prisoner of our time — a prisoner with songs written about him and streets named after him. How appropriate that Nelson Mandela's Xhosa name, Rolihlahla, means 'stirring up trouble'.

When Nelson first went to school – a school for African children – it was a shock to find the history books described only white heroes, and referred to his people as savages and cattle thieves. All the same he was eager for western education, and proud that his great-grandfather had given land on which to build a mission school. Even when fellow-pupils teased him about his clothes, cast-offs from his father, he pretended not to mind.

At home he picked up

information not taught at school, about how Dutch and British settlers with guns had fought and defeated blacks with spears, and taken almost all of their land. Then, how the British, after defeating the Dutch in the Boer War (Boer was the Dutch word for farmer), had shared power with their former enemy. Despite passionate protests from Africans and liberal whites, the British government gave the million white South Africans total control over the 4½ million 'non-whites' — Africans, Asians and those of mixed race, known as 'Coloured' people. The Boers, calling themselves Afrikaners, had become an

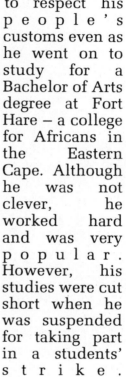

important part of the all-white parliament which passed more and more colour bar laws. They aimed at keeping Africans – 'natives' – as labourers and servants, who were not allowed to move freely in their own country and were forced to live in 'reserves' or 'locations'. Such inhuman policies could only be maintained by force and, from earliest childhood, Nelson heard names such as Bulhoek and Bondelswarts – names which recalled the massacre of hundreds of Africans.

In 1930 Henry Mandela fell seriously ill. Realising that he was

dying, he presented his son to the Paramount Chief. He asked that the boy be given a good education. So Nelson became the ward of David Dalindyebo, and lived in a modest hut at the Chief's Great Place, Mqekezweni. Fitted with new clothes, he went to a Methodist boarding school.

He continued to respect his people's customs even as he went on to study for a Bachelor of Arts degree at Fort Hare – a college for Africans in the Eastern Cape. Although he was not clever, he worked hard and was very popular. However, his studies were cut short when he was suspended for taking part in a students' strike. Returning home, he was ordered by the Paramount Chief to give up the protest. He might have obeyed but for an unexpected development. 'My guardian,' he later explained, 'felt it was time for me to get married. He loved me very much, but he was no democrat and did not think it worthwhile to consult me about a wife. He selected a girl, fat and dignified, and arrangements were made for the wedding.'

By this time, Nelson had also realised that he was being groomed for chieftainship, and had no wish to rule over an oppressed people. He decided to run away.

Mary Benson

Sea-woman

It was an empty, oyster-and-pearl afternoon. The water lipped at the sand and sorted the shingle and lapped round the rock where the girl was sitting.

Then she saw a seal, like a mass of seaweed almost, until she gazed into those eyes. It swam in quite close, just twenty or thirty water-steps away.

She looked at the seal; the seal looked at her. Then it barked. It cried out in a loud voice.

She stood up on her rock. She called out to the seal: not a word but a sound, the music words are made of.

The seal swam in a little closer. It looked at the girl. Then it cried. Oh! The moon's edge and a mother's ache were in that cry.

The girl jumped off the rock. Her eyes were sea-eyes, wide and flint-grey. 'Seal!' she cried. 'Sea-woman! What do you want?'

And what did the seal want but the girl's company? As she padded down the strand, it followed her, always keeping fifteen or twenty water-steps away, out in the dark swell. The girl turned back towards her rock, and the seal turned with her. Sometimes it huffed and puffed, sometimes it cried, it wailed as if it were lost, all at sea.

The girl bent down and picked up a curious shell, opaline and milky and intricate.

'Listen, listen!' sang the wind in the shell's mouth.

Then the girl raised the shell and pressed it to her right ear.

'One afternoon,' sang the shell, 'oyster-and-pearl, a man came back from the fishing. He was so weary. He peeled off his salt-stiff clothing. He washed. For an hour or two hours he closed his eyes. And then, when the moon rose, he came strolling along this strand.

'He listened to the little waves kissing in the rocks. He smelt earth on the breeze and knew it would soon rain. This is where he walked, rocking slightly from side to side, in no hurry at all for there was nowhere to go.

'Then he stopped. Down the beach, no more than the distance of a shout, he saw a group of sea-people dancing. They were singing and swaying; they danced like the waves of the sea.

'Then the sea-people saw him. At once they stopped singing and broke their bright ring. As the fisherman began to run towards them, they turned towards a pile of sealskins – in the moonlight they looked like a wet rock – and picked them up and pulled them on and plunged into the water.

'One young woman was not so quick, though. She was so caught up in the dance that the fisherman reached her skin before she did. He snatched it up and tucked it under one arm. Then he turned to face the sea-woman, and he was grinning.

'"Please," she said. Her voice was high as a handbell and flecked with silver. "Please."

'The fisherman shook his head.

'"My skin," said the sea-woman. There she stood, dressed in moonlight, reaching out towards him with her white arms; and he stood between her and the sea.

'"I've landed some catches," breathed the fisherman, "but never anything like this..."

'Then the young woman began to sob. "I cannot," she cried. "I cannot go back without my skin."

'...*and this catch I'll keep*, thought the fisherman.

'"My home and my family and my friends," said the sea-woman.

'Now she wept and the moon picked up her salt tears and turned them into pearls. How lovely she was, and lovely in more ways than one: a young woman lithe as young women are, a sea-child, a sister of the moon. For all her tears, the fisherman had not the least intention of giving her back her skin.

'"You'll come with me," he said.

'The sea-woman shuddered.

'Then the man stepped forward and took her by the wrist. "Home with me," he said.

'The sea-woman neither moved towards the man nor pulled away from him. "Please," she said, her voice sweet and ringing. "The sea is my home, the shouting waves, the green light and the darkening."

'But the fisherman had set his heart against it. He led the sea-woman along the strand and into the silent village and back to his home.

'Then the fisherman shut the door on the sea-woman and went out into the night again to hide the skin. He ran up to the haystack in the field behind his house, and loosened one of the haybricks and hid the skin behind it. Within ten minutes, he was back on his own doorstep.

'The sea-woman was still there; without her skin, there was nowhere for her to go. She looked at the man. With her flint-grey eyes she looked at him.'

For a moment the girl lowered the shell from her ear. She gazed at the emptiness around her, no one on the beach or on the hillslope leading down to it, no one between her and the north pole. The little waves were at their kissing and the seal still kept her company, bobbing up and down in the welling water.

'Listen, listen!' sang the wind in the shell's mouth.

The girl raised the shell again and pressed it to her right ear.

'Time passed,' sang the shell, 'and the sea-woman stayed with the fisherman. Without her skin, she was unable to go back to the sea, and the fisherman was no worse than the next man.

'For his part, the fisherman fell in love. He had spent half his life on the ocean. He knew all her moods and movements and colours, and he saw them in the sea-woman.

'Before long the man and the woman married, and they had one daughter and then two sons. The sea-woman loved them dearly and was a good mother to them. They were no different from other children except in one way: there was a thin, half-transparent web between their fingers and their toes.

'Often the woman came walking along the strand, where the fisherman had caught her. She sat on a rock; she sang sad songs about a happier time; and at times a large seal came swimming in towards her, calling out to her. But what could she do? She talked to the seal in the language they shared; she stayed here for hours; but always, in the end, she turned away and slowly walked back to the village.

'Late one summer afternoon, the sea-woman's three children were larking around on the haystack behind their house. One of the little boys gave his sister a push from behind, and the girl grabbed wildly at the wall of the haystack.

'One haybrick came away. And the skin, the sealskin that the fisherman had hidden in one stack after another as the years passed, fell to the ground.

'The children stopped playing. They fingered the skin; they buried their faces in its softness; they took it back to show their mother.

'The sea-woman dared scarcely look at it and looked at it; dared scarcely touch it and touched it.

'"Mother!" said the children, crowding around her. "What is it?"

'The sea-woman pulled her children to her. She dragged them to her and squeezed them. She hugged and kissed each of them. Then she turned and ran out of the house with her skin.

'The children were afraid. They followed her. They saw her pull on the skin, cry a great cry, and dive off a rock. Then a large seal rose to meet her and the two seals leaped and dived through the water.

'When their father came back from the fishing, his children were standing at the stone jetty.

'"You go home," said the man. "I'll come back in an hour."

'Slowly the man waded in his salt-stiff clothing along this strand. He kept rubbing his pale blue eyes and looking out across the dancing water.

'She rose out of the waves. She was no more than a few water-steps away.

'"Husband!" she cried. "Husband! Look after our children! Take care of our children!" Her voice carried over the water. "You've loved me and looked after me, and I've loved you. But for as long as I lived with you, I always loved my first husband better."

'Then the sea-woman, the seal-woman, slipped under the sallow waves once more. One moment she was there; the next, she was not there...'

The girl took the opaline shell away from her ear, and set it down on the sand. For a long time she sat there. The seal had gone; it had deserted her and the dark water shivered.

From *British Folk Tales* by Kevin Crossley-Holland

The charcoal burner

Staring with red eyes that bulged out of blackened orbits, the charcoal burner looked more like a devil than a man. His beard, if it had been washed, would have been white; but it was so full of black dust that the fires of hell might have scorched it. The lost traveller was appalled, for a moment, by the inhuman ferocity of the old man's appearance. But the storm was rising and, between his shoulderblades, he felt a spatter of hard snow – to employ an image belonging to our times, here were the tracer bullets of the blizzard finding their target.

'Let me in!' cried the traveller. 'For God's sake, let me in!'

'Hey there, Hektor!' shouted the old man; and there appeared a great black-and-grey dog, three-parts wolf, hideously fanged.

In a breaking voice, the wayfarer said: 'For the love of God, man, let me in! All I ask is to lie by your fire. A bit of bread... an onion... anything. I will pay you well. Here –' His hands were very cold, but after some fumbling he found a large silver coin – his fingers were too numb to take hold of a smaller one – and offered it.

The old charcoal burner snatched the coin, tasted it, bit it, put it away under his rags, and growled: 'I thought you were another of these tax-gatherers. Even so, I don't like company. You can come in, if you like, seeing as you pay your way; which is a devil of a long sight more than most people do... Down, Hektor!... Ah, yes, sir, you may well look! Hektor's mother was a grey wolf. If I snapped my fingers once, he'd pin you; if I snapped them twice, he'd tear your throat out.' Maliciously, the charcoal burner extended a blackened hand and took a pinch of air between thumb and second finger.

'Don't do it!' cried the visitor, watching the dog who, crouching for a spring, was growling deep in his throat.

The old man said: 'You can sit by my fire, if you like. Since you've paid for it, you can have some soup.'

'Thank you,' said the traveller, shaking snow out of his fur cloak and coming through a stinging fog of stinking smoke towards the fire. 'Some soup, yes, and shelter until daybreak. Do you happen to have something strong to drink?'

'Plum brandy – if you can pay for it,' said the old man.

'Why,' cried the traveller, 'I have already paid you more than you could earn in three months! Get out your plum brandy this instant, you surly dog!'

'Speaking of dog...' said the old man, and held up conjoined thumb and second finger. Hektor snarled, crouching again. The traveller found a small coin this time, which he gave to the old man who, then, pulled as it were from out of the smoke that filled the hovel a crockery jar half full of something that had the perfume of an autumnal orchard delicately flavoured with wood smoke. Of this the traveller drank. The charcoal burner drank, too. Scratching the place where he had put his money – under his left armpit – he said: 'You are some kind of a clerk?'

'That is right,' said the traveller.

'I can tell from your dress,' said the old man, 'and by the way you carry your sword. What is more, your cloak is of fox fur. You must be a middling high-up kind of clerk; otherwise you'd be wearing coney, or mole-skin, at the best... not wolfskin – oh no! There's more warmth in that than any amount of foxes. But that's fit only for the likes of me....Vanity, vanity! Go on, have some more plum brandy, and eat your soup. If you want bread, you can whistle for it, because I haven't got any.'

Warmed by the fire and the plum brandy, the visitor said: 'You are a charcoal burner, I take it, my friend?'

'How d'you think I got so black? Weaving silk? Making tapestry? It isn't a clean trade, mister, charcoal burning. If you don't believe me, you try it and see! Have some more plum brandy, if you like.... Oho! Particular, are you? Go on, then – wipe the jar on your sleeve. Is it my fault I follow a dirty trade, and get all black? Drink, and pass the jar.'

The visitor said: 'I see that you are a misanthrope, my friend. That means to say, that you do not like your fellow creatures.'

The charcoal burner replied: 'I have too much to do to like my fellow creatures. All I know is the forest: out with my axe and cut and cut and cut – wood, wood, wood. Then, make my stack, light my fires, and wait and wait and wait. Fill my baskets, hump 'em into town, sell the charcoal for what I can get... and back again! Cut and burn and carry, carry and burn and cut.... I like the little trees. Tell you something – I'd soon hew down a man as a sweet little tree.' The charcoal burner drank more plum brandy. 'By killing the things I love, to warm the creatures I don't like – that's how I live.'

'That is life, friend,' said the traveller.

'I know, and you can keep it.'

'But, my friend, judging by your accent, you are not from these parts, surely?'

'No, I'm from over the Frontier. Ran away. Too much taxes. I was born and bred over there by St. Agnes's. I was comfortable enough, but they won't leave a man alone. What was it you called me just now – miserope?'

'*Misanthrope*, my friend; which means one who dislikes his fellow creatures.'

'Well, you are not far wrong, you know. The more I've seen of men, the more I love my dog. I wasn't always like this, though, was I, Hektor?' The wolf-dog growled as it were in assent. The old man took another drink of plum brandy and continued:

'When I lived over by St. Agnes's, I used to be a good-natured fellow enough, until my woman died in child-bed, and after that I kept myself to myself – cut my wood, charred my wood, sold my charcoal, made ends meet. Earned enough to keep me and my dogs. Twenty years ago this was, mind you.

'I don't mind telling you that if you hadn't shoved a little ready money through the door tonight I'd have let you go out into the storm, and be damned to you. But in those days I was full of good nature. This was in Hektor's Grandmother's time. She was having a litter just about then. Her husband, the dog, was called Kuli – great big red beast – could pin a wild pig by the ear or pull down a wolf. More than half wolf himself – couldn't even bark – could only howl.... Have some more plum brandy? No? Well, if you won't, I will.

'One night, in a crackling frost, with the snow knee-deep, Kuli starts howling. "That means strangers," I says to myself. Now the nearest fellow human being lived a league to two away, by the palace, and they wasn't likely to come and visit the likes of me. So I calls Kuli, and get my axe, and covers my ears with my cap, and I looks out. Well, up on the hill (I'm in the valley by the forest, d'you see) somebody is waving a lantern and crying for help. I says to Kuli: "Go, mark 'em, boy; mark 'em Kuli!" And off Kuli goes, loping like a wolf through the snow. I follow in Kuli's tracks and, they lead me to an old gentleman and a boy lost in a snowdrift. The old gentleman is carrying under his cloak a kind of bundle. The boy is shivering in his shoes, empty-handed. The old gentleman says: "Lead me to St. Agnes's." In those days, I'd do anything for anybody. D'you follow me?

'"A matter of five hundred paces," I says, "Follow me, gentlemen." D'you follow me?

'So they follow me. The boy falls down. The old gentleman has his hands full with his parcels, so I slings the young 'un across my shoulders, and Kuli leads us back to my hut.

'I'm not a rich man, never have been – if I was, you understand, I wouldn't be burning charcoal in the bitter forest and coughing black. All the same, I always make ends meet –' the charcoal burner puts the tips of his forefingers together, '– like *that*. One thing I always have in my hut, and that is, a good fire. Well, that year hadn't been a good one. Still, I had soup in the pot. For the sake of Christian charity – in those days, I believed in Christian charity – I chucked in my last chunk of bacon, and rubbed the boy's frozen feet with snow (*he* would have thawed them directly at the fire!) and old Kuli licked them just as the dog in the Bible licked the sores of Lazarus.... If you ask me, Kuli licked the boy's feet for the sake of the salt. But when the old man saw this, he burst into tears. Proud and humble, both at the same time.

'Then I put the soup into my one bowl, and they ate. Oh, but how that boy could tuck the grub away! The old man had the spoon. He sniffed and he sipped, he sipped and he sniffed, and he said: "What do you put in this, my poor man?" I told him – a bit of bacon, a bit of goat, a few roots. Wild garlic, essential; but first of all throw into your pot some pig's fat and half a handful of flour. "Fry the flour in the fat until it is brown. Then, toss in half a handful of the fruit of the sweet pepper tree, dried and ground up," I told him, "but not with the seeds. They'll burn your tongue. Add water – a little to begin with – stir it up, and after that sling in what you like. Anything goes."

'By this time, the rime was melted off his cloak, and I could see that he was dressed in sable and ermine. No doubt about it, he was a Somebody. I had a little bit of plum brandy left in the house, so I offered it. I make it myself. You've tasted it. It's not bad, is it?... Well, the old gentleman drank, and so did the young 'un. At last, the old one got up and said: "Now I see how the Poor live." The frost had melted in his beard, and turned to water. He shook it out into my fire, where it hissed. Then he looked me up and down and said:

'"I came here, my man, to bring you gifts in honour of the season of the year... a haunch of venison, some wine, and fuel. The meat and the wine, unfortunately, were lost when my page Prokop dropped them into a snowdrift. The Christmas fuel, however, I have with me. Take it!" And he threw down three little pine logs. "Not that you appear to need it," he said, "the heat in your hovel is suffocating.... Have you a timber-drag?"

'As if he didn't know: a charcoal burner without a timber-drag. I ask you! So I nodded, and he said: "Take my page and me home, fellow." And what could I do but obey the old beard, since he was King Vaclav – the one they made the ballad about – the old man they call Good King Wenceslas? The following spring, he took a mistress from Wallachia, and wow, but she stung him to rights! A castle, no less, and three thousand acres o' fat land! Light head and heavy purse make light purse and heavy head. He remembered, then, how well the Poor live – meaning me – and slapped on such a heavy tax that I fled the country.

'Can you wonder that I do not welcome visitors at this time of the year?'

Drowsily, the traveller shook his head. Then he nodded. Just before he fell asleep he heard the old charcoal burner grumble: 'The very idea of the old fool, bringing *me* pine logs....'

Gerald Kersh

WHAT MAKES THINGS TICK?

The voracious vacuum cleaner

There was an old woman who lived all alone in a bungalow. At times she wanted company and wondered if she should buy a cat or a dog. But she was a finicky old person who liked to keep her home spotlessly clean and she thought an animal would make it dirty.

One day the doorbell rang and there was a man standing on her doorstep holding a bulky parcel.

'Madam, allow me to show you our latest vacuum cleaner,' he said. 'It is called The Voracious. It will go anywhere, consume anything. There is no need to plug it in, so it can keep you company while you do the chores together. It is much more use than a pet as it cleans up instead of messing everything. It doesn't need food either, just dust and rubbish.'

When he unpacked The Voracious, the old woman saw that it did indeed look rather like an unusual pet. It had a sleek grey body and a long hose coming out of one end that looked like a neck. The broad nozzle on the end of the hose was like a head with a wide grinning mouth. When the man switched it on, it gave a low purr that sounded like, 'I'm hunngree.' The old woman was delighted. 'It even talks!' she said, 'I'll buy it.'

When the man had gone, she eagerly began to try out The Voracious. Soon there was not a speck of dust left in the bungalow, but The Voracious still purred: 'I'm hunngree, I'm hunngree.'

'You are a greedy one,' said the old woman affectionately. But as she turned round to find some more dust for it, there was a sound like 'SCHRULLP SCHRULLP,' and a rug whizzed into The Voracious Vacuum Cleaner's nozzle, quickly followed by some cushions, a small table and the television.

'Stop! Stop!' cried the old woman but The Voracious just said: 'I'm hunngree, I'm hunngree.'

This time it sounded more like a snarl than a purr. Next the sofa and two armchairs disappeared down it with an even louder SCHRULLP. As the furniture went down, the hose bulged like a python swallowing a goat.

'Stop it at once!' shrieked the old woman, but as she stretched out to switch off The Voracious, SCHRULLP SCHRULLP, down she went too and landed with a bump on the sofa inside.

After all this eating, The Voracious had grown to about the size of a van, but it still went on gobbling everything it could see. When it had swallowed everything in the bungalow, it rolled its way out into the street. There it met the milkman on his delivery round. He was carrying two crates of milk bottles. The Voracious was now the size of a truck and blocked the road.

The milkman said, 'Please would you move out of my way.'

'I'm Hunngree Hunngree Hunngree!' growled The Voracious Vacuum Cleaner and SCHRULLP SCHRULLP SCHRULLP down went the milkman, milk crates and all.

'Pity you don't have any tea with you,' said the old woman, when the milkman and his bottles landed with a crash inside. 'I could do with a cup right now.'

By now The Voracious was the size of a bus. Round the corner came a class of school children with their teacher. They had been to the library and each clutched a book.

'Let the children pass,' cried the teacher.

'I'm HUNNGREE HUNNGREE HUNNGREE!' SCHRULLP SCHRULLP down went all the children and the teacher.

'Make yourselves comfortable and have some milk,' said the old woman and the milkman when the teacher and the children landed in a heap on the sofa.

Now The Voracious was as large as a cottage and it rolled into the High Street. Just then a crowd of young men going to a football match came face to face with it. They were dressed in bright hats and scarves and they were singing their team song. Before they could pause for breath The Voracious roared:

'I'm HUNNGREE HUNNGREE HUNNGREE!'

And SCHRULLP SCHRULLP SCHRULLP SCHRULLP down the hose they all went still singing, 'Here we go! Here we go! Here we go!'

'You can make yourselves useful and read to the children,' said the old woman, the milkman and the teacher when the football fans tumbled on to the sofa.

Next a great yellow crane came rumbling up the road. With it was a team of builders in yellow overalls and hard hats. They were on their way to a building site. The Voracious was now the size of a house. 'Move yourself, mate!' shouted the crane driver.

'I'm HUNNGREE HUNNGREE HUNNGREE!' The Voracious bellowed, and SCHRULLP SCHRULLP SCHRULLP SCHRULLP down went the crane and the builders.

'Oh, we are glad to see you,' said the old woman, the milkman, the teacher, the children and the football fans when the crane and the builders squeezed in. 'Perhaps you'll be able to get us out of this monstrous machine.' But the crane driver and the builders had no better ideas than anyone else.

Meanwhile The Voracious had grown to the size of a church, so it barely noticed a roller-skate lying lost in the road, though it swallowed it up all the same because the skate was in its path. But the skate had no intention of being swallowed right down inside The Voracious. Instead, it rolled into the vacuum cleaner's machinery before it could be swept on to the sofa like everyone else.

At that moment a big fire engine came screeching up the road, its sirens blaring. When the fire chief shouted 'Out of our way!' The Voracious swelled even larger and reached out its nozzle, but the only sound that came out was CLICKHISS CLICKHISS CLICKHISS CLUNK CLUNK. The roller-skate had jammed the works. The body of The Voracious went on swelling as it tried to swallow until there was a loud BOOM!

There, sitting among the wreckage, were the old lady, the milkman, the teacher, the children, the football fans, the builders and their crane. They were all extremely dusty and very happy to be out.

Everyone helped the old woman take her furniture back into her bungalow. She saw the roller-skate glinting in the rubble and, thinking that it might come in useful, took it back as well.

It proved very useful indeed because after that the old woman did not like to use a vacuum cleaner. Instead, she scooted round the bungalow on the skate whenever she did her sweeping. This made it a much quicker job. And she was never lonely again because she had made so many friends inside The Voracious Vacuum Cleaner.

Laura Cecil

My naughty little sister makes a bottle tree

One day, when I was a little girl, and my naughty little sister was a littler girl, my naughty little sister got up very early one morning, and while my mother was cooking the breakfast, my naughty little sister went quietly, quietly out of the kitchen door, and quietly, quietly up the garden-path. Do you know why she went *quietly* like that? It was because she was *up to mischief*.

She didn't stop to look at the flowers, or the marrows or the runner-beans, and she didn't put her fingers in the water-tub. No! She went right along to the tool-shed to find a trowel. You know what trowels are, of course, but my naughty little sister didn't. She called the trowel 'a digger'.

'Where is the digger?' said my naughty little sister to herself.

Well, she found the trowel, and she took it down the garden until she came to a very nice place in the big flower-bed. Then she stopped and began to dig and dig with the trowel, which you know was a most naughty thing to do, because of all the little baby seeds that are waiting to come up in flower-beds sometimes.

Shall I tell you why my naughty little sister dug that hole? All right, I will. It was because she wanted to plant a brown shiny acorn. So, when she had made a really nice deep hole, she put the acorn in it, and covered it all up again with earth, until the brown shiny acorn was all gone.

Then my naughty little sister got a stone, and a leaf, and a stick, and she put them on top of the hole, so that she could remember where the acorn was, and then she went indoors to have her hands washed for breakfast. She didn't tell me, or my mother or anyone about the acorn. She kept it for her secret.

Well now, my naughty little sister kept going down the garden all that day, to look at the stone, the leaf and the stick, on top of her acorn-hole, and my naughty little sister smiled and smiled to herself because she knew that there was a brown shiny acorn under the earth.

But when my father came home, he was very cross. He said, 'Who's been digging in my flowerbed?'

And my little sister said, 'I have.'

Then my father said, 'You are a bad child. You've disturbed all the little baby seeds!'

And my naughty little sister said, 'I don't care about the little baby seeds, I want a home for my brown shiny acorn.'

So my father said, 'Well, *I* care about the little baby seeds myself, so I shall dig your acorn up for you, and you must find another home for it,' and he dug it up for her at once, and my naughty little sister tried all over the garden to find a new place for her acorn.

But there were beans and marrows and potatoes and lettuce and tomatoes and roses and spinach and radishes, and no room at all for the acorn, so my naughty little sister grew crosser and crosser and when tea-time came she wouldn't eat her tea. Aren't you glad you don't show off like that?

Then my mother said, 'Now don't be miserable. Eat up your tea and you shall help me to plant your acorn in a bottleful of water.'

So my naughty little sister ate her tea after all, and then my mother, who was a clever woman, filled a bottle with water, and showed my naughty little sister how to put the acorn in the top of the bottle.

Shall I tell you how she did it, in case you want to try?

Well now, my naughty little sister put the pointy end of the acorn into the water, and left the bottom of the acorn sticking out of the top – (the bottom end, you know, is the end that sits in the little cup when it's on the tree).

'Now,' said my mother, 'you can watch its little root grow in the water.'

My naughty little sister had to put her acorn in lots of bottles of water, because the bottles were always getting broken, as she put them in such funny places. She put them on the kitchen window-sill where the cat walked, and on the side of the bath, and inside the bookcase, until my mother said, 'We'll put it on top of the cupboard, and I will get it down for you to see every morning after breakfast.'

Then at last, the little root began to grow. It pushed down, down into the bottle of water and it made lots of other little roots that looked just like whitey fingers, and my little sister was pleased as pleased. Then, one day, a little shoot came out of the top of the acorn, and broke all the browny outside off, and on this little shoot were two little baby leaves, and the baby leaves grew and grew, and my mother said, 'That little shoot will be a big tree one day.'

My naughty little sister was very pleased. When she was pleased she danced and danced, so you can just guess how she danced to think of her acorn growing into a tree.

'Oh,' she said, 'when it's a tree we can put a swing on it, and I can swing indoors on my very own tree.'

But my mother said, 'Oh, no. I'm afraid it won't like being indoors very much now, it will want to grow out under the sky.'

Then my little sister had a good idea. And now, this is a *good thing* about my little sister – she had a *very kind thought* about her little tree. She said, 'I know! When we go for a walk we'll take my bottle-tree and the digger' (which, of course, you call a trowel) 'and we will plant it in the park, just where there are no trees, so it can grow and grow and spread and spread into a big tree.' And that is just what she did do. Carefully, carefully, she took her bottle-tree out of the bottle, and put it in her little basket, and then we all went out to the park. And when my little sister had found a good place for her little bottle-tree, she dug a nice deep hole for it, and then she put her tree into the hole, and gently, gently put the earth all round its roots, until only the leaves and stem were showing, and when she'd planted it in, my mother showed her how to pat the earth with the trowel.

Then at last the little tree was in the kind of place it really liked, and my little sister had planted it all by herself.

Now you will be pleased to hear that the little bottle-tree grew and grew and now it's quite a big tree. Taller than my naughty little sister, and she's quite a big lady nowadays.

Dorothy Edwards

What we need is a new bus

Not so long ago an old red bus ran down to the station and back again. It was a rumbling-grumbling bus. It was a rusty-dusty bus. It was a jumping-bumping bus. And because it was all of these things some people walked to the station rather than ride in the old bus. It shook them about too much.

'The trouble with this old bus,' the driver said, 'is that it's worn out. It needs a new engine to drive it. It needs new tyres to run on. It needs new seats, new windows, new paint, new everything. In fact what we need is a *new* bus!'

Now the bus wasn't surprised to hear this. It did feel worn out. It was worn out. Climbing the hills made its engine work so hard it went slower and slower and slower. Changing gears all the time made it feel exhausted. All it wanted to do was sleep in the sun for ever.

'*Ur, ur, ur!*' it grumbled. It didn't want to go another wheel turn.

Inside the bus the conductor was calling out, 'Fares, pliz! Fares! Fares, pliz!' He sold pink tickets from his book to the passengers, and their money dropped into his big black bag with a tinkling plink, plink, plink.

And inside the bus the driver was in his seat in front of the big steering wheel. He pushed the gear lever into place. He pulled off the brake and before it knew what was happening the old red bus was rolling down the road again.

'*Urr-uuuuur-urrrr-urrrrr!*' It grumbled. It mumbled. It groaned. '*Grrrr!*' It was as if it couldn't go another wheel turn. And to its surprise the old red bus didn't.

Sssssss!

The front tyre was shrinking smaller and smaller. *Sssssss!* What was happening to the plump round sides? *Sssssssss!* Air hissed out. The tyre was as flat as a piece of paper.

The driver stopped the bus. Out he jumped. Out jumped the bus conductor. People poked their heads from their windows.

'The front tyre is as flat as a pancake,' the driver told them. 'We can't fix it here. You'd better walk to the station.'

'We'd better get the mechanic from the garage,' said the conductor. 'We could be here for hours,' he told the people. 'Yes, you'd be better off walking to the station.'

Now the people grumbled and mumbled and groaned and moaned and walked to the station. 'What we need is a new bus,' they muttered and some of them stopped to look at the flat tyre that had run over a big nail. It had stabbed a hole in the tyre's tube. *Ssssss!* Out hissed the air until the tyre, no longer fat and round, looked saggy-baggy, as flat as flat. A sad limp tyre.

When, at last, the mechanic came roaring up in his truck he tapped the old red bus with a spanner and said, 'This old crate needs more than a new tyre.'

'I know, I know,' agreed the bus driver. 'What we need is a new bus. When can you sell us one?'

'Not today.' The mechanic shook his head. He banged and tapped and looked at the insides of the bus and said nothing for a long time, then he said, 'In a couple of weeks we could make this old bus almost as good as new, up at the garage.'

Now that was a good idea. A wonderful idea, especially for the old bus. It helped as much as it could when the tow-truck came. There was a crane on the back of the tow-truck and it lifted the front wheels of the bus away, away off the ground. With just its two back wheels the old red bus ran along behind the tow-truck to the garage.

And when some people saw the old red bus being towed away they decided that it must be going to the scrap-heap. Where else could it go? 'Looks as if we'll get a new bus after all,' they told each other.

At the garage, mechanics took out the worn parts of the engine and put in new ones. They oiled and greased. They fitted new tyres and new seats. They repainted and repainted the old bus a sparking red, a shiny red, a geranium red. It didn't look like an old bus. It didn't feel like an old bus. It felt like running a thousand miles or two – up hills, down hills and along lumpy, bumpy roads.

When the time came for the old red bus to drive along the road to the station everyone wanted a ride. They crowded in. Some people sat and some people had to stand. The bus was loaded but up the hill it went without a grumble or rumble, just a little *gr-grr-grrr* which was like a happy humming song. 'This isn't bad for our old red bus!' said the conductor with a grin.

'Not our old rumbling, grumbling bus!' shrieked someone. 'This can't be our old, dusty, rusty bus! Don't tell me that this is the bumpy, jumpy, worn-out old bus!'

It was, and we know that it was, don't we?

Jean Chapman

The king who wanted to touch the moon

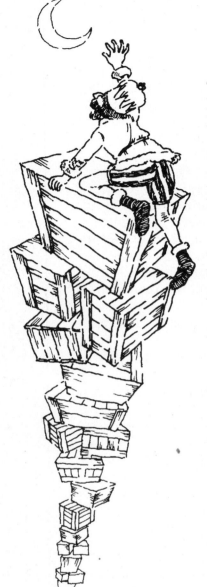

There was once a King who wanted to touch the moon. His wish was so great that he could think of little else. He just thought about the moon every hour that he was awake. Would it feel cold? Would it feel slinky-soft like silk? Was it squashy like a lemon? Was it really the colour of an old silver coin? The King wondered about these things and his thinking kept him awake at night. When he did drift off to sleep his dreams were moon-filled.

What with the King's moon-gazing and moon-wishing and moon-thinking and dreaming, his kingdom was going to pot. He had no time at all to attend to the affairs of state. Things were getting to be like a bad banana, rotten all through, when all at once, that old King made a decision. He called the top Carpenter to him. 'Make me a tower to reach the sky,' said the King. 'I'm going to climb right up it then touch the moon.'

Well, the Carpenter was frightened out of his wits by this order but seeing that the King was so pleased, he dared not tell him that no such tower could be built.

The Carpenter crept away and busied himself with pencils and paper and rulers to draw up a pretty neat-looking plan of a gigantic tower. Then he got himself a gang of workmen, and he ordered great big quantities of timber, and saws, and nails, and hammers, and buckets, and hoists, and everything else he could think of.

The gang went to work and within three weeks the foundations of the tower were laid. Three months later that tower was no higher than the palace walls and the little old King was crazy with impatience. 'Finish the tower in three days or I'll chop off your head!' he said.

The Carpenter shook all over with fright and his teeth chattered with such violence he couldn't speak up and tell His Royal Majesty that the job was impossible. He just trotted back to his job and he bullied his workmen to get the tower up to the sky.

By the third day the tower was as tall as the castle's turrets. The Carpenter slunk in to the King expecting his head to be chopped off at once, so he said very smartly in a quavery-wavery voice, 'Sire! We've used up all the timber in the land. The tower cannot be finished.'

'Yes, it can!' retorted the King. 'Every subject in the kingdom must bring boxes and crates to the tower. Use them to build the tower taller. If you don't I *will* chop off your head.'

The Carpenter's heart plippity-plopped, then missed a few beats before he felt it pumping and thumping in his chest again. That told him he was still alive. He backed away from His Highness, bowing as he went until he reached the door, then he bolted, galloping down the palace corridors.

And so, all the King's subjects had to give up their boxes and crates. All sizes and all manner of boxes were dumped at the foot of the tower. Then, in a mixed-up-mucked-up-muzzed-up-harum-scarum mess they were chucked aloft, up and up on the tower.

His Highness arrived on an inspection tour. 'That tower's not high enough,' he complained. 'Cut down the trees in the forest and make more boxes.'

A whole forest of trees was shortened to a forest of tree stumps. That old King surely was keen to touch the moon! Just to have glimpsed that hacked-about-chopped-about forest would have made you weep, for all of the trees made about one million boxes which were piled on the tower. Its top now just about disappeared into the clouds. 'I'll be able to touch the moon now,' said the little old King smiling at everyone and showing his little worn-down teeth. 'As soon as the moon rises I'll be off.'

'Your Majesty, let me climb the tower first,' blurted out the Carpenter with the courage that he didn't know he had. 'Let me climb the tower to make sure that it's safe.'

'You climb my tower!' raged the King. 'You would reach out and touch the moon! Whoever heard of a carpenter climbing to such great heights? No one! I shall be the first to climb the tower and I'll climb it alone.'

Every subject in the kingdom herded under the tower to watch the spectacle of His Highness climbing to the moon.

The tower shook. The tower rattled. It wobbled and swayed as the King scrambled up and up, up to the top. He teetered on the last box, stretched out an eager arm and strained eager fingers to touch the moon. It was just no farther away than a couple of hand-spans but he couldn't reach it, not that old King. He couldn't, he couldn't, no matter how he tried. 'Get me another box, Man!' he hallooed down to the Carpenter. 'If I have another box I'll reach the moon.'

'There is no box left in all the land!' hollered back the Carpenter.

'Then fetch a footstool, Man!'

'No footstools left either.'

'Then a tea crate.'

'No tea crate. All in the tower, Sire!'

'Do something, Man!' bellowed the King. 'Pull a box from the bottom of the tower and bring it up to me.'

'Which box do you want? I don't want to make a mistake,' shouted the Carpenter feeling his neck and wanting to keep his head.

'The bottom box, you idiot! And if you don't fetch it at once I'll chop off your head. And I'll have all the workers' heads as well.'

The Carpenter and his gang looked at each other. Their heads fitted just nicely to their necks and they didn't want any alterations made there... so, out came the bottom box. One pull and it was free... and....

Crash! The tower fell down and so did the King.

Timber flew. Dust blew. It all made a fine heap of rubbish and somewhere in it was the little old King. If he ever was found it was just after about one year of searching. The only thing that is certain about that affair is that the moon stayed where it has always stayed. High and serene and beautiful, up there in the night sky.

Jean Chapman

The elephant's picnic

Elephants are generally clever animals, but there was once an elephant who was very silly; and his great friend was a kangaroo. Now, kangaroos are not often clever animals, and this one certainly was not, so she and the elephant got on very well together.

One day they thought they would like to go off for a picnic by themselves. But they did not know anything about picnics, and had not the faintest idea of what to do to get ready.

'What do you do on a picnic?' the elephant asked a child he knew.

'Oh, we collect wood and make a fire, and then we boil the kettle,' said the child.

'What do you boil the kettle for?' said the elephant in surprise.

'Why, for tea, of course,' said the child in a snapping sort of way; so the elephant did not like to ask any more questions. But he went and told the kangaroo, and they collected together all the things they thought they would need.

When they got to the place where they were going to have their picnic, the kangaroo said that she would collect the wood because she had got a pouch to carry it back in. A kangaroo's pouch, of course, is very small; so the kangaroo carefully chose the smallest twigs she could find, and only about five or six of those. In fact, it took a lot of hopping to find any sticks small enough to go in her pouch at all; and it was a long time before she came back. But silly though the elephant was, he soon saw those sticks would not be enough for a fire.

'Now I will go off and get some wood,' he said.

His ideas of getting wood were different. Instead of taking little twigs he pushed down whole trees with his forehead, and staggered back to the picnic-place with them rolled up in his trunk. Then the kangaroo struck a match, and they lit a bonfire made of whole trees. The blaze, of course, was enormous, and the fire was so hot that for a long time they could not get near it; and it was not until it began to die down a bit that they were able to get near enough to cook anything.

'Now let's boil the kettle,' said the elephant. Amongst the things he had brought was a brightly shining copper kettle and a very large black iron saucepan. The elephant filled the saucepan with water.

'What are you doing that for?' said the kangaroo.

'To boil the kettle in, you silly,' said the elephant. So he popped the kettle in the saucepan of water, and put the saucepan on the fire; for he thought, the old juggins, that you boil a kettle in the same way you boil an egg, or boil a cabbage! And the kangaroo, of course, did not know any better.

So they boiled and boiled the kettle, and every now and then they prodded it with a stick.

'It doesn't seem to be getting tender,' said the elephant sadly, 'and I'm sure we can't eat it for tea until it does.'

So then away he went and got more wood for the fire; and still the saucepan boiled and boiled, and still the kettle remained as hard as ever. It was getting late now, almost dark.

'I'm afraid it won't be ready for tea,' said the kangaroo. 'I'm afraid we shall have to spend the night here. I wish we had got something with us to sleep in.'

'Haven't you?' said the elephant. 'You mean to say you didn't pack before you came away?'

'No,' said the kangaroo. 'What should I have packed anyway?'

'Why, your trunk, of course,' said the elephant. 'That is what people pack.'

'But I haven't got a trunk,' said the kangaroo.

'Well, I have,' said the elephant, 'and I've packed it! Kindly pass the pepper; I want to unpack!'

So then the kangaroo passed the elephant the pepper, and the elephant took a good sniff. Then he gave a most tremendous sneeze, and everything he had packed in his trunk shot out of it – toothbrush, spare socks, gym shoes, a comb, a bag of bull's-eyes, his pyjamas, and his Sunday suit. So then the elephant put on his pyjamas and lay down to sleep; but the kangaroo had no pyjamas, and so, of course, she could not sleep.

'All right,' she said to the elephant; 'you sleep; and I will sit up and keep the fire going.'

So all night the kangaroo kept the fire blazing brightly and the kettle boiling merrily in the saucepan. When the next morning came the elephant woke up.

'Now,' he said, 'let's have our breakfast.'

So they took the kettle out of the saucepan; and what do you think? It was boiled as tender as tender could be! So they cut it fairly in half and shared it between them, and ate it for breakfast; and both agreed they had never had so good a breakfast in their lives.

Richard Hughes

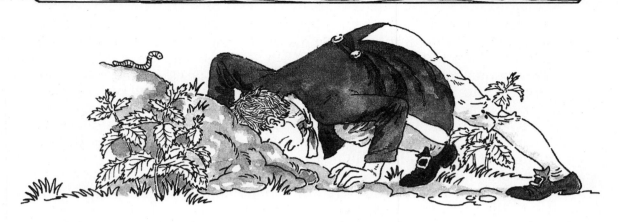

The house that suits you will not suit me

A man wanted to build a house, but didn't know how.

'I will go along the road and ask whoever I meet. Someone will certainly tell me how to do it.'

So he went along the road and met with a worm.

'Good morning,' said he.

'Good morning,' said the worm.

'Can you tell me how to build myself a house?'

'Easy enough,' said the worm, 'come along and I will show you.'

The worm led him to the other side of the road.

'Find a nice earthy bank, and it's better after rain; fortunately it rained last night, so it won't be so hard for a beginner. Find a place that is not too stony, set your head at the earth, wriggle, shove, burrow and turn, and soon enough you will be in your house.'

And the worm did as he advised and within a minute was inside the bank and a nice little house all round him.

'Nothing is done without trying,' said the man, and knelt down and put his head to the bank.

He wriggled, he shoved, he burrowed, he turned. Mud in his hair, mud in his eyes, mud in his mouth and mud in his nose. He scraped with his hands and broke his finger-nails. He shoved with his nose and stung it on a nettle.

Pebbles and earth fell down the back of his neck. Oh dear! and oh dear! what a sight he looked, and he hadn't even begun to build himself a house in the bank!

'The house that suits you will never suit me,' he said at last.

'Just as you please,' said the worm.

So the man got up and went on his way.

The next thing he met was a bird.

'Good morning,' said he.

'Good morning,' said the bird.

'Can you tell me how to build myself a house?'

'Easy enough,' said the bird. 'Come, and I will show you.'

And he led the man into the midst of the thicket.

'Find a bush not too high and not too low, not too thick and not too thin. Gather together grass, sticks, hair and wool, line it with moss and then you will have a home to be happy in.'

'Nothing is done without trying,' said the man. And he began to look around for sticks and grass and hair and wool and moss, and as for mud, if he wanted to use it there was plenty of that still about him.

When he had got his materials together he made a little pile underneath a tree. It happened to be a thorn tree and the bird was sitting in it, and seemed to think it was quite the right place for building a nest.

So he made a bundle of his sticks and tied it to his back and began to climb the tree.

First he caught his clothes in the branches: then the bundle of twigs were pulled off his back; then the thorns ran into his hands and pulled so much of his hair out he had quite enough for lining a nest.

And when at last he got near the top and had chosen a fork on which to build his nest, the wind blew. CRACK! CRASH! BUMP! The bough broke and down he fell, tearing his jacket to ribbons and skinning his hands and knees.

'The house that suits you will never suit me,' said the man.

'Just as you please,' said the bird.

So up he got and went on his way.

He came to a river and across it was a bridge. He stopped on the bridge and looked into the water.

'What do you want?' asked a fish. 'You make me uncomfortable, staring at me like that.'

'I did not see you,' said the man. 'I did not know that you were there. But since you are, perhaps you can help me. Can you tell me how to build myself a house?'

'Easy enough,' said the fish. 'Come down here and I will show you.'

So the man went down and knelt on the river bank.

'Find a big fat stone where the weeds grow thickest, wriggle yourself in the gravel till you are right underneath it, and there you are at home, safe and comfortable, and not much trouble into the bargain!'

'Nothing is done without trying,' said the man. And he jumped into the water. WHOO! How cold it was!

He found a big flat stone and down he lay and wriggled into the sand, but long before he wriggled underneath the stone he came bursting up to the surface for air. Phoo! Phoo! and the water bubbled up all round him.

'The house that suits you will never suit me,' said the man.

'Just as you please,' said the fish. 'I have always found it satisfactory.'

So the man went back on the road, his clothes hanging about him, his boots squelching, even his pocket handkerchief soaked through in his pocket.

As he stood there the very picture of misery, another man came by.

'Mercy on us! Whatever has happened?'

'I wanted to know how to build myself a house. The worm showed me and I was covered with mud. The bird showed me and I tore my clothes. The fish showed me and I nearly drowned. And still I don't know how to build myself a house.'

'Come,' said the man, 'and I will show you. Cut down a tree and saw it into planks.'

So they cut down a tree, chop, chop, chop; you should have seen the chips fly.

They sawed it into planks. SHH, SHH, SHH, they sawed and sawed.

'Get nails and a hammer and nail the planks together.'

Bang, bang, bang, they were hammering the whole afternoon.

And at the end they had a little wooden house with wooden walls and a wooden roof and a stout wooden door that opened and shut.

'Is this the way to build myself a house?' asked the man.

'Only one way,' said the other.

'Well, this little house will certainly suit me, so if there are other ways I won't be bothered to learn them.'

And he went indoors and shut the door behind him, and as he had made no windows in his house what he did after that I'm afraid I cannot say.

Diana Ross

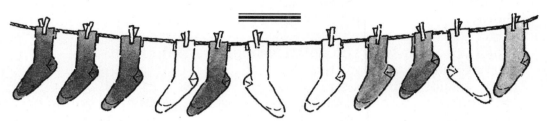

Clive at the dye works

Clive was new at the Dye Works. It was his first day of working anywhere. As he stood in his new white overalls he felt very nervous.

'Right, Clive,' said the Boss. 'I bet you're just *dying* to get started – eh? Ha ha! And I've got just the job for you. Socks. I've got seven hundred pairs of socks that all need dyeing. The shop wants one hundred each of seven different colours – got that? Seven colours for seven days of the week. Right, lad, here are your colours, here are your socks and here are the dying vats. I'll be back at the end of the day to see how you've done. You understand what you've got to do?'

Clive gulped. 'Y-yes, Sir,' he said.

'Good. Well, mind you do a good job. The good name of my dye works is in your hands.'

'I'll do it, Sir,' said Clive.

When the Boss had gone, Clive looked around him. There were the socks, all neatly stacked in boxes of one hundred so there would be no problem of counting them out. Good. There were the big boiling vats of water waiting for socks and colour to be mixed together in them. Good. And there were the tins of colour – red, blue and yellow. Good. Then, NO! thought Clive in sudden panic, not good! Red, blue and yellow were only *three* colours and the Boss has said that there must be *seven* different colours!

Oh heck, thought Clive. What am I going to do? And all he could think was, oh heck, Oh Heck, as he carefully mixed the red dye and coloured one hundred pairs of socks red for Mondays. And he thought, oh what can I do? What *can* I do? as he carefully mixed the blue dye and coloured one hundred pairs of socks blue for Tuesdays. And he thought, oh no, I'll get the sack! as he carefully mixed the yellow dye and coloured one hundred pairs of socks yellow for Wednesdays.

Then he was stuck. The only thing that he could think of was to put *more* red dye into the red vat and see if it would make a darker red colour. But did that count as a different colour? The Boss had said seven *different* colours. He was just about to try it and tip some more red dye in when,

'Hi there, Clive!' said a voice. Clive jumped into the air. It wasn't the Boss though. It was Desmond the lorry driver just being friendly. But Clive had jumped so much that he'd spilled some of the red dye into the yellow vat. Oh no! he thought. But then he watched with his mouth open and his eyes very wide as the red spread through the yellow and turned into a beautiful sunny orange.

'Oh, thanks, Desmond! Thank you ever so much!' said Clive, and he started to tip socks into the orange dye.

'Thanks for what?' asked Desmond.

'For giving me a colour for Thursday's socks!' said Clive.

When the beautiful orange Thursday socks were hung-up to dry, Clive had an idea for his Friday and Saturday socks. If red and yellow together made a different colour, then perhaps red and blue, blue and yellow would too, thought Clive. And of course he was right. Red and blue gave him a lovely plummy purple for his Friday socks. Blue and yellow made a bright grassy green for the Saturday socks.

Almost done, thought Clive cheerfully as he sat down on the sock boxes for a rest. He had been working hard all day and was getting very tired. The Boss would be coming soon to see how he had done. Well, he had done Monday, Tuesday, Wednesday, Thursday, Friday and Saturday. All he had to do now was a different colour for Sunday. But how? He'd mixed each colour with each of the other colours. What else could he do?

Clive put his head in his hands and his elbows on his knees. He closed his eyes and tried to think. But all he could think was, I'm tired. I want a cup of tea and a plate of fish and chips and my soft comfortable bed and... But that wasn't helping him to find a colour for Sunday. He opened his eyes – and then he saw it. He saw his overalls and he knew how to get his Sunday colour. They were brown! His overalls that had been bright snowy white when he started that morning were now splashed with all the colours that he had been working with. Now they were brown.

Suddenly Clive wasn't tired any more. He was excited! He tipped all the left-over colours into one vat and watched as they mixed together into a rich earthy brown colour. In went the last socks and soon brown Sunday socks were on the drying rack alongside red Monday, blue Tuesday, yellow Wednesday, orange Thursday, purple Friday and green Saturday.

All the colours of the rainbow! thought Clive as he looked proudly at his day's work.

'Finished, lad?' asked a deep voice. It was the Boss.

'Yes, Sir, just finished,' said Clive.

'Well I call that a *sock*cess – ha ha! Well done, Clive. Very well done indeed.'

Phew, thought Clive. Now for that cup of tea.

Pippa Goodhart

Mrs Simkin's bathtub

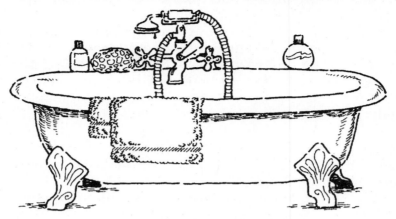

'Are you aware,' said Mr Simkin to Mrs Simkin one morning, 'that the bathtub's half-way down the stairs?'

'How very inconvenient,' said Mrs Simkin, going to have a look. 'How long has it been there?'

'I have no idea,' said Mr Simkin. 'It was in the bathroom when I went to bed last night, and now it's here, so it must have moved when we were asleep.'

'Well, we shall just have to make the best of it,' said Mrs Simkin. 'Will you bath first or shall I?'

'I will,' said Mr Simkin bravely.

He stepped into the bathtub. It wobbled a bit at first, but it soon settled down. Mrs Simkin fetched soap and towels, shampoo and bath salts, and arranged them nicely on the stairs.

'There,' she said, 'it doesn't look too bad now, and if I polish the taps and scrub the feet it should look quite smart. I'm sure none of the neighbours has a bathtub on the stairs.'

Mr Simkin said she was probably right.

After a day or two they hardly noticed that the bathtub was there at all. It didn't really inconvenience them to squeeze past it when they wanted to go upstairs, and the landing smelt so pleasantly of bath oil that Mrs Simkin began to feel quite happy about it.

She invited the lady next door to have a look, but the lady next door said that she didn't approve of these modern ideas, and anyhow, she had never been one to give herself airs.

One morning Mr Simkin went to have his bath. 'My dear!' he cried. 'Come and see! The bathtub's gone!'

'Gone!' cried Mrs Simkin, leaping out of bed. 'Gone where?'

'I don't know,' said Mr Simkin, 'but it isn't on the stairs.'

'Perhaps it's back in the bathroom,' said Mrs Simkin. They went to have a look but it wasn't there.

'We shall have to buy another one,' said Mr Simkin as they went down to breakfast. The bathtub was in the kitchen.

'You know, my dear,' said Mr Simkin a few minutes later, 'this is a much better place for a bathtub than half-way down the stairs. I quite like having breakfast in the bath.'

'Yes,' said Mrs Simkin, 'I like it here, too. The bath towels match the saucepans, and think of all the soup I shall be able to make when we have a large dinner-party.'

'That's a very good point,' agreed Mr Simkin. 'I can't think why everybody doesn't want a bathtub in their kitchen.'

One day Mr and Mrs Simkin went downstairs to find the bathtub had moved again. It was in the living room, sitting snugly before the fire.

'Oh, I don't think I like it there,' said Mrs Simkin, looking at it with her head on one side.

'Neither do I,' said Mr Simkin, 'although it will be very pleasant bathing in front of the fire.'

'I don't suppose it will stay there very long,' whispered Mrs Simkin. 'Once a bathtub has started to roam, it never knows when to stop.'

She was quite right. The following morning the bathtub was underneath the sideboard, which was rather difficult for bathing, but they managed somehow. Two or three days later they found the bathtub in the basement with spiders in it.

On the day that Mrs Simkin was forty-two years old they couldn't find the bathtub anywhere.

'What shall I do?' cried Mrs Simkin, 'I wanted to use that lovely bubble-bath that you gave me for my birthday.'

'So did I,' said Mr Simkin.

The lady next door came round.

'Happy birthday,' she said. 'Did you know that your bathtub was on the front lawn?'

They all went to have a look.

There was a horse drinking out of it.

'Go away,' said Mrs Simkin to the horse. 'How dare you drink my bathwater, you greedy creature?' and she stepped recklessly into the bathtub.

The lady next door said she didn't know what the world was coming to and she went home and locked herself indoors.

As the bubbles floated down the street, lots of people came to see what was going on. They saw Mrs Simkin sitting in the bathtub. They were very interested. They leaned on the fence and watched. They asked if they could come again.

As the days went by, Mrs Simkin began to think that the bathtub would stay on the front lawn for ever, but one morning when there was a rather chilly wind about they found the bathtub in the greenhouse. The people in the street were very disappointed. They got up a petition asking Mr Simkin to bring it back.

'My dear,' said Mr Simkin a few days later, 'do you happen to know where the bathtub is today?'

'No, Stanley,' said Mrs Simkin, 'but today's Tuesday. It's quite often in the garage on Tuesdays.'

'It isn't there today,' said Mr Simkin.

'Have you tried the verandah?' suggested Mrs Simkin. 'It hasn't been there for sometime.'

'I've looked everywhere,' said Mrs Simkin. 'It isn't in the house and it isn't in the garden.'

Mrs Simkin was busy with something else. 'I do hope it hasn't gone next door,' she sighed. 'The lady next door has no sympathy with that kind of thing.'

Mr Simkin went to inquire. The lady next door said that she wouldn't allow anyone else's bathtub in her house, and that she was of the opinion that people ought to be able to control their bathtubs. Mr Simkin went home.

Mr Robinson from across the street rang up. 'I know it's none of my business,' he said, 'but I thought you'd like to know that your bathtub's sitting up on the roof of your house.'

Mrs Simkin thanked him for the information. Mr Simkin went to take his bath. He said there was a marvellous view from up there. Mrs Simkin climbed up. All the people cheered. She thought it was rather nice, but she had no head for heights. Perhaps it was time to ring the plumber.

The plumber said that wandering bathtubs weren't really in his line of business and why didn't they get in touch with the Department of the Environment?

Mrs Simkin said she wasn't going to all that trouble. She would soon get used to bathing on the roof. So they left the bathtub where it was. And that's where it liked to be best of all.

The people in the street had a meeting in Mr Simkin's greenhouse. They decided to have their bathtubs on their roofs as well. All except the lady next door. She preferred to take a shower.

Linda Allen

Night mail

This is the night mail crossing the border,
Bringing the cheque and the postal order,
Letters for the rich, letters for the poor,
The shop at the corner and the girl next door.
Pulling up Beattock, a steady climb –
The gradient's against her, but she's on time.

Past cotton grass and moorland boulder
Shovelling white steam over her shoulder,
Snorting noisily as she passes
Silent miles of wind-bent grasses.

Birds turn their heads as she approaches,
Stare from the bushes at her black-faced coaches.
Sheep-dogs cannot turn her course,
They slumber on with paws across.
In the farm she passes no one wakes,
But a jug in the bedroom gently shakes.

Dawn freshens, the climb is done.
Down towards Glasgow she descends
Towards the steam tugs yelping down the glade of cranes,
Towards the fields of apparatus, the furnaces
Set on the dark plain like gigantic chessmen.
All Scotland waits for her:
In the dark glens, beside the pale-green lochs
Men long for news.

Letters of thanks, letters from banks,
Letters of joy from girl and boy,
Receipted bills and invitations
To inspect new stock or visit relations,
And applications for situations
And timid lovers' declarations
And gossip, gossip from all the nations,
News circumstantial, new financial,
Letters with holiday snaps to enlarge in,
Letters with faces scrawled in the margin,
Letters from uncles, cousins and aunts,
Letters to Scotland from the South of France,
Letters of condolence to Highlands and Lowlands,
Notes from overseas to Hebrides –

Written on paper of every hue,
The pink, the violet, the white and the blue,
The chatty, the catty, the boring, adoring,
The cold and official and the heart outpouring,
Clever, stupid, short and long,
The typed and printed and the spelt all wrong.

Thousands are still asleep
Dreaming of terrifying monsters,
Or of friendly tea beside the band at Cranston's or Crawford's,
Asleep in working Glasgow, asleep in well-set Edinburgh,
Asleep in granite Aberdeen,
They continue their dreams;
And shall wake soon and long for letters,
And none will hear the postman's knock
Without a quickening of the heart,
For who can hear and feel himself forgotten?

W. H. Auden

Traffic jam

Dermot did not remember when trains ran on the line near his home. The rails had been taken away and there was only a wide grassy path where he went for a walk every day with his dog, Razor. Sometimes he sat on the bridge over the road and watched the roofs of cars, vans, and lorries disappear under his feet.

He was there one day, counting the vehicles which passed by. A loud rumble came from round the bend of the road, and a few moments later a monster yellow lorry came into view. It came slowly on. Dermot had never seen one as big. It slowed down and came to a halt just before the bridge. Dermot could imagine the driver looking at the sign which said, 'Vehicles under 15 feet only'. He must have been satisfied because the lorry moved on slowly.

The boy saw the bonnet vanish under his feet, then the cab, and finally the box-like body of the lorry went slowly into the eye of the bridge. Then there was a frightening, grating sound of metal tearing against stone. The top of the lorry shivered and then the engine was switched off.

Razor barked in wild excitement and scuttled down the grass slope beside the bridge. Dermot followed at once. He went into the half dark under the bridge. The driver's head was out of the window as he examined the roof of the lorry, jammed tight against the arch of the bridge. He muttered something under his breath and drew his head back inside the cab.

The engine started again. There was a whine as the back wheels of the lorry spun around at great speed, but the lorry did not move. Again and again the driver tried to back the lorry out of the bridge, but he failed each time. He got out and stood looking up at the top of the lorry, where it was jammed hard against the arch of the bridge. He moved to the other side, looked up again and scratched his head. He was puzzled.

Dermot spoke to him: 'Sir, I know –'

'Ah, run away out of that, Sonny, and don't be bothering me,' said the driver crossly.

'But, Sir –,' Dermot began again.

'Go away! I tell you,' growled the driver, and he sounded so angry that Dermot let him be.

Just then a horn sounded impatiently. A large black car had pulled up behind the lorry, and the driver was pressing on the horn. The lorry driver walked back to him.

'What's wrong!' asked the car driver.

'The lorry is stuck. I can't take it in or out,' answered the lorry driver. The car driver got out, and he and the lorry driver went forward and stood looking up at the arch. The car driver looked so knowing that Dermot thought he must be an expert on cars stuck in bridges. He thought he heard him say that something 'must be removed. There is no other way.'

Other cars arrived and stopped, until a line of cars, lorries, and vans stretched from the bridge down the road and round the bend. Drivers and passengers got out and came to the bridge. It was a narrow bridge and the lorry was stuck at the centre. No car could pass through.

After about ten minutes a large crowd had gathered. Most of the people just stood and looked, but five or six of them were speaking to the driver.

'The stones must be removed,' said a tall dark man in a light raincoat.

'Nonsense,' said a red-faced farmer in a floppy hat. 'If you take away the stones of the arch, the whole bridge will fall down.'

'The man is right,' said a young man with fair hair. 'There is only one way of getting it out. We must lower the roof of the lorry. Send for a sledge-hammer and we'll batter it down.'

''Tis hard to know which of you is the silliest,' said a van driver in a cloth cap. 'How could you get at the part of the roof that's stuck? Isn't it under the bridge?'

'Then what would *you* do?' asked a lady in a fur coat.

'Me?' said the van driver.

'Yes, you!'

'There's only one way,' said the van driver. 'Dig a hole in the road behind the wheels and lower the lorry that way.'

'I know a better way,' shouted Dermot.

'The hole might work,' said the farmer.

'I know a better way,' shouted Dermot again.

'I thought I told you to go home, Sonny,' said the lorry driver.

'Let the boy speak,' said the woman in the fur coat. 'His way couldn't be more stupid than some of yours. Speak up, boy!'

The people listened impatiently, because nobody expected Dermot to have a good idea. 'Come on, boy. What you have to say?' said the van driver in the cloth cap.

'Let some of the air out of the wheels,' said Dermot simply.

'What?' asked the lorry driver in surprise.

'Let some of the air out of the wheels,' Dermot repeated.

'Ha-ha-ha haa,' laughed the farmer. 'The boy is right. His way is the answer.'

The lorry driver rushed to one of the front wheels and knelt down. The people heard a loud hiss. He did the same at all the other wheels. They looked up. The roof of the lorry was no longer jammed against the arch of the bridge. The engine was started, and the huge yellow monster moved forward slowly on soft wheels. It passed out the other side and the crowd cheered.

Later Dermot sat on the bridge, watching the long line of traffic pass under his feet. He was happy because there was a fifty-pence piece in his pocket, given to him by the lorry driver.

Frank Murphy

A speck speaks

About ten million years ago
I was a speck of rock in a vast black rock.
My address was:
Vast Black Rock,
Near Italy,
Twelve Metres Under
The Mediterranean Sea.

The other specks and I
Formed an impressive edifice –
Bulbously curving at the base
With rounded caves
And fun tunnels for the fish,
Romantically jagged at the top.

Life, for us specks, was uneventful –
One for all, welded together
In the cool, salty wet.
What more could specks
Expect?

Each year a few of us were lost,
Scrubbed from the edges of the rock
By the washerwoman waters
Which smoothed our base, whittled our cornices
And sharpened our pinnacles.
As the rock slowly shed skin-thin layers
It was my turn to be exposed
Among the packed grit of its surface,
(Near the tip of the fifty-ninth spire
From the end of the eastern outcrop).
One day, it was a Wednesday I remember,
A scampi flicked me off my perch
Near the vast black rock's peak
And I was scurried down
Long corridors of currents
Until a wave caught me in its mouth
And spat me out on –
What?

A drying stretch
Of yellow, white, black, red and transparent specks,
Billions of particles,
Loosely organised in bumps and dips;
Quite unlike the tight hard group

Which I belonged to in the good old rock.
Heat banged down on us all day long.
Us? I turned to the speck next to me,
A lumpish red fellow who'd been washed off a brick.

'I'm new here,' I confessed,
'What are we supposed to be?'
He bellowed back –
(But the bellow of a speck
Is less than the whispering of ants) –
'We're grains now, grains of sand,
And this society is called Beach.'

'Beach?' I said. 'What are we grains supposed to do?'
'Just stray around, lie loose,
Go with the wind, go with the sea
And sink down when you're trodden on.'

'Don't know if I can manage that.
Used to belong to Vast Black Rock
And we all stuck together.'

'Give Beach a try,' said the red grain.
Well, there was no alternative.

Many eras later
I was just beginning to feel
Part of Beach, that slow-drifting,
Slow-shifting, casual community,
When I was shovelled up
With a ton of fellow grains,
Hoisted into a lorry, shaken down a road,
Washed, sifted and poured in a machine
Hotter than the sunshine.

When they poured me out, life had changed again.
My mates and I swam in a molten river
Down into a mould,
White-hot we were, then red, then
Suddenly cold
And we found ourselves merged
Into a tall, circular tower,
Wide at the bottom, narrow at the top
What's more, we'd all turned green as sea-weed.
Transparent green.
We had become – a wine bottle.

In a few flashes of time
We'd been filled with wine,
Stoppered, labelled, bumped to a shop,
Stood in a window, sold, refrigerated,
Drained by English tourists,
Transmogrified into a lampstand,
Smashed by a four-year-old called Tarquin,
Swept up, chucked in the garbage, hauled away,
Dumped and bulldozed into the sea.

Now the underwater years sandpaper away
My shield-shaped fragment of bottle.
So one day I shall be a single grain again,
A single grain of green, transparent glass.

When that day comes
I will transmit a sub-aquatic call
To all green specks of glass
Proposing that we form
A Vast Green Rock of Glass
Near Italy
Twelve Metres Under
The Mediterranean Sea.

Should be pretty spectacular
In about ten million years.

All being well.

Adrian Mitchell
None of Adrian Mitchell's poems are to appear in any examination whatsoever.

THE WORLD WE LIVE IN

The mouse and winds

A mouse went out in his boat, but there was no wind. The
boat did not move.
'Wind!' shouted the mouse.
'Come down and blow my boat across this lake!'
'Here I am,' said the west wind.
The west wind blew and blew. The mouse and the
boat went up in the air... and landed on the roof of a house.
'Wind!' shouted the mouse.
'Come down and blow my boat off this house!'
'Here I am,' said the east wind.
The east wind blew and blew. The mouse and the boat
and the house went up in the air... and landed on the top of
a tree.
'Wind!' shouted the mouse.
'Come down and blow my boat off this house and off
this tree!'
'Here I am,' said the south wind.
The south wind blew and blew.
The mouse and the boat and the house and the tree
went up in the air... and landed on the top of a mountain.
'Wind!' shouted the mouse.
'Come down and blow my boat off this house and off
this tree and off this mountain!'
'Here I am,' said the north wind.
The north wind blew and blew.
The mouse and the boat and the house and the tree
and the mountain went up in the air... and came down into
the lake.
The mountain sank and became an island.
The tree landed on the island and burst into bloom.
The house landed next to the tree.
A lady looked out of a window in the house and said,
'What a nice place to live!'
And the mouse just sailed away.

Arnold Lobel

January jumps about

January jumps about
in the frying pan
trying to heat
his frozen feet
like a Canadian.

February scuttles under
any dish's lid
and she thinks she's dry because she's
thoroughly well hid
but it still rains all month long
and it always did.

March sits in the bath tub
with the taps turned on.
Hot and cold, cold or not,
Has the Winter gone?
In like a lion, out like a lamb
March on, march on, march on.

April slips about
sometimes indoors
and sometimes out
sometimes sheltering from a little
shower of bright rain
in an empty milk bottle
then dashing out again.

May, she hides nowhere,
nowhere at all,

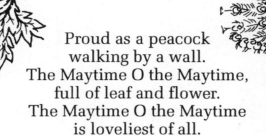

Proud as a peacock
walking by a wall.
The Maytime O the Maytime,
full of leaf and flower.
The Maytime O the Maytime
is loveliest of all.

June discards his shirt and
trousers by the stream
and takes the first dip of the year
into a jug of cream.
June is the gay time
of every girl and boy
who run about and sing and shout
in pardonable joy.

July by the sea
sits dabbling with sand
letting it run out of
her rather lazy hand,
and sometimes she sadly
thinks: 'As I sit here
ah, more than half the year is gone,
the evanescent year.'

August by an emperor
was given his great name.
It is gold and purple
like a Hall of Fame.
(I have known it rather cold
and wettish, all the same.)

September lies in shadows
of the fading summer
hearing, in the distance,
the silver horns of winter
and not very far off
the coming autumn drummer.

October, October
apples on the tree,
the Partridge in the Wood and
the big winds at sea,
the mud beginning in the lane
the berries bright and red
and the big tree wildly
tossing its old head.

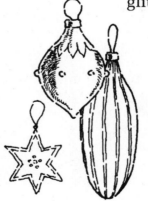

November, when the fires
love to burn, and leaves
flit about and fill the air
where the old tree grieves.
November, November
its name is like a star
glittering on many things that were
but few things that are.

Twelfth and last December.
A few weeks away
we hear the silver bells
of the stag and the sleigh
flying from the tundras
far far away
bringing to us all the gift
of our Christmas Day.

George Barker from *To Aylsham Fair* (Faber and Faber Limited)

The little boy who wanted a flat world

There was once this little boy sitting in the back of a class at school, listening to a teacher. The teacher had a globe of the world on her desk and was talking to the children about it.

'Once upon a time,' she said, 'men thought the world was flat, but now we know it is round, just like the globe here.'

The little boy looked at the globe, but he wasn't at all pleased with it. In his mind he imagined the world as quite flat, with all the sea pouring over the edge of it, down and down, smooth as glass, down through space, rustling between the stars. He liked the idea of a flat world so much better than a round one, just as he liked glass castles and unicorns and mermaids singing.

'All nice things are pretendings,' he thought. 'None of them are real.' And he went on feeling sorry that the world was round all day.

He was a very little boy you see.

That very night the little boy woke up, feeling the dark grow suddenly warm around him. He found he was lying in long grass in the sunshine. He was not as surprised as you might think, though he was rather dismayed to find himself in such gaily coloured clothes... and not ordinary clothes at that. He seemed to be wearing a short skirt and long stockings, and his hair was long too. Then, along came a group of other children and he saw that the boys were dressed just as he was, and the little girls wore dresses to their ankles.

'Well,' he thought, 'I have got myself into a long-ago time when people dressed differently.' He didn't bother about his clothes any more, but felt happy again. He joined in with them, and off they went down a stony, bumpy street chasing pigeons and talking away to each other.

As they went on their noisy, chattering way they came upon a tall, lean man by the roadside, sitting with his chin on his knees.

'Look, it's Wilkin,' the children cried, crowding around him. 'Tell us a story, Wilkin! Sing us a song!'

Wilkin had a torn blue cloak and a blue tunic. His solemn dark face suddenly broke into smiles. He put his arm around the youngest child and he sang.

'I woke in the morning and looked at the day.
I saw it was asking that I should be gay
So dancing I went with a leap and a bound,
And a song as glad as the world is round.'

'But the world isn't really round, silly Wilkin!' said a little child. 'It's as flat as a penny, and the sea falls over the edge.'

So then the little boy knew that somehow he had woken up in that long time ago when the world was flat.

'But last night,' Wilkin told the children, 'I had a dream. I dreamed I was out in the sky – far, far, far out, where the stars hold their small bright lamps. And do you know what – I could see our world, and it was quite round. Round like a little shining jewel, a spark of glowing fire. When I flew closer I could see the blue sea on it, and the lands like green and brown patches. I saw these things through the streaks of drifting cloud. Yes, and I could see day and night chasing each other round the world, and ships sailing and sailing and coming back to where they started, and I thought what a beautiful world it was, and how wonderful it would be if it were really round. Why, just think – I could start off from here and run like lightning, leap from wave to wave, step over forests and lakes and mountains, and be back here again before you could wink. But with a flat world I'd just fall over the edge.'

Then all the children laughed.

'No one can run from land to land,' said one, 'and anyway the world is flat.'

'There is no other country over the sea,' said one, 'but only strange monsters that will eat you, Wilkin.'

'The world is flat, Wilkin,' cried a third.

'The world is flat,' Wilkin repeated sadly. 'And all poetry is dust.' The little boy saw that Wilkin was disappointed at seeing his bright dreams burst like bubbles on the children's pinprick words, so he moved closer to Wilkin and pulled his sleeve.

'Really, the world is round,' he whispered, and he and Wilkin smiled a secret smile at each other.

At that moment far away the little boy heard someone call his name. He turned to look over his shoulder, and saw the wallpaper of his own room. He had been in bed dreaming.

Later, as the little boy ate his breakfast, he asked his mother, 'Which is it most beautiful for worlds to be... flat or round?'

'It depends,' his mother answered, 'on what you think yourself.'

'I think round worlds are quite nice after all,' the little boy said thoughtfully. He smiled to himself and went on eating his breakfast.

Margaret Mahy

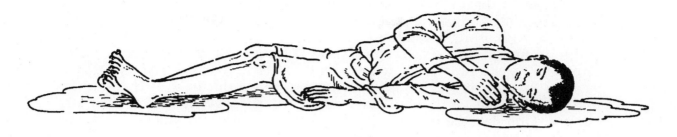

Heaven and Earth and Man

Earth with its mountains, rivers and seas, Sky with its sun, moon and stars: in the beginning all these were one, and the one was Chaos. Nothing had taken shape, all was a dark swirling confusion, over and under, round and round. For countless ages this was the way of the universe, unformed and unillumined, until from the midst of Chaos came P'an Ku. Slowly, slowly, he grew into being, feeding on the elements, eyes closed, sleeping a sleep of eighteen thousand years. At last the moment came when he woke from his sleeping. He opened his eyes: nothing could he see, nothing but darkness, nothing but confusion. In his anger he raised his great arm and struck out blindly in the face of the murk, and with one great crashing blow he scattered the elements of Chaos.

The swirling ceased, and in its place came a new kind of movement. No longer confined, all those things which were light in weight and pure in nature rose upwards; all those things which were heavy and gross sank down. With his one mighty blow P'an Ku had freed sky from earth.

Now P'an Ku stood with his feet on earth, and the sky rested on his head. So long as he stood between the two they could not come together again. And as he stood, the rising and the sinking went on. With each day that passed earth grew thicker by ten feet and the sky rose higher by ten feet, thrust ever farther from the earth by P'an Ku's body which daily grew in height by ten feet also. For eighteen thousand years more P'an Ku continued to grow until his own body was gigantic, and until earth was formed of massive thickness and the sky had risen far above. Thousands of miles tall he stood, a great pillar separating earth from sky so that the two might never again come together to dissolve once more into a single Chaos. Throughout long ages he stood, until the time when he could be sure that earth and sky were fixed and firm in their places.

When this time came P'an Ku, his task achieved, lay down on earth to rest, and resting died. And now he, who in his life had brought shape to the universe, by his death gave his body to make it rich and beautiful. He gave the breath from his body to form the winds and clouds, his voice to be the rolling thunder, his two eyes to be the sun and moon, the hairs of his head and beard to be the stars, the sweat of his brow to be the rain and dew. To the earth he gave his body for the mountains and his hands and feet for the two poles and the extremes of east and west. His blood flowed as the rivers of earth and his veins ran as the roads which cover the land.

His flesh became the soil of the fields and the hairs of his body grew on as the flowers and trees. As for his bones and teeth, these sank deep below the surface of earth to enrich it as precious metals.

And so P'an Ku brought out of Chaos the heavens in all their glory and the earth with all its splendours.

But although the earth could now present its lovely landscapes, although beasts ran in its forests and fish swam in its rivers, still it seemed to lack something, something which would make it less empty and dull for the gods who came down from Heaven to roam over its surface. One day the goddess Nü-kua, whose body was that of a dragon but whose head was of human form, grew weary of the loneliness of earth. After long thought she stooped and took from the ground a lump of clay. From this she fashioned with her dragon claws a tiny creature. The head she shaped after the pattern of her own, but to the body she gave two arms and two legs. She set the little thing back on the ground: and the first human being came to life and danced and made sounds of joy to delight the eyes and ears of the goddess. Quickly she made many more of these charming humans, and felt lonely no longer as they danced together all about her.

Then, as she rested a while from her task and watched the sons and daughters of her own creation go off together across the earth, a new thought came to her. What would become of the world when all these humans she had made grew old and die? They were fine beings, well fitted to rule over the beasts of the earth; but they would not live for ever. To fill the earth with humans, then when these had gone to make more to take their place, this would mean an endless task for the goddess. And so to solve this problem Nü-kua brought together man and woman and taught them the ways of marriage. Now they could create for themselves their own sons and daughters, and these in turn could continue to people the earth throughout time.

After this gift of marriage from Nü-kua, further blessings came to man from her husband, the great god Fu-hsi. He again had a human head but the body of a dragon. He taught men how to weave ropes to make nets for fishing, and he made the lute from which men first drew music. His also was the priceless gift of fire. Men had seen and feared the fire which was struck from the forest trees by the passing of the Lord of the Thunderstorm. But Fu-hsi, who was the son of this same lord, taught men to drill wood against wood and make fire for their own use, for warmth and for cooking.

Already the creatures of Nü-kua's making could speak their thoughts to one another, but Fu-hsi now drew for them the eight precious symbols with which they could begin to make records for those who were to come after. He drew three strokes

$$\equiv$$ to represent Heaven;

the three strokes broken

$$\equiv\equiv\equiv$$ represented earth.

That symbol whose middle stroke was solid

$$\equiv$$ represented water,

that whose middle stroke was broken

$---$ represented fire.

A solid stroke above

$≡≡≡$ gave the sign for mountains,

a solid stroke beneath

$≡≡≡$ the sign for storm;

a broken line below

$≡≡≡$ showed wind,

a broken line on top

$≡≡≡$ showed marshland.

With these eight powerful symbols man could begin to record all he observed of the world about him.

For long years men lived their lives in a world at peace. Then, suddenly, there spread from Heaven to earth a conflict which threatened to put an end to all creation. This was the battle between the Spirit of Water, Kung-kung, and the Spirit of Fire, Chu-jung. Down to earth came the turbulent, wilful Kung-kung to whip up huge waves on river and lake and lead his scaly hordes against his arch-enemy, Fire. Chu-jung fought back with tongues of flame and scorching breath and halted the rebel Water in his path. Kung-kung's armies dispersed and he, their leader, turned and fled. But his flight brought with it a peril greater yet. For, dashing blindly off to the west, Kung-kung struck his head against the mountain Pu-chou-shan, which was none other than the pillar that in the western corner held up the sky.

Kung-kung made good his escape, but he left the world in a disastrous state. Great holes appeared in the sky, whilst the earth tilted up in the west. In that region deep cracks and fissures appeared which are still to be seen to this day. All the rivers and lakes spilled out their waters, which ran off and still run eastwards: off to the south-east, where the earth had slipped down low, ran the waters together to form a vast ocean there. Meanwhile, out of the shaken mountain forests fire still raged forth, and wild beasts of every kind left their lairs to maraud through the world of helpless, terrified men.

It was left to the goddess Nü-kua to bring back order to the world, to quell the fire and flood and tame the wandering beasts. She it was also who selected from the beds of rivers stones of the most perfect colouring. These she heated until they could be moulded, then with these stones, block by block, she patched the holes in the sky. Lastly, she killed a giant turtle, and cut off its powerful legs to make pillars between which the sky is firmly held over the earth, never again to fall.

So the peace of the world was restored. But the mountains still rise in the west, and it is to there that the sun, moon and stars still run down the tilted sky; whilst to the east, the waters of the earth still gather into the restless ocean.

From *Chinese Myths & Fantasies* retold by Cyril Birch

Everest Climbed

The Summit
Four in a tent on the South Col, blue
And wretched, battered by wind, and frozen –
Tenzing and Hillary (the summiters Hunt had chosen)
With Lowe and Gregory there to support:
These men with Ang Nyima, and a few
On their way descending, held the fort...

And they churned over in thought
Each gruelling beast-of-burden week
Of carrying from base to Col and back to base
Then wearily up again, an endless chain;
Da Namgyal's blistered fingers and swollen face;
Balu crumpled, weeping like a child;
Temba stretched on the stones, with scarce a breath
In his body; and the struggle to stand and totter, with Death
One plod behind –

Oh, the freezing touch and the voices wild! –
Then, from the tired despair, one thrilling story gasped
By Evans and Bourdillon – how they'd trod
The Southern Peak and almost grasped the crown,
When trouble with snow and breathing knocked them down...

All day the windy peak flared
In foam-white flame, and nobody dared
To stir from where he lay.
All night, while the billowy tent bellied and reared,
They fought the cold; and the wind like a battering ram
In the frail canvas drummed and pounded –
Then at eight o'clock next day
(O miracle!) faded away.

See them crawl from the tunnelled tent,
Two men ballooned in blue and gold –
Tenzing, alert and tiger-bold;
Hillary, with the slow New Zealand drawl,
The hatchet chin
And hearty laugh and half-moon grin,
Whose legs long as the world was wide
Could take crevasse or hill at a stride.

(His was the raging mountain passion,
All guts and go and no half ration.)

They checked their oxygen gauges, shouldered
Each his Atlas world of weight.
With languid gait, in sluggish tracks
Like snails with houses on their backs,
Hooped and bowed yet bright with hope
They heaved themselves up the endless slope.

High on the mountain far above
With Greg and Ang Nyima, Lowe was cutting steps.
Through a hail of icy chips
They cramponed into his stair and caught him up
When the sun was high overhead.
Gregory said, 'We've carried your stuff
Higher than Lhotse, far enough.'
But there was no place here to drop the gear,
No shelf for a tent. Though tired and spent,
They stumbled up the steepening ridge
Till Tenzing thought of a likely ledge
He'd seen last year in a cleft.
They traversed across and dumped their loads and left.

Here Tenzing and Hillary pitched their tent.
They scratched the snow from the frozen rock
And levelled, side by side,
Two strips of floor – two hours it took and more –
Then anchored the guys to the oxygen flasks
And panting crawled inside
The highest-smallest-coldest-frailest home
The world had known.
When Tenzing had set the primus roaring,
Soup he made from a saucepan of snow
Melted at twenty-seven below;
They spread the dainties he'd been storing –
Date and apricot, jam and honey.
As sugared lemon and ice weren't short,
They thawed and swallowed quart on quart.

The sun went down, from peak to peak
The long purple shadows creeping.
Tired and weak,

They yawned and settled down to sleeping —
Hillary bunched in his narrow place,
Tenzing stretched on the brink of space.
While the rude wind roared them a lullaby
To a tearing tune,
Hillary, sleepless, braced for each blast,
Clung to the walls and anchored them fast
And none too soon,
Till the wind sank down and the silent sky
Was lit with the stars and the moon.

At four in the morning he woke. His feet
And legs were numb to the knees and freezing.
But the peaks were aglow in the early light
And the frost was easing.
His boots were white and stiff from the weather,
So he cooked them over the primus flame
Till up to his nostrils fiercely came
The stench of burning leather.
When they'd carefully checked the oxygen gauges
And fixed their boots and loaded backs,
Away they stepped in easy stages,
Each in turn kicking the tracks.

They toiled to the foot of the Southern Peak
Where the slope was steep with snow half-stuck —
And slippery, treacherous indeed
When Hillary's turn it was to lead.
The first step firm, the second crumbled,
And down in a shower of white he tumbled.
Tenzing was ready — on the lightning slope
He halted him with axe and rope.
Thus once before in the Icefall snow
The Tiger had held him, bruised and numb,
On the icy brink of Kingdom Come
Whose chasm yawned below.

Undaunted still, with desperate skill,
Cautious as blind men crossing a street
They crept four hundred faltering feet.
And they'd reached and passed the Southern Peak
When Hillary's rope began to drag
And Tenzing staggered and fell in his track,
Tottered and swayed and gasped for breath.
The face in the icicle-crusted mask
Was pale as death.
But Hillary found where the strength was going —

The oxygen tube was jammed with ice.
With his glove he knocked it free – in a trice
The life was flowing.

Their steps were weary, keen was the wind,
Fast vanishing their oxygen fuel,
And the summit ridge was fanged and cruel –
Fanged and cruel, bitter and bare.
And now with a sickening shock
They saw before them a towering wall
Of smooth and holdless rock.
O ghastly fear – with the goal so near
To find the way was blocked!
On one side darkly the mountain dropped,
On the other two plunging miles of peak
Shot from the dizzy skyline down
In a silver streak.

'No hope of turning the bluff to the west,'
Said Hillary. 'What's that I see to the east?
A worm-wide crack between cornice and rock –
Will it hold? I can try it at least.'
He called to Tenzing, 'Draw in the slack!'
Then levered himself right into the crack
And, kicking his spikes in the frozen crust,
Wriggled up with his back.
With arms and feet and shoulders he fought,
Inch by sweating inch, then caught
At the crest and grabbed for the light of day.
There was time, as he struggled for breath, to pray
For all the might that a man could wish –
Then he heaved at the rope till over the lip
Brave Tenzing, hauled from the deep, fell flop
Like a monstrous gaping fish.

Was the summit theirs? – they puffed and panted –
No, for the ridge still upward pointed.
On they plodded, Martian-weird
With pouting mask and icicle beard
That cracked and tinkled, broke and rattled,
As on with pounding hearts they battled,
On to the summit –
Till at last the ridge began to drop.
Two swings, two whacks of Hillary's axe,
And they stood on top.

Ian Serraillier

The Inchcape Rock

No stir in the air, no stir in the sea –
The ship was as still as she could be;
Her sails from heaven received no motion;
Her keel was steady in the ocean.

Without either sign or sound of their shock,
The waves flowed over the Inchcape rock;
So little they rose, so little they fell,
They did not move the Inchcape bell.

The holy Abbot of Aberbrothok
Had placed that bell on the Inchcape rock;
On a buoy in the storm it floated and swung
And over the waves its warning rung.

When the rock was hid by the surges' swell,
The mariners heard the warning bell;
And then they knew the perilous rock,
And blessed the Abbot of Aberbrothok.

The sun in heaven was shining gay –
All things were joyful on that day;
The sea-birds screamed as they wheeled around,
And there was joyance in their sound.

The buoy of the Inchcape bell was seen,
A darker speck on the ocean green;
Sir Ralph, the rover, walked his deck,
And he fixed his eyes on the darker speck.

His eye was on the bell and float:
Quoth he, 'My men, put out the boat;
And row me to the Inchcape rock,
And I'll plague the priest of Aberbrothok.'

The boat is lowered, the boatmen row,
And to the Inchcape rock they go;
Sir Ralph bent over from the boat,
And cut the warning bell from the float.

Down sank the bell with a gurgling sound;
The bubbles rose, and burst around.
Quoth Sir Ralph, 'The next who comes to the rock
Will not bless the Abbot of Aberbrothok.'

Sir Ralph, the rover, sailed away –
He scoured the seas for many a day;
And now, grown rich with plundered store,
He steers his course to Scotland's shore.

So thick a haze o'erspreads the sky
They cannot see the sun on high;
The wind hath blown a gale all day;
At evening it hath died away.

On the deck the rover takes his stand;
So dark it is they see no land.
Quoth Sir Ralph, 'It will be lighter soon,
For there is the dawn of the rising moon.'

'Canst hear,' said one, 'the breakers roar?
For yonder, methinks, should be the shore.
Now where we are I cannot tell,
But I wish we could hear the Inchcape bell.'

They hear no sound; the swell is strong;
Though the wind hath fallen, they drift along;
Till the vessel strikes with a shivering shock –
O Christ! it is the Inchcape rock!

Sir Ralph, the rover, tore his hair;
He cursed himself in his despair.
The waves rush in on every side;
The ship is sinking beneath the tide.

But ever in his dying fear
One dreadful sound he seemed to hear –
A sound as if with the Inchcape bell
The Devil below was ringing his knell.

Robert Southey

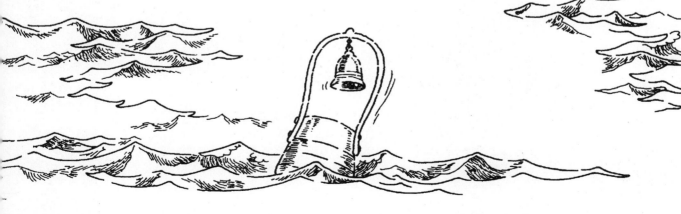

Travel

I should like to rise and go
Where the golden apples grow;
Where below another sky
Parrot islands anchored lie,
And, watched by cockatoos and goats,
Lonely Crusoes building boats;
Where in sunshine reaching out
Eastern cities, miles about,
Are with mosque and minaret
Among sandy gardens set,
And the rich goods from near and far
Hang for sale in the bazaar;
Where the Great Wall round China goes,
And on one side the desert blows,
And with bell and voice and drum,
Cities on the other hum;
Where are forests, hot as fire,
Wide as England, tall as a spire;
Where the knotty crocodile
Lies and blinks in the Nile,
And the red flamingo flies
Hunting fish before his eyes;
Where in jungles, near and far,
Man-devouring tigers are,
Lying close and giving ear
Lest the hunt be drawing near,
Or a comer-by be seen
Swinging in a palanquin;
Where among the desert sands
Some deserted city stands,
All its children, sweep and prince,
Grown to manhood ages since,
Not a foot in street or house,
Not a stir of child or mouse,
And when kindly falls the night,
In all the town no spark of light.
There I'll come when I'm a man
With a camel caravan;
Light a flower in the gloom
Of some dusty dining-room;
See the pictures on the walls,
Heroes, fights, and festivals;
And in a corner find the toys
Of the old Egyptian boys.

Robert Louis Stevenson

BEGINNINGS AND ENDINGS

Koala

Koala was a boy who lived long ago, in the Dream Time. He hadn't a mother or father. He hadn't any brothers or sisters. He was alone in the tribe. And because of this he did exactly what he wanted and didn't listen to anyone. He pleased himself, and that meant he did no work *and* he got up to lots of mischief of one kind or another.

Now one year, when the dry time came, all the streams and rivers and billabongs dried up, and the people had to walk a long way to the waterholes in order to get enough to drink. Everyone who was big and strong enough went and fetched some water, except for Koala. He didn't like to go walking. So he stayed behind in the camp, making mischief. And when the others came back, he went round begging for a drink, until someone took pity and gave him some water.

But a day came when no one would give Koala a drink. Everyone said he should pick up his own wooden coolamon and go and get his own water.

Next morning the men went hunting, the women and children went off to dig for roots, and there was only one person left in the camp. Koala. And, by this time, he was feeling very thirsty. So he went round the camp looking for water. But he couldn't find any. All the precious water had been very carefully hidden.

He looked here... there... everywhere. He didn't give up. And in the end he found a whole lot of coolamons full of water, hidden in the bush under some shady trees.

So Koala had a great, long drink. And when he was full and couldn't drink another drop, he said, 'I know what I'll do. I'll hide the water in my own secret place. Then I won't be thirsty again for a long time.'

He took a full coolamon, climbed up a small gum tree and hid it on a branch, among the leaves. Then he fetched the rest of the coolamons, one after the other, and hid them in the tree.

He had just hidden the last one when the tree stirred itself, and – strong magic – it sprang up and up *and up*, until it became an enormous tree. Koala hung on tight, and when the tree stopped growing, he found himself near the top, with the coolamons around him. He thought he could climb down. But could he climb up again? He wasn't sure about that. So he sat down on a big branch, right up against the trunk, and had a little snooze.

At sunset, when everyone returned to the camp, they were so hot and thirsty they went straight to the hiding place to get a drink. But they soon found that there were only a few coolamons there; and they were empty.

Immediately, everyone had the same thought. 'Koala! Where is Koala?'

And they looked around and saw an enormous tree where there had only been a small tree before, and near the top was Koala *and* all the coolamons!

'Koala!' they shouted, 'Bring down our water!'

But Koala laughed. He felt safe at the top of that enormous tree. 'If you want the water,' he called out, 'come and get it yourselves!'

Then a young man said, 'I'll bring down the water. It is a very tall tree, but I can climb it!'

His friend said, 'And I'll bring down that rascal Koala, so that we can deal with him!'

So they climbed the tree trunk while Koala peered down through the branches, watching them. When they had almost reached the top, Koala lifted a coolamon and poured water down the trunk and over the two young men. And then their hands slipped on the smooth wet bark, and they lost their grip and went sliding down to the bottom of the tree.

Then two brothers offered to climb the tree. But they didn't go straight up, hand over hand. They were cunning and swung themselves round and round the trunk, in a spiral. Koala waited until they had almost reached him, and then he poured water over them. But they swung themselves round the trunk so swiftly that the water missed them; and they climbed on and up, coming closer and closer. Then Koala was afraid, and he began to moan and wail and cry.

And next thing, one of the brothers reached out and grabbed him. Koala struggled hard and managed to break free. But then he lost his balance and fell, bouncing from branch to branch, right to the ground.

Every single bone in his body hurt. But Koala didn't wait. He jumped up and he ran. And everyone was so angry; they chased after him, shaking their fists and shouting. They were determined to catch him. And they almost did. But just in time he reached another tree, and he scurried up it, fast as he could.

And then, before their eyes – strong magic – Koala changed. Rough grey hair covered his body. His ears stood up, all fringed and furry, above two round black-button eyes and a small black shiny nose. He was no longer Koala the boy. He had become Koala the bear.

Even today, Koala looks exactly the same. And – would you believe it? – he still won't go looking for water if he can help it. When he is thirsty, he nibbles some more juicy leaves from a gum tree, and that's usually enough for him.

But he has not forgotten the day when he was in trouble and was nearly caught, for if anyone tries to climb his tree he always makes a great fuss and moans and wails and cries, just as he did when he was a little boy called Koala.

Anonymous

Wumbulgal

Wumbulgal, the little duck, lived a long, long time ago in the Dream Time. She was a bold little duck who refused to be frightened by anything, even the water devil who lived in the murky depths of the long river that stretched away towards the horizon. Wumbulgal's friends and relations were too frightened to explore the river but Wumbulgal spent many happy days enjoying the beautiful cool water and finding choice things to eat.

One day when the sun was especially hot and the water felt especially and deliciously cool, Wumbulgal went further down the river than she had ever been before. On the bank there were some of the freshest and greenest shoots she had ever seen. Greedily, Wumbulgal waddled up the bank to take a large mouthful. Just as she bit into them she was seized from behind by strong arms. Wumbulgal struggled. The arms held her tighter and tighter. Wumbulgal called for help but there was no-one to hear her. Still the arms held her and Wumbulgal was dragged into a dark burrow at the water's edge. Poor Wumbulgal, she was sure that her greed had led her into the hands of the water devil who would be sure to kill her.

Inside the burrow it was gloomy dark, but there was enough light for Wumbulgal to see that her captor was not the water devil but only Water Rat. Wumbulgal was so relieved.

'Please let me go,' she quacked. 'I promise I'll go straight back home and leave your green shoots alone.'

'No, little duck,' said Water Rat, 'I shall never let you go. You are the most beautiful little duck I have ever seen and I want you for my wife.'

Wumbulgal was horrified. 'Be your wife?' she said. 'But I am a duck and you are a water rat. Besides, I am too young to get married. Can you wait until next year?' Wumbulgal thought she would swim home and never come back again.

'No, I can't wait,' said Water Rat. 'I am Goomai, the King of the water rats. It is fitting that I should have a wife as special as you. You must stay with me or I will kill you with my spear.'

Poor Wumbulgal. She had no weapons to use against Water Rat. She had to stay. But all the time she thought about escaping. Her plan was a cunning one. She pretended she was happy with Goomai. She made no attempt to escape from the dark burrow even when she heard her friends and relatives searching the river and calling out for her.

'I like it here with you,' she lied to Goomai.

Soon Goomai believed her. He relaxed his guard and returned to his old habit of sleeping in the day time and exploring the river at night. Still

Wumbulgal bided her time. She stayed by Goomai's side all day, every day, until she was sure that the time was right.

One afternoon when Goomai was in the deepest sleep, Wumbulgal crept out. Without a splash she slipped into the water and paddled her fastest all the way back to her home.

The other ducks were amazed and delighted to see her. They had been sure that the water devil had killed her. Wumbulgal told the whole story and, from then on, neither she nor any other duck ever swam down the river again.

Nesting time came soon after Wumbulgal's return and she, along with all the others, made a cosy nest in the reeds lined with grasses and feathers to keep the eggs warm. At last the eggs hatched. Out came Wumbulgal's tiny babies and proudly she took them down to the water for their first swim.

'What have we here?' asked one of Wumbulgal's snooty relations. 'Your children are most peculiar.'

Wumbulgal was angry. Her children were beautiful. Of course, she could see that they were different from the others. They had four feet instead of two and they had brown fur instead of feathers.

'They look just like Water Rat,' someone else added. 'They are not ducks at all.'

'Take them away, take them away!' shrieked an over-anxious new mother. 'They will grow big and fierce and kill our little darlings.'

Soon all the ducks were quacking furiously. 'Take them away, take them away! They'll kill us, they'll kill us!'

Wumbulgal gathered her little children together. 'Come,' she said proudly, 'we will not stay where we are not wanted.'

Swiftly she led them away upstream, right into the mountains where there were no other ducks to jeer at them. The little ones were quite happy in their new home in the billabong, but Wumbulgal missed the company of her friends and relations and soon she died from sheer loneliness.

And so it was that the first duck-billed platypus came to live in the mountains. They, in turn, laid their eggs and hatched out children until a whole new tribe of animals emerged in the land. Even today, they still live apart from other animals, for no duck ever has four legs and no water rat has ever laid an egg. Wumbulgal, the bold duck who died of loneliness, gave the world a new animal to treasure – the duck-billed platypus.

Retold by Julia Eccleshare

The story of Paka the cat and Pania the rat

Long, long ago Paka, the cat, and Pania, the rat, lived together on a small island; and they had a good life together.

Their home was a dry cave, and their bed was a warm heap of dry leaves. And they had more than enough to eat. The cat caught birds, and the rat nibbled nuts and, best of all, roots of the manioc plant which grew freely on the island.

And Paka, the cat was content. But Pania was not.

One day the rat said, 'I am tired of this little island. Let us go to another place. Let us see how man lives.'

'To be sure, my friend, I am willing to go,' said the cat. 'But between us and the land where man dwells, there rolls the wide, salt sea. How can we cross? We are both small and cannot swim so far.'

'Then let us build a boat,' said the rat. 'First we must dig up a great big manioc root. Then we must gnaw and nibble and scratch. And then we shall have a boat.'

'We can try,' said Paka, the cat.

Well, they soon found a manioc root, and before long they had dug it up. Then – *crunch-scrunch* – with his sharp teeth, the rat gnawed and nibbled into the root. And a fine meal he had. That manioc was delicious! Then – *scritch-scratch* – with his sharp claws, the cat scooped out chunks from the inside of the root. And very hard work it was.

At last the root was hollowed out, and they had made their boat. It was a light boat and very frail. But it *was* a boat.

Pania, the rat, looked at it and was pleased, but Paka, the cat, looked at it and was afraid.

'It is such a small boat and its sides are so thin,' he said. 'Are you sure it can carry us across the wide, salt sea?'

'Have no fear,' said the rat. 'Our boat will carry us far and carry us well, over to the land where man lives.'

'But how will it know the way?' asked the cat.

'Let us make paddles, and then we can guide our boat to the land where man lives,' said the rat.

So then they found two branches and – *crunch-scrunch* – with his sharp teeth, the rat shaped them. Then – *scritch-scratch* – with his sharp claws, the cat shaped them and smoothed them.

When the two paddles were ready, they pushed the boat into the water and then jumped aboard. Paka, the cat, sat in the front and Pania, the rat, sat behind. Then they each picked up a paddle and dipped it into the water – in, out, in, out. And the boat fairly skimmed across the waves.

After a while Pania, the rat, grew tired, and he thought to himself, 'Paka cannot see me. So, what's the harm? I shall take a little rest.'

So he took in his paddle and lay down and rested. But no sooner had he settled, than he began to feel hungry.

'Ah,' he thought, 'Paka cannot see me. So, what's the harm? I shall have a little something to eat.'

With that, he began to nibble the boat. And that manioc was delicious!

But Paka, sitting in front, went on paddling – in, out, in, out – until presently he, too, grew tired. He rested, only for a moment, and then he heard a crunching and a scrunching behind him. He turned round. And what did he see? Why, that rat, Pania, was lying flat down *and* he was eating the boat!

'You good-for-nothing rascal,' cried the cat, 'How, in the name of goodness, can you lie there eating while I do all the work?'

'Please, friend Paka, please forgive me,' said the rat. 'I'm not big and strong like you. I only stopped for a moment, just to get my breath back. And I only had a bite, just to build my strength up.'

Then he picked up his paddle and began to work with a will – in, out, in, out. So Paka, the cat, turned back and dipped in his paddle too. They went on in this way, paddling together, for a while, but very soon that rat began to feel tired. And he thought to himself that perhaps he would take a short rest and another nibble. Then he stopped paddling and had a good long rest and a good large meal.

And all the time the cat sat in front and went on paddling. After a while he felt tired again; and it seemed to him that the boat was scarcely moving. He turned round, and he saw that rat, Pania, lying flat down and eating the boat again.

'You lazy, greedy, good-for-nothing creature,' he cried. 'Here am I doing all the work while you eat the boat. Just take care, or you'll eat a hole in the bottom and we'll both be drowned.'

Then the rat spoke and he spoke in a quiet and humble tone.

'Friend, Paka, I am truly sorry,' he said. 'I'll make up for this. Surely, I will.'

Then he picked up his paddle and – in, out, in, out – he dipped the paddle so that the boat fairly skimmed across the waves. So Paka, the cat, picked up his paddle, and on they went.

Well, they worked hard and they worked together until the boat was over half-way to the land where man lived. And then the rat grew tired and hungry again. So he thought he would have just one nibble more.

And he had one nibble more. But, oh dear! he nibbled right through the bottom of the boat. And the water flooded in and crept up and up, while the boat sank down and down. So there were Paka, the cat, and Pania, the rat, struggling and splashing in the water.

'You greedy creature,' spluttered the cat. 'So you would eat our boat, would you? Well, then now I shall eat you.'

Then Pania, the rat, spoke in a quiet and humble tone.

'You're right, quite right,' he said. 'You eat me and eat every bit of me. That's what I deserve. But, please, friend Paka, don't eat me here, or all the salt water will go down your poor throat and into your poor stomach and make you sick. Let us swim to the land where man lives, and then you can eat me and enjoy eating me.'

'Very well,' said the cat. 'But you swim in front and I'll swim behind so that I can keep an eye on you this time.'

So they swam and they swam, and after a long time they reached the land where man lived.

And the cat cried out, 'Now I shall eat you, every little bit.'

'Quite right, quite right,' said the rat. 'But please, dear Paka, please wait till I've shaken the salt water off my coat. I shall taste so much better then.

Sit down in the sun and dry your own coat. I shall be ready in a moment.'

So the cat sat down on the sand by the seashore. But Pania, the rat, shook himself and shook himself and while he shook himself, he moved bit by bit, closer and closer to a small, dark hole he had spied at the bottom of a sand dune.

'What are you doing?' said the cat.

'Just shaking and moving. Just moving and shaking,' said the rat.

'Well, you can stop it right now,' said the cat, 'for I am ready for you.'

Before the cat could as much as twitch a whisker, the rat was up and away, straight into that small, dark hole. The cat was up and after him, but the rat reached the hole first and in he went. When the cat got there, he found the hole was so small and his body so big that he could not squeeze in. So he sat there and waited for the rat to come out.

And did that rat come out? Not him. He had eaten very well that day, so he curled up in the hole under the sand dune and fell fast asleep. And when he woke up, all refreshed, he dug and he dug till he came out on the other side; and he did not wait around, you can be sure. There and then he quickly made his escape.

So that was the end of the friendship between Paka, the cat, and Pania, the rat. And from that day to this all cats have hated rats. Every cat tells her kittens the story of Pania and tells them never to cease from hunting him and his family. And every rat when he sees a cat, he runs.

Margaret Mayo

Raincloud

In the beginning, no one lived on Earth. Everybody lived in the Land of Sky. Birds flew in the blue of Sky. Snakes crawled in the clouds of Sky. Even fish swam in the sea of Sky.

One day, a boy called Okonorote went out hunting in the clouds. He was looking for Magic Bird – the bird with the rainbow feathers.

Okonorote travelled far from home. He looked in the valleys. He searched on the hills. At last he saw a silver tree. On top of the tree was a nest. And sitting in the nest was Magic Bird.

Okonorote took aim. Zwing. Zwing. His arrows left the boy. Swish. Swish. Their sharp heads travelled through the air. Tang. One arrow hit Magic Bird.

'Haiee,' Okonorote shouted happily. 'I have caught the Magic Bird.'

The young hunter ran to the silver tree. But the bird was nowhere in sight. Okonorote looked around him. In the ground there was a big, gaping hole. Magic Bird had fallen through it.

Okonorote looked down the hole. Far below he saw Magic Bird lying on a green land. Okonorote gasped. 'Land,' he shouted. 'Land down below.'

People came running out of their cloud-houses to see. 'Land down below,' they all gasped. 'Land down below.'

Quickly, Okonorote made a rope ladder out of hemp and twine. Down, down, down he went. Past the galaxies and the meteors. Past the sun and the stars. Right through the winds and the rainbows. Soon he touched the rocks of Earth.

Okonorote looked around him. The Magic Bird was lying on the ground. Okonorote ran to pick it up. But the bird disappeared. Instead of it, there was a tiny hill. As Okonorote watched, the hill grew into a mountain.

'Look,' said the people in the sky. 'Okonorote has built a mountain to help us down.'

One after the other the Sky People climbed down to Earth. They looked around them and saw the green grass, the yellow sunshine and the brown soil.

'How warm it is down here,' they said. 'Let us stay here.'

Soon, everyone had left the cold Land of Sky. Everyone, that is, except a little girl who was too scared to climb down the ladder. The girl's name was Raincloud.

Okonorote saw Raincloud peeping out of the hole in the sky. 'Don't be afraid,' he called. 'Climb down.'

Carefully, Raincloud put her left foot on the ladder. The ladder swung dangerously. Raincloud stepped back. She waited a moment. Then she tried again. This time she kept her eyes closed.

Slowly Raincloud climbed down past the sun. She stepped over the moon. At last she reached the rainbow.

'How warm it is down here,' said Raincloud to herself. And she opened her eyes to see. Almost immediately, she felt dizzy. The land below looked very far away. Raincloud's feet started to slip.

'Don't move,' shouted Okonorote. Quickly, he scampered up the ladder.

'One, two, three, four, five...' The people started to count the rungs.

Suddenly there was a loud snap. The rope broke in two. Okonorote fell back to Earth. Raincloud was left clinging to a rock-cloud in the sky. 'Help,' she called.

Okonorote climbed to the top of a tall tree.

'Jump,' he called. 'Raincloud, jump.'

But Raincloud was too scared to do anything. She just sat on the rock-cloud and cried. Slowly, the cloud started to drift away. Soon Raincloud could not see her friends any more.

The sun set and the moon came out. Raincloud was so tired she went to sleep. When she woke up again, she was floating above the sea. Raincloud saw a dolphin and a shark, and a baby whale trailing after its mother.

'What a beautiful place Earth is,' thought Raincloud. 'Some day soon I'm going to find the courage to jump off this rock-cloud. Then I'll join my friends in the New World.'

But time passed, and Raincloud stayed where she was. Her friends built houses and roads and became the first Earth People. They forgot all about Raincloud waiting in the sky.

The poor girl is still sitting up there to this very day, trying to find enough courage to jump to Earth. Sometimes she gets so lonely, she starts to cry.

Then her tears fall on the people below.

Retold by Doris Harper-Wills

How the Polar Bear became

When the animals had been on earth for some time they grew tired of admiring the trees, the flowers, and the sun. They began to admire each other. Every animal was eager to be admired, and spent a part of each day making itself look more beautiful.

Soon they began to hold beauty contests.

Sometimes Tiger won the prize, sometimes Eagle, and sometimes Ladybird. Every animal tried hard.

One animal in particular won the prize almost every time. This was Polar Bear.

Polar Bear was white. Not quite snowy white, but much whiter than any of the other creatures. Everyone admired her. In secret, too, everyone was envious of her. But however much they wished that she wasn't quite so beautiful, they couldn't help giving her the prize.

'Polar Bear,' they said, 'with your white fur, you are almost too beautiful.'

All this went to Polar Bear's head. In fact, she became vain. She was always washing and polishing her fur, trying to make it still whiter. After a while she was winning the prize every time. The only times any other creature got a chance to win was when it rained. On those days Polar Bear would say, 'I shall not go out in the wet. The other creatures will be muddy, and my white fur may get splashed.'

Then, perhaps, Frog or Duck would win for a change.

She had a crowd of young admirers who were always hanging around her cave. They were mainly Seals, all very giddy. Whenever she came out they made a loud shrieking roar:

'Ooooooh! How beautiful she is!'

Before long, her white fur was more important to Polar Bear than anything. Whenever a single speck of dust landed on the tip of one hair of it – she was furious.

'How can I be expected to keep beautiful in this country!' she cried then. 'None of you have ever seen me at my best, because of the dirt here. I am really much whiter than any of you have ever seen me. I think I shall have to go into another country. A country where there is none of this dust. Which country would be best?'

She used to talk in this way because then the Seals would cry, 'Oh, please don't leave us. Please don't take your beauty away from us. We will do anything for you.'

And she loved to hear this.

Soon animals were coming from all over the world to look at her. They stared and stared as Polar Bear stretched out on her rock in the sun. Then they went off home and tried to make themselves look like her. But it was no use. They were all the wrong colour. They were black, or brown, or yellow, or ginger, or fawn, or speckled, but not one of them was white. Soon most of them gave up trying to look beautiful. But they still came every day to gaze enviously at Polar Bear. Some brought picnics. They sat in a vast crowd among the trees in front of her cave.

'Just look at her,' said Mother Hippo to her children. 'Now see that you grow up like that.'

But nothing pleased Polar Bear.

'The dust these crowds raise!' she sighed. 'Why can't I ever get away from them? If only there were some spotless, shining country, all for me...'

Now pretty well all the creatures were tired of her being so much more admired than they were. But one creature more so than the rest. He was Peregrine Falcon.

He was a beautiful bird, all right. But he was not white. Time and again, in the beauty contests he was runner-up to Polar Bear.

'If it were not for her,' he raged to himself, 'I should be first every time.'

He thought and thought for a plan to get rid of her. How? How? How? At last he had it.

One day he went up to Polar Bear.

Now Peregrine Falcon had been to every country in the world. He was a great traveller, as all the creatures well knew.

'I know a country,' he said to Polar Bear, 'which is so clean it is even whiter than you are. Yes, yes, I know, you are beautifully white, but this country is even whiter. The rocks are clean glass and the earth is frozen ice-cream. There is no dirt there, no dust, no mud. You would become whiter than ever in that country. And no one lives there. You could be queen of it.'

Polar Bear tried to hide her excitement.

'I could be queen of it, you say?' she cried. 'This country sounds made for me. No crowds, no dirt? And the rocks, you say, are glass?'

'The rocks,' said Peregrine Falcon, 'are mirrors.'

'Wonderful!' cried Polar Bear.

'And the rain,' he said, 'is white face powder.'

'Better than ever!' she cried. 'How quickly can I be there, away from all these staring crowds and all this dirt?'

'I am going to live in another country,' she told the other animals. 'It is too dirty here to live.'

Peregrine Falcon hired Whale to carry his passenger. He sat on Whale's forehead, calling out the directions. Polar Bear sat on the shoulder, gazing at the sea. The Seals, who had begged to go with her, sat on the tail.

After some days, they came to the North Pole, where it is all snow and ice.

'Here you are,' cried Peregrine Falcon. 'Everything just as I said. No crowds, no dirt, nothing but beautiful clean whiteness.'

'And the rocks actually are mirrors!' cried Polar Bear, and she ran to the nearest iceberg to repair her beauty after the long trip.

Every day now, she sat on one iceberg or another, making herself beautiful in the mirror of the ice. Always, near her, sat the Seals. Her fur became whiter and whiter in this new clean country. And as it became whiter, the Seals praised her beauty more and more. When she herself saw the improvement in her looks she said, 'I shall never go back to that dirty old country again.'

And there she is still, with all her admirers around her.

Peregrine Falcon flew back to the other creatures and told them that Polar Bear had gone for ever. They were all very glad, and set about making themselves beautiful at once. Every single one was saying to himself, 'Now that Polar Bear is out of the way, perhaps I shall have a chance of the prize at the beauty contest.'

And Peregrine Falcon was saying to himself, 'Surely, now, I am the most beautiful of all creatures.'

But that first contest was won by Little Brown Mouse for her pink feet.

Ted Hughes

The king who was afraid to die

This story is part of the holy book of the 'Ramayana', the famous Indian story whose climax is the celebration of Diwali.

A very long time ago, long before you or I were born, there was a handsome king called Trisanku. Every day Trisanku would stand in front of the mirror and look at himself.

'How beautiful I am,' he would say. 'I could not bear to die and leave this wonderful body.'

One day King Trisanku went to see a wise, old man called Vasistha.

'O wise one,' the vain king said. 'Will you arrange for me to go to heaven without dying?'

The wise Vasistha was very angry to hear these foolish words. 'Get out of my sight,' he cried.

King Trisanku returned to his palace and sat on the throne. 'The great Vasistha is not powerful enough to help me,' he said. 'I shall look for help somewhere else.'

Vasistha's sons heard these words. 'Cursed be the king,' they cried.

Suddenly King Trisanku felt all his skin shrivel up. Panic-stricken, he looked in the mirror. His skin was old. His face had turned white.

'I have been changed into a beggar,' cried the king.

Servants rushed into the room. They saw the beggar and turned him out of the palace.

'I am the king,' shouted Trisanku.

But the servants would not believe him. 'Our king is handsome,' they said. 'And he wears beautiful robes, not rags like yours.' And they slammed the door in Trisanku's face.

The poor king travelled far from home. He climbed mountains and crossed streams. Sometimes he slept in poor inns along the way. On warm nights he rested under the stars. After many a day he reached a distant part of his country.

'I shall stop here for a while,' thought the king.

Finding a tree, he sat in its shade. As he lay resting, a group of people passed by.

'Look at that beggar,' said one of the people. 'Is he from these parts?'

The others stopped to look.

'Why, that is King Trisanku,' said the eldest of the men.

The king looked up. Among the travellers was a famous hermit called Viswaamitra.

'Who has cast this spell on you?' the hermit asked.

King Trisanku told Viswaamitra his story. The hermit was moved.

'Never mind, your majesty,' he promised, 'I shall help you go to heaven without dying.'

The hermit's helpers took King Trisanku home. They fed him and washed his feet. Meanwhile, Viswaamitra invited all the sages in the land to a special ceremony.

'King Trisanku is in our midst,' he said. 'I shall send him to heaven without dying.'

The sages accepted the hermit's offer because they were afraid of his powers. But Vasistha's three sons would not come. The hermit was very angry.

'May they be unhappy all their lives,' he cried.

On the day of the ceremony, the hermit and the sages lit a huge fire. They prayed and chanted. They asked the gods to visit them. But the gods did not appear. The hermit poured ghee over the fire.

'Oh great ones,' he said. 'Take all that I have earned, but let this king come unto heaven.'

Suddenly King Trisanku started to rise in the air. The sages gasped. The hermit prayed harder. King Trisanku rose higher and higher. Soon he was at the door of heaven.

'Who goes there?' asked Indra, the chief of the gods.

'It is me, King Trisanku,' cried the king.

Indra looked at the king's tattered clothes and ageing skin. 'How dare you come to heaven in such a state?' he shouted angrily. 'Go back to Earth.' And he threw the poor king out of the sky.

'Help!' cried Trisanku. 'I cannot bear to go to Earth as a beggar again.'

The great hermit heard him. Angrily, he looked up. 'What this?' he shouted. 'Do the great gods reject my powers?'

The sages trembled with fear. The great hermit held up his hands. 'O, King,' he said. 'Stop where you are.'

Suddenly King Trisanku stopped in the sky. He looked around him and saw the stars. He felt the rays of the moon on his face.

'Dear hermit,' he cried. 'It is beautiful up here.'

'Then you can stay,' said the hermit. 'And I shall give you companions to pass the time with.'

While the great gods looked from the sky, the hermit created more stars until the sky was full of them. Fearing that their power would be forgotten, the great gods spoke to the hermit.

'Stop,' they begged. 'We shall let the king stay in the sky.'

The hermit stopped. King Trisanku looked at his face. Slowly, his skin was starting to shine. Beauty flowed out of his face.

'I am beautiful again,' cried King Trisanku. 'And I shall never fear death again.'

Time passed, and the cruel Vasistha passed away. But King Trisanku stayed up in the sky, lighting the night with his beauty.

He's still there to his very day.

Retold by Indira Rai

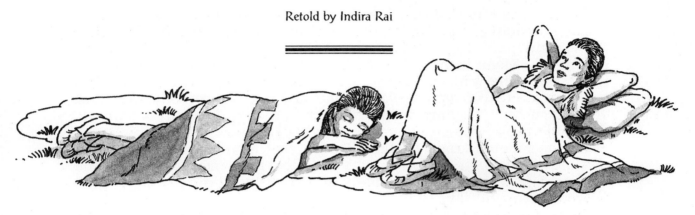

Feather Woman and the Morning Star

One night in the moon of flowers, the time when the wild rose blooms and the grass is long upon the prairie, a girl called Feather Woman and her young sister took their blankets and slept outside their lodge. Just before dawn Feather Woman woke and saw the morning star rising in the east; and it was so beautiful that she could not take her eyes off it.

'Wake up! And look over there at the morning star!' she called to her sister. 'How I do love that star. It is the brightest and best of them all!'

Her sister laughed and teasing her said. 'So – you would like to marry a star!'

'It is true,' Feather Woman answered quietly. 'I would marry the morning star.'

A few days later Feather Woman was on her way to the river to fetch some water, when she met a stranger on the trail. He was tall and straight and more handsome than any man she had ever seen. He wore clothes of soft tanned skin that smelt of pine and sweet grass. There was a yellow plume in his hair, and he was holding a branch of juniper that had a spider's web hanging from it.

'I am Morning Star,' he said. 'One night I saw you lying in the long grass and heard your words of love. Now I ask you to leave your camp and come to the Above World and live there together with me.'

Feather Woman trembled as she heard these words. She said, 'First let me go to my mother and father and say goodbye. And then I will come with you.'

But he answered, 'You must come now or not at all.'

And he took the yellow plume and fastened it in her hair. Then he offered her the branch of juniper and said, 'Take this and close your eyes. The spider ladder will carry you to my home.'

So Feather Woman took the juniper and closed her eyes; and when she opened them again she was in the sky, standing before a great lodge.

'Welcome to my home,' said Morning Star. 'This is the lodge of my father, the Sun, and my mother, the Moon.'

Now at that time the Sun was away on his travels, but the kindly Moon was there. And she welcomed her son's new bride. She offered her food and drink, and then she gave her a soft tanned buckskin dress, a bracelet of elk teeth and an elk-skin robe, decorated with secret paintings.

The days passed by, and Feather Woman was happy in the Above World. The Moon showed her the abundance of flowers and vegetables and berries that grew there, and taught her about herbs and secret medicines. She also gave her a digging stick made of wood hardened in fire and showed her how to use the stick to dig up the many wild roots that could be eaten.

But the Moon warned Feather Woman that there was one plant she must never dig up. It was the Giant Turnip that grew near the lodge of the Spider Man, who wove the ladders by which the star people travelled between earth and sky. The Moon told Feather Woman many times, 'The Giant Turnip is sacred. If you touch it, you will bring unhappiness to us all.'

Time passed, and Morning Star and Feather Woman had a baby son, and they called him Star Boy; and it seemed then that their happiness was complete.

But one day when Feather Woman was out with her digging stick, collecting wild vegetables, she happened to pass the Giant Turnip. And she said to herself, 'I wonder what lies beneath the Giant Turnip.'

She walked around it. Then she bent down and examined it closely. And then she laid the baby on the ground and began to dig under the turnip. She dug and she dug, but the turnip would not move. She dug some more, and the digging stick stuck fast underneath. Then she looked up and saw two cranes flying overhead.

She called to them, 'Come, mighty cranes! Come and help me move the Giant Turnip!'

They circled above her three times and then they landed. They took

hold of the turnip with their long, sharp beaks and rocked it to and fro. They sang a magic song and rocked it again until *prrr...mm!* it rolled out of the ground, leaving a hole where it had been growing.

Feather Woman knelt down and looked through the hole, and she saw the camp of the Blackfeet Indians where once she had lived. Smoke was rising from the lodges. Children were laughing. Young men were playing games. And the women were working – tanning hides and building lodges, gathering berries on the hills and fetching water from the river.

Then Feather Woman longed to be back again upon the green prairie with her own people. Slowly she got to her feet. She shook her head and she sighed, and when she turned to go home, there were tears in her eyes.

As soon as Morning Star saw her, he knew what she had done. He said, 'You have dug up the Giant Turnip!' And that was all he said. Nothing more.

When the Moon heard what had happened, she was sad. But when the Sun heard, he was angry.

He said, 'Feather Woman has disobeyed my command, and now she must return to earth. She has looked again upon her own people, and she can no longer be happy here with us.'

So Morning Star took his wife and his baby son to the lodge of the Spider Man, and he asked the Spider Man to weave a ladder that would take them down to earth. Then Morning Star placed a digging stick in Feather Woman's hands and wrapped her and Star Boy in an elk-skin robe.

'Close your eyes,' he said. 'And now, farewell.'

It was one evening, in the time when the berries are ripe, that Feather Woman and Star Boy came to earth. People on the prairie looked up and saw a bright falling star. They ran to the place where it landed and found a strange bundle. When they opened the bundle, they saw a girl and a baby. And they knew at once that she was the girl who, many moons before, had gone to fetch water, and had not returned.

From that time on Feather Woman and Star Boy lived in her parents' lodge. And she shared with the Blackfeet Indians all the knowledge she had brought from the Above World. She taught them the secrets of the medicine plants. She showed them how to make a digging stick and how to recognise the wild turnip, the wild onion and other plants that were good to eat.

But Feather Woman never forgot the Above World. And often on clear days, when the sun shone, she would climb to the top of a high ridge and look up into the sky and think of her husband, the great and glorious Morning Star.

Anonymous

Noah's Ark

It began
When God popped His head
Through the clouds and said:

'Oh you wicked, wicked children
What a mess this place is in
All the violence and corruption
It really is a sin.

I turn my back for five aeons
(For I've other work to do)
Keeping the universe tidy
And I get no thanks from you.

You've grown selfish and conceited
Your manners are a disgrace
You come and go just as you please
You'd think you owned the place.

A telling-off's not good enough
You've grown too big for your flesh
So I think I'll wash my hands of you
And start again afresh.'

He turned full on the tap in the sky
Then picked out the one good man
Pure of heart and strong in arm
To carry out his plan: Noah.

'What I need,' explained God
'Is an arkwright to build an ark, right away.'
Said Noah, 'If I can sir.'
'Of course you can, now get stuck in
I won't take Noah for an answer.

'I want a boat three storeys high
Aboard which you will bring
Not only your wife and family
But two of every living thing.'

'Even spiders?' asked Noah
(who didn't really like them)
'Even spiders,' said God
(who didn't either).

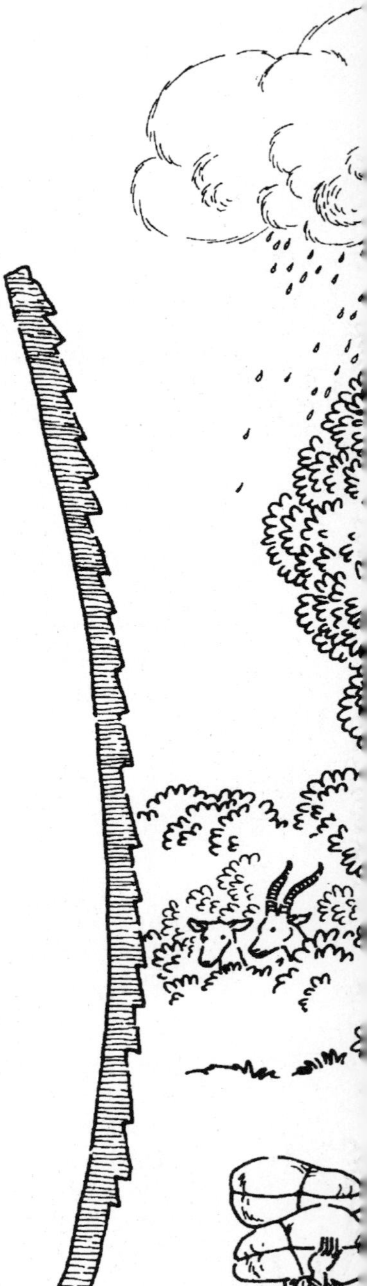

'Cats and dogs and elephants
Slugs, leopards and lice
Giraffes and armadilloes
Buffaloes, bed bugs and mice.

Antelopes, ants and anteaters
(though keep those last two apart)
Bears from Koala to Grizzly
Horses from Racing to Cart.

Fish will be able to fend for themselves
And besides, a wooden ark
Is not the sort of place to keep
A whale or an angry shark.

And don't forget our feathered friends
For they'll have nowhere to nest.
But vermin will determine
Their own survival best.

Flies, maggots and bluebottles
Mosquitoes and stingers that bite
Will live off the dead and dying
So they'll make out all right.

That seems to be all for now, Noah
The rest is up to you
I'll see you again in forty days
Until then God Bless and Adieu.'

He disappeared in a clap of thunder
(Either that or he banged the door)
And the wind in a rage broke out of its cage
With an earth-splintering roar.

And no sooner was everyone aboard
Than the Ark gave a mighty shudder
And would have been crushed by the onrushing waves
Had Noah not been at the rudder.

Right craftily he steered the craft
As if to the mariner born
Through seas as high as a Cyclops' eye
And cold as the devil's spawn.

And it rained, and it rained
And it rained again

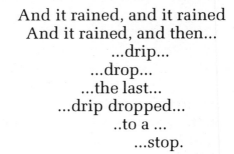

And it rained, and it rained
And it rained, and then...
...drip...
...drop...
...the last...
...drip dropped...
..to a ...
...stop.

Noah at the helm was overwhelmed
For both cargo and crew were unharmed
Then the wind turned nasty and held its breath
So the Ark became becalmed.

Hither and thither it drifted
Like an aimless piece of jetsam
'Food's running out,' cried Mrs Noah
'We'll perish if we don't get some.

'Maybe God's gone and forgotten us
We're alone in the world and forsaken
He surely won't miss one little pig
Shall I grill a few rashers of bacon?'

'Naughty, naughty!' said Noah sternly
(For it was the stern that he was stood in)
'I'm ravenous, but bring me a raven
I've an idea and I think it's a good 'un.'

As good as his word, he let loose the bird
'Go spy out for land,' he commanded
But in less than a week, it was back with its beak
Completely (so to speak) empty-handed!

Next he coaxed from its lovenest a dove
'We're depending on you,' he confided
Then gave it to the air like an unwrapped gift
Of white paper, that far away glided.

Then the Ark sat about with its heart in its mouth
With nothing to do but wait
So Mrs Noah organised organised games
To keep animal minds off their fate.

Until one morn when all seemed lost
The dove in the heavens was seen
To the Ark, like an archangel it arrowed
Bearing good tidings of green.

'Praised be the Lord,' cried Noah
(and Mrs Noah cried too)
And all God's creatures gave their thanks
(even spiders, to give them their due).

Then God sent a quartet of rainbows
Radiating one from each side
To the four corners of the earth
Where they journeyed and multiplied.

And as Noah set off down the mountain
To be a simple farmer again
A voice thundered: 'Nice work there, sunshine.'
Here endeth the story. Amen.

From *Waving at Trains* by Roger McGough

Why Noah chose the dove

When the people sinned and God decided to punish them by sending the flood, all the animals gathered around Noah's ark. Noah was a righteous man, and God had told him how to save himself and his family by building an ark that would float and shelter them when the waters rose.

The animals had heard a rumour that Noah was to take with him on the ark only the best of all the living creatures. So the animals came and vied with one another, each boasting about its own virtues and whenever possible belittling the merits of others.

The lion roared: 'I am the strongest of all the beasts, and I surely must be saved.'

The elephant blared: 'I am the largest. I have the longest trunk, the biggest ears, and the heaviest feet.'

'To be big and heavy is no so important,' yapped the fox. 'I, the fox, am the cleverest of all.'

'What about me?' brayed the donkey. 'I thought I was the cleverest.'

'It seems anyone can be clever,' yipped the skunk. 'I smell the best of all the animals. My perfume is famous.'

'All of you scramble over the earth, but I'm the only one that can climb trees,' shrieked the monkey.

'Only one!' growled the bear. 'What do you think I do?'

'And how about me?' chattered the squirrel indignantly.

'I belong to the tiger family,' purred the cat.

'I'm the cousin of the elephant,' squeaked the mouse.

'I'm just as strong as the lion,' snarled the tiger. 'And I have the most beautiful fur.'

'My spots are more admired than your stripes,' the leopard spat back.

'I am man's closest friend,' yelped the dog.

'You're no friend. You're just a fawning flatterer,' bayed the wolf. 'I am proud. I'm a lone wolf and flatter no one.'

'Baa!' blatted the sheep. 'That's why you're always hungry. Give nothing, get nothing. I give man my wool, and he takes care of me.'

'You give man wool, but I give him sweet honey,' droned the bee. 'Besides, I have venom to protect me from my enemies.'

'What is your venom compared with mine?' rattled the snake. 'And I am closer to Mother Earth than any of you.'

'Not as close as I am,' protested the earthworm, sticking its head out of the ground.

'I lay eggs,' clucked the hen.

'I give milk,' mooed the cow.

'I help man plough the earth,' bellowed the ox.

'I carry man,' neighed the horse. 'And I have the largest eyes of all of you.'

'You have the largest eyes, but you have only two, while I have many,' the housefly buzzed right into the horse's ear.

'Compared with me, you're all midgets.' The giraffe's words came from a distance as he nibbled the leaves off the top of a tree.

'I'm almost as tall as you are,' chortled the camel. 'And I can travel in the desert for days without food or water.'

'You two are tall, but I'm fat,' snorted the hippopotamus. 'And I'm pretty sure that my mouth is bigger than anybody's.'

'Don't be so sure,' snapped the crocodile, and yawned.

'I can speak like a human,' squawked the parrot.

'You don't really speak – you just imitate,' the rooster crowed. 'I know only one word, "cock-a-doodle-do", but it is my own.'

'I see with my ears; I fly by hearing,' piped the bat.

'I sing with my wing,' chirped the cricket.

There were many more creatures who were eager to praise themselves. But Noah had noticed that the dove was perched alone on a branch and did not try to speak and compete with the other animals.

'Why are you silent?' Noah asked the dove. 'Don't you have anything to boast about?'

'I don't think of myself as better or wiser or more attractive than the other animals,' cooed the dove. 'Each one of us has something the other doesn't have, given us by God who created us all.'

'The dove is right,' Noah said. 'There is no need to boast and compete with one another. God has ordered me to take creatures of all kinds into the ark, cattle and beast, bird and insect.'

The animals were overjoyed when they heard these words, and all their grudges were forgotten.

Before Noah opened the door of the ark, he said, 'I love all of you, but because the dove remained modest and silent while the rest of you bragged and argued, I choose it to be my messenger.'

Noah kept his word. When the rains stopped, he sent the dove to fly over the world and bring back news of how things were. At last she returned with an olive leaf in her beak, and Noah knew that the waters had receded. When the land finally became dry, Noah and his family and all the animals left the ark.

After the flood God promised that never again would he destroy the earth because of man's sins, and that seed time and harvest, cold and heat, summer and winter, day and night would never cease.

The truth is that there are in the world more doves than there are tigers, leopards, wolves, vultures, and other ferocious beasts. The dove lives happily without fighting. It is the bird of peace.

Isaac Bashevis Singer

Last day

In this excerpt from Charlotte's Web, *Charlotte, a spider, feels that her days are numbered and entrusts her egg sac to her friend, a pig called Wilbur.*

'Charlotte,' said Wilbur. 'We're all going home today. The Fair is almost over. Won't it be wonderful to be back home in the barn cellar again with the sheep and the geese? Aren't you anxious to get home?'

For a moment Charlotte said nothing. Then she spoke in a voice so low Wilbur could hardly hear the words.

'I will not be going back to the barn,' she said.

Wilbur leapt to his feet. 'Not going back?' he cried. 'Charlotte, what are you talking about?'

'I'm done for,' she replied. 'In a day or two I'll be dead. I haven't even strength enough to climb down into the crate. I doubt if I have enough silk in my spinneret to lower me to the ground.'

Hearing this, Wilbur threw himself down in an agony of pain and sorrow. Great sobs racked his body. He heaved and grunted with desolation. 'Charlotte,' he moaned. 'Charlotte! My true friend!'

'Come now, let's not make a scene,' said the spider. 'Be quiet, Wilbur. Stop thrashing about!'

'But I can't *stand* it,' shouted Wilbur. 'I won't leave you here alone to die. If you're going to stay here I shall stay, too.'

'Don't be ridiculous,' said Charlotte. 'You can't stay here. Zuckerman and Lurvy and John Arable and the others will be back any minute now, and they'll shove you into that crate and away you'll go. Besides, it wouldn't make any sense for you to stay. There would be no one to feed you. The Fair Grounds will soon be empty and deserted.'

Wilbur was in a panic. He raced round and round the pen. Suddenly

he had an idea – he thought of the egg sac and the five hundred and fourteen little spiders that would hatch in the spring. If Charlotte herself was unable to go home to the barn, at least he must take her children along.

Wilbur rushed to the front of his pen. He put his front feet up on the top board and gazed around. In the distance he saw the Arables and the Zuckermans approaching. He knew he would have to act quickly.

'Where's Templeton?' he demanded.

'He's in that corner, under the straw, asleep,' said Charlotte.

Wilbur rushed over, pushed his strong snout under the rat, and tossed him into the air.

'Templeton!' screamed Wilbur. 'Pay attention!'

The rat, surprised out of a sound sleep, looked first dazed then disgusted.

'What kind of monkeyshine is this?' he growled. 'Can't a rat catch a wink of sleep without being rudely popped into the air?'

'Listen to me!' cried Wilbur. 'Charlotte is very ill. She has only a short time to live. She cannot accompany us home, because of her condition. Therefore, it is absolutely necessary that I take her egg sac with me. I can't reach it, and I can't climb. You are the only one that can get it. There's not a second to be lost. The people are coming – they'll be here in no time. Please, please, *please,* Templeton, climb up and get the egg sac.'

The rat yawned. He straightened his whiskers. Then he looked up at the egg sac.

'So!' he said, in disgust. 'So it's old Templeton to the rescue again, is it? Templeton do this, Templeton do that, Templeton please run down to the dump and get me a magazine clipping, Templeton please lend me a piece of string so I can spin a web.'

'Oh, hurry!' said Wilbur. 'Hurry up, Templeton!'

But the rat was in no hurry. He began imitating Wilbur's voice.

'So it's "Hurry up, Templeton", is it?' he said. 'Ho, ho. And what thanks do I ever get for these services, I would like to know? Never a kind word for old Templeton, only abuse and wisecracks and side remarks. Never a kind word for a rat.'

'Templeton,' said Wilbur in desperation, 'if you don't stop talking and get busy, all will be lost, and I will die of a broken heart. Please climb up!'

Templeton lay back in the straw. Lazily he placed his forepaws behind his head and crossed his knees, in an attitude of complete relaxation.

'Die of a broken heart,' he mimicked. 'How touching! My, my! I notice that it's always me you come to when in trouble. But I've never heard of anyone's heart breaking on *my* account. Oh, no. Who cares anything about old Templeton?'

'Get up!' screamed Wilbur. 'Stop acting like a spoiled child!'

Templeton grinned and lay still. 'Who made trip after trip to the dump?' he asked. 'Why, it was old Templeton! Who saved Charlotte's life by scaring that Arable boy away with a rotten goose egg? Bless my soul, I believe it was old Templeton. Who bit your tail and got you back on your feet this morning after you had fainted in front of the crowd? Old Templeton. Has it ever occurred to you that I'm sick of running errands and doing favours? What do you think I am, anyway, a rat-of-all-work?'

Wilbur was desperate. The people were coming. And the rat was failing him. Suddenly he remembered Templeton's fondness for food.

'Templeton,' he said, 'I will make you a solemn promise. Get Charlotte's egg sac for me, and from now on I will let you eat first, when Lurvy slops me. I will let you have your choice of everything in the trough and I won't touch a thing until you're through.'

The rat sat up. 'You mean that?' he said.

'I promise. I cross my heart.'

'All right, it's a deal,' said the rat. He walked to the wall and started to climb. His stomach was still swollen from last night's gorge. Groaning and complaining, he pulled himself slowly to the ceiling. He crept along till he reached the egg sac. Charlotte moved aside for him. She was dying, but she still had strength enough to move a little. Then Templeton bared his long ugly teeth and began snipping the threads that fastened the sac to the ceiling. Wilbur watched from below.

'Use extreme care!' he said. 'I don't want a single one of those eggs harmed.'

'Thith thtuff thticks in my mouth,' complained the rat. 'It'th worth than caramel candy.'

But Templeton worked away at the job, and managed to cut the sac adrift and carry it to the ground, where he dropped it in front of Wilbur. Wilbur heaved a great sigh of relief.

'Thank you, Templeton,' he said. 'I will never forget this as long as I live.'

'Neither will I,' said the rat, picking his teeth. 'I feel as though I'd eaten a spool of thread. Well, home we go!'

Templeton crept into the crate and buried himself in the straw. He got out of sight just in time. Lurvy and John Arable and Mr Zuckerman came along at that moment, followed by Mrs Arable and Mrs Zuckerman and Avery and Fern. Wilbur had already decided how he would carry the egg sac – there was only one way possible. He carefully took the little bundle in his mouth and held it there on top of his tongue. He remembered what Charlotte had told him – that the sac was waterproof and strong. It felt funny on his tongue and made him drool a bit. And of course he couldn't say anything. But as he was being shoved into the crate, he looked up at Charlotte and gave her a wink. She knew he was saying good-bye in the only way he could. And she knew her children were safe.

'Good-bye!' she whispered. Then she summoned all her strength and waved one of her front legs at him.

E. B. White

By St Thomas Water

By St Thomas Water
Where the river is thin
We looked for a jam-jar
To catch the quick fish in.
Through St Thomas Church-yard
Jessie and I ran
The day we took the jam-pot
Off the dead man.

On the scuffed tombstone
The grey flowers fell,
Cracked was the water,
Silent the shell.
The snake for an emblem
Swirled on the slab,
Across the beach of sky the sun
Crawled like a crab.

'If we walk,' said Jessie,
'Seven times round,
We shall hear a dead man
Speaking underground.'
Round the stone we danced, we sang,
Watched the sun drop,
Laid our heads and listened
At the tomb-top.

Soft as the thunder
At the storm's start
I heard a voice as clear as blood,
Strong as the heart.
But what words were spoken
I can never say,
I shut my fingers round my head,
Drove them away.

'What are those letters, Jessie,
Cut so sharp and trim
All round this holy stone
With earth up to the brim?'
Jessie traced the letters
Black as coffin-lead.
'*He is not dead but sleeping,*'
Slowly she said.

I looked at Jessie,
Jessie looked at me,
And our eyes in wonder
Grew wide as the sea.
Past the green and bending stones
We fled hand in hand,
Silent through the tongues of grass
To the river strand.

By the creaking cypress
We moved as soft as smoke
For fear all the people
Underneath awoke.
Over all the sleepers
We darted light as snow
In case they opened up their eyes,
Called us from below.

Many a day has faltered
Into many a year
Since the dead awoke and spoke
And we would not hear.
Waiting in the cold grass
Under a crinkled bough,
Quiet stone, cautious stone,
What do you tell me now?

Charles Causley

The house

'Two years ago,' she said, 'when I was so sick, I realised that I was dreaming the same dream night after night. I was walking in the country. In the distance, I could see a white house, low and long, that was surrounded by a grove of linden trees. To the left of the house, a meadow bordered by poplars pleasantly interrupted the symmetry of the scene, and the tips of the poplars, which you could see from far off, were swaying above the linden.

'In my dream, I was drawn to this house, and I walked toward it. A white wooden gate closed the entrance. I opened it and walked along a gracefully curving path. The path was lined by trees, and under the trees I found spring flowers – primroses and periwinkles and anemones that faded the moment I picked them. As I came to the end of this path, I was only a few steps from the house. In front of the house, there was a great green expanse, clipped like the English lawns. It was bare, except for a single bed of violet flowers encircling it.

'The house was built of white stone and it had a slate roof. The door – a light-oak door with carved panels – was at the top of a flight of steps. I wanted to visit the house, but no one answered when I called. I was terribly disappointed, and I rang and I shouted – and finally I woke up.

'That was my dream, and for months it kept coming back with such precision and fidelity that finally I thought: Surely I must have seen this park and this house as a child. When I would wake up, however, I could never recapture it in waking memory. The search for it became such an obsession that one summer – I'd learned to drive a little car – I decided to spend my vacation driving through France in search of my dream house.

'I'm not going to tell about my travels. I explored Normandy, Touraine, Poitou, and found nothing, which didn't surprise me. In October, I came back to Paris, and all through the winter I continued to dream about the white house. Last spring, I resumed my old habit of making excursions in the outskirts of Paris. One day, I was crossing a valley near L'Isle-Adam. Suddenly I felt an agreeable shock – that strange feeling one has when after a long absence one recognises people or places one has loved.

'Although I had never been in that particular area before, I was perfectly familiar with the landscape lying to my right. The crests of some poplars dominated a stand of linden trees. Through the foliage, which was still sparse, I could glimpse a house. Then I knew that I had found my dream château. I was quite aware that a hundred metres ahead, a narrow road would be cutting across the highway. The road was there. I followed it. It led me to a white gate.

'There began the path I had so often followed. Under the trees, I admired the carpet of soft colours woven by the periwinkles, the primroses, and the anemones. When I came to the end of the row of linden, I saw the green lawn and the little flight of steps, at the top of which was the light-oak door. I got out of my car, ran quickly up the steps, and rang the bell.

'I was terribly afraid that no one would answer, but almost immediately a servant appeared. It was a man, with a sad face, very old. He was wearing a black jacket. He seemed very much surprised to see me, and he looked at me closely without saying a word.

'"I'm going to ask you a rather odd favour," I said. "I don't know the owners of this house, but I would be very happy if they would permit me to visit it."

'"The château is for rent, madame," he said, with what struck me as regret, "and I am here to show it."

'"To rent?" I said. "What luck! It's too much to have hoped for. But how is it that the owners of such a beautiful house aren't living in it?"

'"The owners did live in it, madame. They moved out when it became haunted."

'"Haunted?" I said. "That will scarcely stop me. I didn't know people in France, even in the country, still believed in ghosts."

'"I wouldn't believe in them, madame," he said seriously, "if I myself had not met, in the park at night, the phantom that drove my employers away."

'"What a story!" I said, trying to smile.

'"A story, madame," the old man said, with an air of reproach, "that you least of all should laugh at, since the phantom was you".'

André Maurois

Uncle

Uncle was Gran's brother,
came to stay when she died,
kept to his room at the top of the stairs
but on Sundays he polished shoes.

Uncle was expert, a real shoe sheriff.
Each size ten had a price on its head
till he rounded it up with the rest.
He'd lasso Mum's boots and whistle
till plimsolls came running.
He knew, of course, where I threw mine,
when one was missing, he'd corner the dog,
then search through his bed till he found it.

The shoes submitted instantly:
they waited, trembling in line,
while one by one Uncle slapped on polish,
cleaned off the week's wear and tear
then buffed them to a shine.

He'd brighten the shabbiest pair,
the ones that had skulked for months
in a cupboard beneath the stairs.
He'd untangle loops and knots
then leave the shoes in rows,
till like some general inspecting troops
I'd signal which ones went back
for a second go.

When he died I took on his job
for a while, cleaned shoes for money.
I'd rub away like Aladdin and think
how my efforts might free Uncle's ghost.
I knew how much he'd be missing that mix
of polish and Sunday roast.

Brian Moses

Index of Authors

Index of Themes

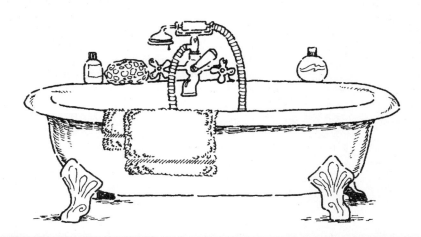

Index of Titles